Deforming American Political Thought

Deforming American
Political Thought

ETHNICITY, FACTICITY, AND GENRE

MICHAEL J. SHAPIRO

THE UNIVERSITY PRESS OF KENTUCKY

Publication of this volume was made possible in part by a grant
from the National Endowment for the Humanities.

Editorial and Sales Offices: The University Press of Kentucky
663 South Limestone Street, Lexington, Kentucky 40508–4008
www.kentuckypress.com

10 09 08 07 06   5 4 3 2 1

Library of Congress Cataloging-in-Publication Data

Shapiro, Michael J.
  Deforming American political thought : ethnicity, facticity, and genre / Michael J.
Shapiro.
    p. cm.
  Includes bibliographical references and index.
  ISBN-13: 978-0-8131-2412-4 (hardcover : alk. paper)
  ISBN-10: 0-8131-2412-3 (hardcover : alk. paper) 1. Political science–United States–
History. 2. Ethnicity–United States. 3. Ethnocentrism–United States. 4. Political
culture–United States–History. 5. Arts–Political aspects–United States. I. Title.
  JA84.U5S514 2006
  320.0973–dc22   2006012956

This book is printed on acid-free recycled paper meeting
the requirements of the American National Standard
for Permanence in Paper for Printed Library Materials.

Manufactured in the United States of America.

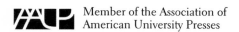

Member of the Association of
American University Presses

To the memory of Jorge Luis Andrade Fernandes
(1968–2004)

Contents

Illustrations

Preface

Many of the ideas incorporated in the investigations in this book were developed during pedagogical plans and their implementation. For several years I have taught a "scope and methods" course for beginning political science graduate students. Most courses under this rubric were invented during the 1960s, when departments of government became departments of political science, a shift reflecting a new preoccupation with "method," as a formerly historical and descriptive discipline was being transformed into a social science. The social scientization of a politics discipline is an ambiguous achievement.[1] While on the one hand, the introduction of rigor in a knowledge practice enables systematic inquiry, on the other, as Sheldon Wolin pointed out in a polemical essay written in the midst of the "behavioral revolution" in political science, a preoccupation with method (which he referred to as "methodism") is incompatible with the vocation of the political theorist, inasmuch as that vocation requires attentiveness to a historically informed and politically engaged knowledge.[2] A reading of Wolin's indictment, which I offer in chapter 2, reveals at a minimum a radical difference between his and mainstream political science perspectives on political theory. Observing this particular disciplinary contention among others, it has been clear to me that there is no unambiguous way to represent political science as a consensual discipline, in terms of either scope or method. Political science, as deployed in American academia, is recalcitrant to a representation as what Thomas Kuhn famously called a paradigm.

As a result, I have encouraged students to explore—borrowing Arjun Appadurai's term—the changing "ideoscape" of political science, as it is reflected in, among other places, the historical trajectory of presidential addresses at annual meetings of the American Political Science Association since its founding in 1903.[3] As I read these along with my students, tracking changes in the designation of political subjects, in the cartography of "the political," in the social imaginaries within which politics has been theorized, and in notions of the ethical responsibilities of the scholar, my imagination was captured by the 1990 address by the first female president of the APSA, the political theorist Judith Shklar. In her address, "Redeeming American Political Thought" (which I analyze in chapters 1 and 2), she explores the epistemological compatibility between influential Euro-American figures in a founding period of American political theory and contemporary social science, seeking to redeem the scientific perspicacity of the "founders."[4] But in addition, she is the first to confess that the existence of "chattel slavery" impugns an unambiguous democratization narrative applied to the American political tradition. Her focus on the concept of redemption has encouraged me to undertake a redemptive project as well, although as will be clear from my discussion in chapter 1, my version of that project is very different from hers. Briefly, rather than attempting to redeem the scientific credentials of Euro-American founders, I redeem other voices.

A second major aspect of my analysis stems from my teaching of the aesthetic-politics relationship. After exposing students to Immanuel Kant's *Critique of Judgment* and treating its implications for approaching facticity, not as something the world simply confers but as what emerges from the way subjects actively apprehend worlds, I go on to emphasize the ways in which Kant's contribution to turning what is sensible into what is knowable is inflected in the thinking of such post-Kantians as Gilles Deleuze, Jean-François Lyotard, and Jacques Rancière. I then encourage students to apply a post-Kantian appreciation of the permeable boundary between epistemological and aesthetic modes of analysis and judgment to the politics of literary, visual, and aural texts.

As my own investigations of diverse genres took shape — in course preparation, in the classroom, and in my writing — I became particularly engaged by critical interpretive approaches edified by concepts of deformation and partitioning. With respect to the former, I implement, while shifting genres, Gilles Deleuze's analysis of the way the painter Francis Bacon deforms the "psychic clichés" and "figurative givens" in the history of painting and Houston A. Baker Jr.'s analysis of the way W. E. B. Du Bois's writing effects a "deformation of mastery" to challenge aspects of the textuality of white dominance.[5] With respect to the latter, I am instructed by Jacques Rancière's conception of the politics of aesthetics, where aesthetics is understood to involve "the partitioning of the sensible." Noting Plato's well-known statement that artisans have no time to do anything but their work, Rancière states:

> Obviously this "lack of time" is not an empirical matter, it is the mere naturalization of a symbolical separation. Politics precisely begins when they who have "no time" to do anything else than their work take that time that they have not in order to make themselves visible as sharing in a common world and prove that their mouth indeed emits common speech instead of merely voicing pleasure or pain. That distribution and re-distribution of times and spaces, places and identities, that way of framing and re-framing the visible and the invisible, of telling speech from noise and so on, is what I call the partition of the sensible. Politics consist in reconfigurating the partition of the sensible, in bringing on the stage new objects and subjects, in making visible that which was not visible, audible as speaking beings they who were merely heard as noisy animals.[6]

This way of formulating the politics-aesthetics relationship influences aspects of most of my chapters and anticipates a third dimension of my analysis, my attempt to make voluble voices that have been neglected in the academic construction of "American political thought." As I have been assembling materials for my American political thought courses, I have been disappointed with the texts that advertise themselves under that rubric. The canon to which traditional political theory approaches defer is chromatically limited (most of the contributions are from white Americans) and genre restricted (most of the texts and course designs I consulted stuck to nonfictional literatures: brief sections from political treatises and/or commentaries on those treatises). Unlike the humanities, where attention to a diversity of thinking, resident in diverse loci of textual production and diverse kinds of genre analysis, abounds, there has been virtually no attention paid to the alternative ethnic American "thought-worlds" that have articulated themselves in, for example, prose fiction, film, music, and architecture, among other genres.

Seeking to render American political thought as a multi-genre as well as multiethnic field of thinking, I have frequently resorted to films and novels in my courses. The film genre is especially important, not only because, as Miriam Hansen puts it, it is "the aesthetic matrix of a particular historical experience,"[7] and as such is the most engaging genre as regards its relevance for contemporary audiences, but also because, as Walter Benjamin noted, it has "a moral shock effect," evoking sensibilities that have slumbered, either because many of the social and political world's most violent effects are veiled or because of the dulling effects of other genres.[8] Most significantly, film's critical capacity inheres in the way it "inscribes the image with moments of temporality and contingency that *dis*figure the representation" and subjects the viewer to "encounters with contingency, lack of control and otherness."[9] And, as Jacques Rancière points out, film is the genre best suited to rendering judgments on the facticity of events unstable because much of the critical capacity of film arises from "*la contradiction que le visible y apporte a la signification narrative* [the contradiction that the visible brings to narrative signification]."[10]

Of course, some other genres can achieve similar effects. For example, as Alain Badiou says of Paul's epistles, they combine "a kind of violent abstraction with ruptures in tone designed to put pressure on the reader, to deprive him of all respite."[11] However, film is perhaps the best example of the contemporary, pluralizing "aesthetic regime of art," which is a departure from the traditional mimetic regime by dint of its reversal of the privileging of "the primacy of the narrative over the descriptive." As Rancière describes it, the aesthetic regime features "a fragmented or proximate mode of focalization, which imposes raw presence to the detriment of the rational sequences of the story" and presents viewers with multiple perspectives rather than a single privileged focus.[12]

Novels can supply a political pedagogy for similar reasons. Unlike conventional political theory tracts and treatises, they are, in M. M. Bakhtin's terms, "heteroglossic": they contain contending voices and exhibit centrifugal forces. As a result, they enact a "verbal-ideological decentering" as they introduce voices from diverse experiential spaces to convey a dissensus rather than a single master view of the world.[13] A remark by Roberto Calasso about the effects of conversations in Franz Kafka's fictional rooms in *The Castle* reflects what a novel, at its micropolitical best, can deliver: "A room can be as charged as a continent."[14]

To pursue Calasso's figuration a bit further, I want to note another charged instance in a novel that finds its way into my recent courses and into the midst of my sentiments and thinking, one that is especially pertinent to the themes of this investigation. It is not possible to achieve a deep appreciation of what slavery was about without heeding the African American voices of the period, hence in chapter 1 I treat the writing of Harriet Jacobs, who escaped from slavery, and David Walker, a free African American who wrote during the slavery period. Nevertheless, a novelistic treatment of plantation space by an African American writer who bears the legacy of that foundational experience is also an apt vehicle for discerning the micropolitics of the "chattel slavery" to which Judith Shklar briefly referred in her provocative address.

Specifically, in an early scene in Edward P. Jones's novel *The Known World*, Henry Townsend, who as an adult becomes a former slave who owns his own slaves, is about to be left behind by his free parents. His father, Augustus Townsend, who had bought himself out of slavery at age twenty-two, has come to collect his wife, Mildred, whom he has just managed to buy four years later. He does not yet have enough saved to buy his son, Henry. As Augustus and Mildred prepare to leave nine-year-old Henry behind, assuring him that "Before you can turn around good . . . you be coming home with us," the text notes that the plantation owner, William Robbins, is watching the scene from astride his horse, Sir Guilderham, which from Henry's perspective appears as "a mountain separating the boy from the fullness of the sun." Henry, who when asked by Robbins why he is crying, does not dare to say, is to be left in the care of another slave, Rita, to whom Robbins says, "You see things go right," meaning that Henry was not to be allowed to run away. At that moment, the third-person narration says: "He would have called Rita by name but she had not distinguished herself enough in his life for him to remember the name he had given her at birth." Among what we learn here are aspects of the micropolitics of plantation space missing in abstract, historical glosses, its multiple dimensions of dominance: a horse with an aristocratic name contrasted with a slave whose name is not regarded as worth recalling, a child being wrenched away from his parents without having the right to voice his misery, and a "master" who remains on horseback, well above the level of those oppressed by the exercise of his prerogatives, all framed by a historical situation in which bodies can be owned and subjected to any exercise of will but their own.[15] Jones's novel, which contains many such charged scenes, thinks continually and profoundly in a powerful, politically relevant way.

It is primarily the novel that inaugurates my study of American political thought. A contrast between Thomas Jefferson's rationalization of continental space and Thomas Pynchon's novelistic treatment of Mason and Dixon's surveying project holds center stage in chapter 1, as I treat the politics of the survey, with a special emphasis on Pynchon's assertion that the Euro-American surveying and recording process was involved in "changing all from subjunctive to declarative, reducing Possibilities to Simplicities that serve the ends of Governments."[16] I then proceed to an analysis of the role of diverse, ethnic novelists/writers in producing alternative American imaginaries in order to loosen the hold of the entrenched "declarative."

In chapter 2, I turn to novels again, in this case to diverse ethnic crime novels, which I treat under the rubric of "the micropolitics of crime." As is the case with other dimensions of my study, I developed the chapter while teaching. As I prepared a course that featured crime novels and film noir, I was struck by the way crime fiction articulates a level of American politics that is fugitive when one focuses on national level issues. Fredric Jameson, whom I quote at length in the chapter, captures much of the political significance of the crime novel in a discussion of the writing of Raymond Chandler. He notes that in contrast with "a glamourous national politics whose distant leading figures are invested with charisma, an unreal, distinguished quality adhering to their foreign policy activities, their economic programs given the appearance of intellectual content by the appropriation of ideologies of liberalism or conservatism," Chandler's novels reveal a "darker concrete reality . . . local politics, with its odium, its ever-present corruption, its deals and perpetual preoccupation with undramatic, materialistic questions such as sewage disposal, zoning regulations, property taxes, and so forth."[17] In the case of the crime novels of other ethnic writers (African American, Native American, Latino American, and Asian American) featured in my courses and in chapter 2, one encounters a micropolitical sensibility that arises from alternative perspectives on history and on racial-spatial orders, in addition to observing the political forces surrounding the "undramatic, materialistic questions" to which Jameson refers.

Since the concept has now been asserted several times, some words about what I mean by "micropolitics" are in order. Certainly I am influenced by Gilles Deleuze and Felix Guattari's approach to the concept. For example, (as I point out in chapters 1 and 6) because there are no natural majorities and minorities resident in the social formation, and thus to designate an assemblage as either requires normative judgment,

Deleuze and Guattari emphasize avenues of escape from such judgments; they focus on "lines of flight," modes of self-fashioning by those
who flee imposed identities in order to achieve a state of non-closural
becoming. Accordingly, I tend to reserve the concept of macropolitics
for the official modes of political assembly that shape national political
formations: governmental groupings, officially warranted citizen subjects, and for familiar dynamics (political processes) as expressed in
mainstream political discourses—policy making and policy influencing by groups recognized as politically qualified, and by those individuals warranted as citizen participants. In contrast, using the concept
more broadly than Deleuze and Guattari, I see the micropolitical level
as emerging when those who tend to be excluded, given the way that
recognizable "politics" is policed, assemble to contest imposed identities, deform conventional modes of intelligibility, struggle to survive
economically, socially, and politically, or articulate, through writing,
sounds, built structures, or images, aspects of a life and thought-world
that are officially unheeded. Attention to micropolitics pervades my
various chapters.

   Deleuze and Guattari's concept of becoming, which is central to
their notion of micropolitics, applies especially well to the political tensions surrounding the meaning of ethnicity, another important focus
of my investigations. At a macro level in the United States (as in many
other state formations), ethnicity is intimately connected with race. For
example, as Toni Morrison has observed, whiteness has constructed
itself as a de-racialized, universalizing presence, while racializing, or
in her words, assigning a "dark abiding presence" to, African Americans.[18] And in general, so-called ethnic minorities are constituted as
assignments by those groupings that enjoy a majoritarian status with
the power to assign a normative centrality to themselves.

   Insofar as these assignments require marking space and time, because they involve both territorial boundaries and narratives that privilege periods of arrival and settlement, to contest an assignment requires
an exercise of counter-memory. Hence, Jamaica Kincaid's story of her
garden (which I review and analyze in chapter 1) is a contribution to
the micropolitics of identity. She connects gardening to a history of
colonization in which peoples in the Caribbean, members of "a conquered class," had meanings imposed on their domains through, among
other things, a botanical imperialism. Because, as she puts it, "in the
beginning the vegetable kingdom was chaos, people everywhere called

the same things by a name that made sense to them,"[19] she decides to construct her Vermont garden in a way that retrieves that beginning and counters the acts of possession and naming that accompanied the agri-colonization of her place of birth, Antigua. Kincaid's place-shaping amounts to a practice of counter-memory that instigates a becoming ethnic, inasmuch as a self-assignment of ethnicity requires that one relocate onself in space/time. Thus, the micropolitics of ethnicity, which I treat throughout this book by recovering "ethnic" loci of enunciation, is the process by which people produce accounts that disturb official identity matrices. By denaturalizing the history of the ethnic assignments involved in nation-building and the continuing cultural governance of established states, formerly abjected or dominated groups create "new ethnicities" with ambiguous and fluid identity boundaries. As a result, they speak from dynamic loci of enunciation, the recognition of which requires a relaxation of the traditional territorial predicates of political discourse.[20]

Much of the material in my third chapter, which attempts to deform the dominant narrative of America's westward-moving ethnogenesis (the whitening of the continent and concomitant racializing of prior inhabitants),[21] was gathered when I prepared and taught a course on western films, which featured many of John Ford's westerns, in New York University's Cinema Studies Department in the spring of 2002. Subsequently, as a result of invitations to write on film for journal monographs and anthologies, I was encouraged to continue thinking both with and against Ford and thus to appreciate how difficult it is to consign his films to mere complicity with Euro-American triumphalism. Following an investigation of crime genres with westerns evinced for me a powerful pedagogy on the shaping of the American ethnoscape and the representational practices through which its fault lines are continually reinscribed. My debts to many writers, primarily in the humanities, who enhanced that pedagogy with their attentiveness to the ethnic and racial troping that pervades both genres, should be abundantly evident in the chapters.

My first recognition that architecture is, among other things, historically situated materialized thinking is owed to my encounter with Erwin Panofsky's demonstration of the way the High Gothic cathedral enacts a Kantian mode of subjectivity and manifests a detail-by-detail material realization of scholastic thinking.[22] Although chapter 4 on diverse American architectural imaginaries provides a brief treatment of his text and rushes on, I owe more to Panofsky's insights than to any other architectural text I reference. The other major motivation to attempt to think about the architecture-thought relationship was encouraged by my visit to Daniel Libeskind's Jewish Museum in Berlin in the summer of 2002. Rather than merely housing a history of the Holocaust, Libeskind's structure, with its oblique axes and other dysnarrative design features, provides no main thoroughfare for the museum visitor. Accordingly, the visitor has to invent a route and as a result is forced to think inconclusively about that historical episode. Rather than allowing one to close in on an interpretation, the museum is designed to disrupt any attempt to consummate a narrative of one of history's most violent periods. It was then providential for me that Libeskind subsequently signed on to a U.S. project, the design of the new World Trade Center, and to undertake the creation of a text (which I analyze in the chapter) aimed in the same direction as mine, an attempt to open up rather than close off thinking about what America has been, is, and could be.

Nevertheless, as in other chapters, Thomas Jefferson, whose intellectual and political profile contains baffling contradictions, is a primary focus. Examining his designs of both his Monticello residence and his University of Virginia impressed me with how much persistence and diverse talent he brought to his overall project of inventing America. At the same time, after reading an account of Jefferson's daily life by one of Monticello's coerced inhabitants, the slave Isaac Jefferson, I was impressed with the minutiae of Jefferson's tyrannical control over his plantation/gulag. Apart from the spatial domination that Jefferson's coercive household community represented—a domain of forced agricultural, domestic, and sex work—the temporal rhythms of the place were also dominated by one kingly inhabitant. That, as Isaac Jefferson notes, Thomas Jefferson never entered his Monticello kitchen for any reason except to wind the clock speaks volumes about how the management of time is integral to structures of domination. I found this Jeffersonian gesture more pertinent to an understanding of early American politics than any testimony Jefferson's writings might provide about his social science acumen. Moreover, Isaac Jefferson's report on the temporal tyranny of Monticello gave me a deeper appreciation of Jacques Rancière's recovery of the role of time in the political initiatives undertaken by French proletarians in the nineteenth century, which influences parts of my investigation.

As I note in chapter 5, Rancière locates a politics of temporality in those historical episodes in which workers used their evenings to make of themselves political subjects. By devoting the night to writing, they turned the night into a political zone, a space within which to invent themselves in a way that resists the worker identity that exhausts the bourgeois conception of them.[23] However, the bulk of chapter 5 is my attempt to trace the way alternative ethnic composers have invented a distinctive American soundscape, which holds in creative tension rhythms, tonalities, and narrative progressions that speak to alternative ethnic American experiences. My debts to the insights about music of others are multiple. My earliest appreciation of how music, as the organization of sound, articulates with political uses and purposes is owed to Jacques Attali's widely read and influential text, *Noise: The Political Economy of Music*.[24] But the pedagogy that most influenced my analysis of the way musical compositions can think differently and thereby challenge entrenched systems of musical intelligibility comes from David Michael Hertz's relatively little-known text *The Tuning of the Word: The Musico-Literary Poetics of the Symbolist Movement*.[25]

Aside from these texts, I am especially indebted to the American jazz tradition—to Toni Morrison's and Nathaniel Mackey's writing, in which a jazz aesthetic migrates into literary forms; to astute commentators on jazz music: Ralph Ellison, Albert Murray, Amiri Baraka, Nathaniel Mackey, and Houston A. Baker Jr.; and to those musicians/composers who have radicalized musical thinking: the versioning of John Coltrane and Thelonious Monk, the musical hybridity of the arrangements of jazz pianist Marcus Roberts, and the innovative orchestral jazz compositions of Duke Ellington, whose musical thinking is the main focus of the chapter. Jazz is central to my focus on "composing America" because it is an exemplary American aesthetic; it is "at once a distinctly black American art form as well as a cultural hybrid."[26]

I am also very indebted to writing that has helped me understand the trajectory of those American musical innovations meant to create distinctive American compositions, especially MacDonald Smith Moore's treatment of the musical culture–American identity relationship, David Schiff's thorough analysis of the multiple genre influences in George Gershwin's *Rhapsody in Blue*, and Maurice Peress's account of the American musical trajectory that runs from Antonin Dvorak to Duke Ellington.[27] Duke Ellington provides the hinge for my transition from chapter 5 on "Composing America" to chapter 6, in which I inaugurate my discussion of radical approaches to thinking democracy with a focus on Jacques Rancière's notion of dissensus.

It is a short move from Ellington's insistence on dissonant chords because, as he puts it, "dissonance is our way of life in America. We are something apart, yet an integral part," to Rancière's insistence that dissensus is essential to the constitution of democracy.[28] While chapter 6 is assembled from diverse prototypes, its first and most basic incarnation was prepared for a conference on the work of Rancière that featured Rancière's reactions to the various papers. I have profited from Jacques's response to my initial version and, as the text of the book as a whole testifies, from his subsequent writing on the politics of aesthetics. Equality is Rancière's presupposition, episodes of dissensus supply his historical focus, and the contingencies involved in the way aesthetic judgment partitions the sensible world frame his approach to the epistemology-politics relationship. As a whole they structure his radical rethinking of democracy and, for my purposes, provide the basis for applications to diverse genres of expression.

Of all those who have developed conceptual frames for thinking about democratic pluralism, William Connolly has developed the most compelling. His scholarship, particularly as it has applied to the American democracy, is a featured influence in chapter 6, especially his extended meditation on the ambiguous achievement of social and symbolic boundaries, along with the way they reflect the contingencies that have shaped and reshaped America's democratic social space, his version of pluralism as a social ontology of discord, and his demonstration that a suppressed nomadism, a way of being-in-the-world that cannot be captured within contemporary society's authorized model of social segments, is the consequence of democracy's contemporary territorial imperatives. This latter insight stands, among other things, as a telling application to the American scene of Deleuze and Guattari's powerful critique of the modern state. Deleuze and Guattari's insight that modern society is a conflictual arena in which a series of micropolitical initiatives are always in tension with the molar politics of the state, that "there is always something that flows or flees, that escapes the binary organizations, the resonance apparatus and the overcoding machine," is a major influence not only on chapter 6 but throughout the book.[29]

Because I was involved in a conference that explored Jacques Derrida's legacy shortly after his death, I was prompted to revisit his late turn to the problem of democracy. Derrida's insights that democracy will always fall short of its promise, that it has heretofore been haunted by the exclusions it fails to acknowledge, and that to begin to approach its promise it must abandon its grip on a strong model of state sovereignty are all significant influences in the version of my work on democracy that became chapter 6. Derrida's insistence that "the democracy to come" must, in a Kantian sense, welcome those who cross state boundaries sets up my reading of the significance of Paul Laverty's film *Bread and Roses*, which focuses on those whose work the American society enjoys while subjecting them to the greatest risks. Finally, at the end of chapter 6, I treat briefly the paradox in which, in the name of democracy, the American government's policies, as I write, are the greatest threats to the American democracy. It is my hope that readers of this preface will be able, in the not too distant future, to regard this remark as hyperbole.

Acknowledgments

I am indebted to many, for the invitations that led to the prototypes of my various chapters, for critical reactions to the different versions of each chapter, and for conversations about the ideas shaping this book. I am grateful to Hayward Alker, Benjamin Arditi, Kazi Ashraf, Jane Bennett, Jodi Byrd, Bill Carroll, Bill Connolly, Bill Chaloupka, Andrew Crampton, Jodi Dean, Tom Dumm, Bob Gooding-Williams, Manfred Henningsen, Randy Martin, Neal Milner, James Philips, Marcus Power, Jacques Rancière, John Rieder, Jeffrey Stahl, Austin Sarat, Hannah Tavares, Nick Vaughan-Williams, Jeremy Valentine, and several anonymous reviewers. I also want to express my gratitude to all of those at and associated with the University Press of Kentucky for a rapid and very well-managed acquisition and production process — especially the director, Steve Wrinn, and his assistant, Anne Dean Watkins, and to Nichole Lainhart in editorial, Leila Salisbury and Mack McCormick in marketing, and my excellent copy editor, Derik Shelor of Shelor & Son Publishing.

My greatest debt is to my late friend, student, and colleague, to whom this book is dedicated, Jorge Fernandes, whose life and promising academic career was cut short when he died in an automobile accident in December of 2004. Jorge and I discussed most of the literatures and films that I treat in this book, and I relied on him for reactions to most of the chapters. For several years he was my closest intellectual companion as well as one of my closest friends. As a teenager, Jorge emigrated from Cape Verde with his family and entered high school in Massachusetts as a senior (while learning English). He subsequently received a B.A. from Brandeis, an M.A. from Howard, and a Ph.D. in Political Science from the University of Hawai'i, after writing a brilliant dissertation that focuses on third world intellectual migrants. He was in his first year as an Assistant Professor in the Department of Ethnic Studies at Bowling Green University in Ohio when he died. But the trajectory of Jorge's resume is a thin representation of what

Jorge was like. His contribution to the world was not exhausted by his scholarship. He was extraordinarily gracious. In Jorge, this characteristic was not merely polite sociability. Jorge made graciousness an ethos. He treated everyone with whom he came in contact with humility, honesty, and receptive attention. Indeed, Jorge—as much as anyone I have known—lived his ethics and politics. His untimely death is an immense loss, especially to his loved ones—wife (Sasha), son (Gabriel), parents, siblings, in-laws, and friends—but also to the world at large, to which he contributed his thinking and gracious humanity. Grief is a powerful hermeneutic. I will always miss him and will continue to benefit from having known him.

1 Securing the American Ethnoscape

Official Surveys and Literary Interventions

These times are unfriendly toward Worlds alternative to this one.
—Thomas Pynchon, *Mason & Dixon*

Every map presses down onto a physical terrain that it, in part, orders and, in part, effaces.
—Philip Fisher, "Democratic Social Space:
Whitman, Melville, and the Promise
of American Transparency"

The "Fact-Minded" Thomas Jefferson

When Judith Shklar, the late and much-revered Harvard political theorist, delivered her presidential address at the American Political Science Association's annual meeting in 1990, she said that she felt her responsibilities "particularly deeply." One aspect of that depth derived from her position as the first female president of the association. The other was associated with her vocation as a political theorist. Entitling her address "Redeeming American Political Thought," Shklar insisted that American political theory, "far from being demeaning and scientifically superfluous," ought to be integrated into a political science that is, in its best incarnation, "fact-minded."[1]

The redemption of American political theory for Shklar was therefore a matter of overcoming its marginal status by challenging the widely held presumption that it has lacked scientific rigor ever since the colonial period. To make her case, Shklar treated what she called "three political sciences in America," developed during America's

revolutionary and founding periods. These belong to Thomas Jefferson, James Madison, and Alexander Hamilton, whose approaches
were "speculative and physiological," "institutional and historical," and
"empirical and behavioral," respectively.[2] Once she cast the "founding
fathers" as political scientists, the bulk of her address treated instances
of their fact-mindedness and scientific rigor.

However, Shklar's desire to integrate the inaugural period of
American political theory into a scientific political science did not exhaust her historical focus. Unlike most of her predecessors, for whom
the American political tradition constituted an unambiguously proud
legacy, Shklar noted that among the "political phenomena" that distinguished the development of American political theory was, "most
deeply . . . the prevalence of chattel slavery." As a result, she asserted,
"this country has embarked upon two experiments simultaneously: one
in democracy, the other in tyranny."[3] Given the dominant tendency of
APSA presidential addresses to celebrate "the American political tradition," this was a stunning departure. But Shklar offered an immediate
palliative. She went on to suggest that the stain of chattel slavery had
been effectively removed, thanks in part to the social sciences within
which "the democratization of values" is implicit. However tyrannical
the institution of slavery was, a "democratic political science was eventually to be expected." And that political science, given to us "in embry-
onic form"[4] by Jefferson, Madison, and Hamilton, helped to sanitize a
besmirched American democratic tradition.

Yet despite her faith in the democratic proclivities of the entire trajectory of American political science, which originated in the "thought-
world"[5] of the framers of the nation-state's founding documents, Shklar
recognized a flawed perspective in, for example, Jefferson's anthropology with which he was able to legitimate the unjust treatment of "Indians" and slaves. But we should not blame social science, she insisted,
only the choice of inquiries. Jefferson's mistake was his attempt to "assimilate social science to natural history."[6] She did admit, however, that
ultimately, despite its important role in the democratization of values,
America's early versions of political science had their limits. Even with
their exemplary ethos, the founding thinkers "could not imagine a
multiracial citizenry."[7] Remarkably, Shklar was undaunted by this failure of imagination. Since things have worked out well—she implied
that America achieved a democratic, multiracial political order, thanks
in part to the scientific orientation of American political theory—she

could comfortably restrict the theorizing to white founders. The period of chattel slavery that Shklar lamented (however "deep") is merely one of the "political phenomena" that provoked, in a seemingly positive way, an American political theory that is strictly the provenance of Euro-Americans. Shklar felt, for example, that she could safely treat Jefferson as "a revered founder of a nation dedicated to the universal principles of human rights and individual liberties," and ignore the Jefferson whom many have seen as "an example of that 'white mythology' which conceals an oppressive racial imperialism in a language of universal philanthropy."[8]

Shklar's claims for the social science probity of all three thinkers are worthy of analysis. However, given the scope of this chapter and my particular concerns with the rationalization and reconfiguration of the American landscape and the levels of political eligibility assigned to different groups in the American ethnoscape, I am confining my reactions to Shklar's claims to Jefferson, who was most concerned with both and was ultimately most responsible for the expansion and reshaping of continental space. I want especially to contest Shklar's restrictive attention to what she regarded as an ultimately benign and progressive Euro-American thought-world and to treat Jefferson et al.'s slaves and Indians (among others inhabiting the Americas) not as mere "phenomena" but as *loci of enunciation*, as situated voices contributing to "American political theory." Such a move invites a very different kind of redemption. The task of recovery becomes not the integration of a narrow range of Euro-American thinking into a "fact-minded," political science, but a recasting of American political theory to include the diversity of thought-worlds that have, since the seventeenth century, collided and alternatively ignored and nourished each other. Native, African, and, more recently, Latino Americans (among others) have participated with Euro-Americans in a process of negotiating what America has been and is about. Heeding a cartography of alternative thought-worlds, with special attention to those articulated across the "colonial divide" imposed by the European conquest and expansion across the American continent, I redeem neglected portions of American political thinking. Instead of appreciating Jefferson's implementation of a proto social science, my emphasis is on recovering modes of thought to which his "science," and the version of those who continue to pursue a scientistic social and political science, have been inattentive.[9]

To prepare the conceptual ground for such a task, I want to note

another remarkable blind spot in Shklar's rendering of "American political theory." In addition to her restrictive approach to the worlds of
thought is her neglect of genre effects. Theory for Shklar is a matter
of the relationship of theorists' empirical propositions to their subject
matter. For example, rather than merely lamenting Jefferson's failure
to recognize the intellectual capabilities of African and Native Americans, while defending his social science (his sure grasp of facticity), one
can read Jefferson's incorporation of natural history into his inquiries as
extra scientific. His drive to create a particular American future turned
him as much into a polemical historian as a scientist. As has been
noted, his work on founding a unique democratic present and future
required an energetic reconstruction of the past.[10] For example, because he was bent on attributing democratic proclivities to Anglo Saxons and, accordingly, on ascribing Euro-American political institutions
to an Anglo-dominated ethnohistory, he picked a quarrel with David
Hume's *History of England*. The "fact-minded" Jefferson was troubled
by Hume's facts, which challenge the view that England's representative democracy derived from an "ancient constitution" developed in
the Anglo Saxon period that pre-dated the Norman conquest.[11]

The past that Jefferson sought to establish was based on ethnohis-
torical mythology rather than scientific inquiry. If we heed his mythic
stories rather than the "data collection" that they encourage, we must
recognize a Jeffersonian thought-world that consisted less in a scientific approach to facticity than in a commitment to narratives, images,
spatio-temporal models, and biopolitical conceits, all of which constituted his facts. As another president of an academic association put it
in *her* presidential address: "We and the cultural milieus in which we
think determine historical significance."[12] Seeking a different kind of
redemption for America's historical thought-worlds, historian Joyce Appleby urges the recovery of "the historic diversity in our past,"[13] which,
instead of turning attention to the scientific perspicacity of America's
revolutionary leaders, requires "giving voice . . . to those men and wom-
en who have been muffled by the celebration of American exceptionalism"[14] and "lift[ing] from obscurity those who have been left behind,
excluded, disinherited from the American heritage."[15]

Thanks to recent scholarship, there are abundant examples of the
unmuffling of voices that reflect the darker side of the plantation economy that Jefferson enjoyed and the imperial expansion that he sponsored. To heed those voices, one needs to accord more recognition to

the bodies from which they come. Or, to articulate the issue within a cinematic idiom, one needs to displace the panoramic master shot with the close-up. Looking outward from his Virginia plantation, Jefferson wrote a comprehensive description of his state's land- and ethnoscape. After treating the contours and elements of the landscape—rivers, vegetation, minerals, contours, and climate—he lists the animals and humans, treating Europeans, Indians, and Africans as distinct species. When he gets to a description of the slaves, whose importation he calls a "great political and moral evil," he first addresses their "natural" intellectual and civilizational inadequacies as a collective type and then simply enumerates them.[16] In this text, Jefferson's "facts" are articulated primarily within the genre of natural history, the soon-to-be-displaced episteme of the eighteenth century, whose method (its meta-facticity) consisted, as Michel Foucault noted, of "nothing more than the nomination of the visible, an arrangement of elements into a grid."[17]

Yet Jefferson's famous *Notes on the State of Virginia* are not only descriptive. In addition to what Myra Jehlen refers to as his "almost aggressive objectivity," one can discern in Jefferson's writings a turn from "fact gathering to political pleading," a case being made for building a nation by heeding the summons of nature.[18] In one telling instance, while describing a landscape seen from his Monticello plantation, Jefferson "constructs a visible scene" not as a dedicated empiricist but as one witnessing "an icon of historical change," and a symbolic narrative of the movement from chaos to pacified order.[19] After he remarks on the "disruption" that nature creates, he has nature promise a pacified locus of possession, asserting that what nature "presents to your eye" is a "smooth" vista "at an infinite distance in the plain country inviting you, as it were from the riot and tumult roaring around, to pass through the breach and participate in the calm below."[20]

Shklar is correct, Jefferson was indeed fact-minded—but not in Shklar's (empiricist) sense that his conclusions were warranted on the basis of objective observations. Rather, he was fact-minded in the sense that he wanted nothing left unclassified. Impatient with enigma, he mobilized the dominant modes of European thinking, especially natural history, to displace contingency with necessity. The American future he sought—ultimately a continent dominated by Euro-American yeoman farmers—was something that the world had been preparing to invite. According to Jefferson's romantic historical narrative, by the eighteenth century nature was beckoning the Euro-Americans:

"[W]e have an immensity of land courting the industry of the husbandmen."[21]

How else can one read a landscape? To cast the issue of seeing and knowing within a different frame and, at the same time, to welcome different observations, we can turn again to a cinematic idiom and contrast film director Alfred Hitchcock's approach to the seen and the known. Like Jefferson, Hitchcock presents landscapes and peoplescapes. But here the similarity ends. While Jefferson remains a remote observer, offering a wide-angle view, "Hitchcock's camera typically only begins by enacting a survey of a seemingly natural scene. Eventually, as the filming proceeds, it becomes evident that there is a perverse element in the landscape" (for example, in *North by Northwest* a biplane crop duster fogging the ground in an area where—a bystander tells Roger Thornhill/Cary Grant—there are no crops to dust). As one commentator astutely puts it, "[t]he film's movement invariably proceeds from landscape to stain, from overall shot to close-up, and this movement invariably prepares the spectator for the event."[22] Through his close-ups, Hitchcock draws the audience's attention to the perversions sequestered within the seemingly benign and conventional scenes (thus, in *North by Northwest* the crop duster changes from a small speck to a threatening presence as it fills the scene in a close-up while attacking Thornhill).

Accordingly, to offer an alternative to Jefferson's large-framed, distancing gaze on his surroundings and, ultimately, westward to America's Euro-dominated future, we can view close-ups of those belonging to alternative thought-worlds. One such close-up that suggests itself is available within the slave narrative genre. For example, observing life from the same plantation space from which Jefferson's observations were generated, Harriet Jacobs, writing in the mid-nineteenth century, addresses herself to the stain or perversity of slavery in Virginia's landscape, describing it as one who has experienced it rather than as one who, like Jefferson, enjoyed its benefits while lamenting its inconsistency with abstract moral and political principles. Living part of her life as a slave with a coerced sexual as well as occupational history, Jacobs wrote to enter a public sphere in which she had no recognized existence. In so doing, she disrupted the story of American democracy that Jefferson and his "fellow" founders were at pains to establish. Lauren Berlant describes the most pertinent implication of Jacobs's narrative: "She opens up a space in which the national politics of corporeal identity becomes displayed on the monarchical body, and thus interferes with the fantasy norms of democratic abstraction."[23]

In contrast with Jefferson's slide from the enumeration of details to disguised polemic, within a single-voiced narration, Jacobs offers a contentious, dialogic approach to facticity. Seeking to undermine the dominant white perspective on the events of slavery, she juxtaposes different voices—for example, providing white slaveholder articulations and then following their versions with different ones, supplied in the narrator's voice.[24] And sensitive to the perils of writing primarily for white female readers in the North, whom she understands to have easily offended sexual sensibilities, Jacobs's text is a mixed genre; it combines "the generic conventions of the slave narrative to those of the sentimental novel."[25]

There are also notable commentaries by Native and African Americans on Jefferson's most famous document, the Declaration of Independence. For example, noting the gap between the Declaration's ideals and application, the eighteenth-century Pequot writer William Apess addresses himself to the contrast between a Native American patriot, King Philip, whose promises were reliable, with the duplicity of the Euro-American founders.[26] And in his autobiography, Apess appropriates Jefferson's terms—for example, "the tree of liberty," as he urges white Americans to apply their principles equally to Indians. Similarly, the African American writer David Walker penned an "*Appeal . . .*" not only to "*the Colored Citizens of the World*" but also "*and very Expressly to Those of the United States of America.*"[27] Published privately in Boston and often confiscated and suppressed during its dissemination, Walker's appeal refers to the "disparity between the condition of people of African descent in the United States and the 'inalienable rights' and republican principles laid out in the Declaration of Independence."[28]

African American contributions to American political theory have since flourished. For example, at the end of the twentieth century, the work of a critical geographer, Clyde Woods, presents a challenge to both the democratic conceits assumed in Jefferson's image of a less racialist American future and Shklar's narrative of the democratizing tendencies of the social sciences. Focusing on the legacy of the plantation, Woods argues that while it may no longer be the only economic unit in the southern region, it retains not only a "monopoly over agricultural manufacturing, banking, land, and water," but also remains a dominant "world view."[29] Over the last century and a half, "plantation bloc explanation" has persisted, aided and abetted by the social sciences. Noting the collusive role of American social science with "the planters' mythical ethno-regional system of explanation,"[30] Woods shows how influential social science texts allowed the "plantation" as a system of explanation to migrate into a general frame of public policy discourse. The plantation's social science epistemological fellow travelers reside in a history of research running from the mid-nineteenth century (for example, George Fitzhugh's *Sociology of the South, or the Future of Free Society*) through the twentieth century—for example, "modernization theory," which supported the "false belief that industrial growth would eliminate racial inequality."[31] In any case, the social science story within which Shklar locates Jefferson looms less large in the history of Euro-American domination than a cartographic story, to which I now turn.

Jefferson the Surveyor

While Jefferson's role in the contentious history of America's democratic founding is usually treated through a focus on the Declaration of Independence and the American Constitution, arguably his role in creating a Euro-American empire is most manifest in his 1784 and 1785 drafts of the Land Ordinance (implemented by the Congress in 1785), which established a rectangular system for surveying the American continent. The act stated that under the aegis of a "Geographer of the United States," a surveyor from each of the states, appointed by the Congress, "shall proceed to divide said territory into townships of six miles square, by lines running due South, and others crossing these at right angles."[32] Effectively, after imposing a European thought-world on Virginia's land- and ethnoscape, and acting with the presumption that nature was summoning a Euro-American future, Jefferson laid the foundation for imposing the Euro-oriented spatial system and practice of valuing westward. His Ordinance turned "nature" into property. Just as he had rendered the continent's ethnocape into a nominal grid (for "natural history" is primarily the "arrangement of elements into a grid"),[33] he turned the American landscape into a geographic grid, rendering it as an abstract commodity. The Land Ordinance of 1785, which created a checker board whose square mile parcels were assembled as the building blocks for townships, after the system that had been established in New England, has been historically far reaching. As Irene de Sousa Santos observes, "[b]y creating it, Thomas Jefferson drew the grid that would map the U.S. territory practically as we know it today."[34]

In his time, the Ordinance was Jefferson's solution to what he regarded as a troubling diversity. Extending a geographically homogeneous, agriculturally oriented nation-state westward, the act served to negate "diversities of geography and population" and impose a unity in the form of a rigid, geometric abstraction, "a homogeneous cellular medium of life."[35] Finitely situated in a particular world of encounter between alternative spatial practices and modes of valuing, Jefferson sought to dissimulate that finitude into an abstract universality rather than negotiate a co-presence among alternative life worlds. As an extension of enlightenment geography, a "geometric rationalization of space," Jefferson's Ordinance instigated a surveying process that began at the Ohio River and on a line between Virginia and Pennsylvania. Once extended, the surveying process eventually imposed a global model on local domains, consummating the encounter in which, as Enrique Dussel puts it, "Indigenous America felt the impact of the first globalization."[36] As a result, "the multiple local spaces of the Indian became simply insignificant."[37] By the 1930s, Black Elk (an Oglala-Sioux) described the consequence in his dictated biography as a radical diminution of the shared biosphere of Native American nations: "Once we were happy in our own country. . . . But the Wasichus [Euro-Americans] came, and they have made little islands for us and the other little islands for the four-leggeds, and always these islands are becoming smaller, for around them surges the gnawing flood of the Wasichu; and it is dirty with lies and greed."[38]

Black Elk's efforts at resisting the white encroachment in the West in the late nineteenth century were preceded in the early part of that century at the Mississippi by the Sauk warrior Black Hawk, whose armed and textual resistance were both notable (in the Black Hawk War and in his biography, respectively).[39] Opposing his fellow Sauk leader Keochuk's passive acceptance of a treaty that pushed his nation west of the Mississippi, Black Hawk was outraged at the idea of abandoning the lands where his ancestors were buried: "When I called to mind the scenes of my youth and those of later days, when I reflected that the theater on which these were acted, had been so long the home of my fathers, who now slept on the hills around it, I could not bring my mind to consent to leave this country to the whites for any earthly consideration."[40] Rather than a grid of exploitable pieces of property,

Black Hawk saw the landscape as embodied national history. Seeking to preserve that legacy, he resolutely crossed to the east of the river with his warriors to reclaim his territory. His text, dictated to a mixed-blood interpreter after his defeat by the militias formed by Illinois governor John Reynolds, offers an extended discourse on dual nationhood. He casts himself as the personification of the Sauk nation, and seeing America as two nations, he wonders why they were not able to meet on equal footing: "What I wanted to say to these people . . . not to settle on our lands, nor trouble our fences, that there was plenty of land in the country for them to settle."[41] And he wonders why the whites (especially the Americans, for the British had been more true to their promises) could not be relied upon to negotiate an equitable co-existence: "I was puzzled to find out how the white people reasoned, and began to doubt whether they had any standard of right and wrong."[42]

Black Hawk's literary resistance to the Euro-American ethnic rationalization of continental space sits near the beginning of a continuing struggle by Native American writers, many of whom articulate alternative cultural geographies. They, along with other "hyphenated" Americans, African-, Latino-, and Caribbean- (among others), reflect a diverse and fractionated social order from which counter-memories emerge to challenge the conventional story of America's freely inaugurated democratic covenant, celebrated by those who restrict "American political theory" to Euro-American founders and subsequent Euro-American political theorists. Before considering some examples of diverse contemporary writers who contribute versions of American political thought by providing counter-memories that issue from diverse historical trajectories, I turn to Thomas Pynchon's parodic treatment of the surveying process (and cultural effacement) that Jefferson helped inaugurate, because it provides an apt critique of Jefferson's enlightenment rationality as well as his diversity-effacing abstractions. Moreover, as a many-voiced genre that exposes the consequences of Jefferson et al.'s imperial ambitions and brings into dialogue many voices that the foundational Euro-American monologue ignores, it provides a threshold for accessing alternative thought-worlds.

An Encounter of Thomases: Pynchon's *Mason & Dixon*

Jefferson's cartographic rationalization of the American continent can be framed within a grammatical metaphor that shapes much of

Pynchon's novel, which is written not only about the late eighteenth century but also in its idioms. Effectively, Jefferson's cartographic initiatives turned the subjunctive into the declarative. Whatever possibilities for alternative articulations of America might have existed, most were effaced as Jefferson's grid made "American geography into a single semiotic system."[43] As Pynchon's novelistic version of the two historical characters Charles Mason (1728–1786) and Jeremiah Dixon (1733–1779) pursue their surveying task westward, "subjunctive hopes" lose their hold on imaginations. Each hope can abide only until "the next Territory to the West be seen and recorded, measur'd and tied in, back into the network of Points already known, that slowly triangulates its Way into the Continent, changing all from subjunctive to declarative, reducing Possibilities to Simplicities that serve the ends of Governments."[44]

While Jefferson's lifelong efforts were aimed at turning contingency into necessity, Pynchon's novel does the reverse. Throughout the narrative, the contingency of America's emerging Euro-American-dominated institutions continually asserts itself. In the novel's opening section on "Latitudes and Departures," the imperial process is signaled as Mason and Dixon are carried from England to the African Cape, following the Atlantic's imperial trade routes. Once they are in America, the juxtaposition between Jefferson's commitment to a predestined American ethnogenesis and the novel's deconstruction of it are displayed in stark relief when Jefferson himself makes a brief appearance. While in Virginia, sitting in Raleigh's Tavern (a place described as "congenial to the unmediated newness of History a-transpiring"), Dixon, a *bon vivant* and reveler (in contrast with the austere Presbyterian Mason), raises his ale-can and offers a toast: "To the pursuit of Happiness." An unnamed Jefferson hears the toast: "Hey, Sir, — that is excellent!" exclaims a tall, red-headed youth at the next table. "Ain't it oh so true. . . . You don't mind if I use the Phrase sometime?" After he borrows a pencil and a scrap of paper to record the historically sacrilized phrase, the "Landlord," recognizing that the drinker is a surveyor, either Mason or Dixon, says: "Tom takes a *Relative* interest in West lines . . . his father having help'd run the one that forms our own southern border."[45]

The word "relative" here serves as more than a pun; it suggests that Jefferson's westward interest is part of his patrimony. In addition to its implied reference to his father (Peter Jefferson was a surveyor and mapmaker), it also implies that the westward expansion of Euro-America is of a piece with the imperial transfer from Europe to the Americas. Sensitive to the confrontation that the imperial surveying process entailed, the novel contrasts Euro- and Native American cultural geographies, mapping aspects of the ground plan that Mason and Dixon's survey effectively overcodes. Initially hired to establish the boundary between Pennsylvania and Maryland, Mason and Dixon discover that "Previous lines run through the supposedly boundless forest."[46] And subsequently, when the two surveyors are "join'd by a Delegation of Indians . . . most of them Mohawk fighters," they reach "a certain Warrior Path," which they are given to understand is as far west as they should proceed.[47]

They are told that this is not a mere Indian trail, not just an "important road," but rather "one of the major High-ways of all inland America." It is in effect a cultural boundary, and the chapter goes on to treat the incommensurate cultural geographies that pertain to various European and indigenous personae — Jesuits, Encyclopedists, members of the Royal Society on the one hand, and Native American nations on the other. Were the Europeans to cross the Warrior Path (which is not clearly visible and has a "sub-audible Hum of . . . Traffic"), they are informed, the result would be "not only the metaphysickal Encounter of Ancient Savagery with Modern Science," but also the imposition of a different "civic Entity."[48] Rather than merely helping to consummate the invention of a predestined nation-state, they are involved, as Mason puts it, in "trespass, each day ever more deeply."[49]

To follow the exploits of Mason and Dixon, then, is not simply to read of the exploits of scientific adventurers. *Mason & Dixon* is a (novelistic) historico-philosophical-political treatise. As the narrative of their surveying proceeds, the reader must become less convinced that Mason and Dixon are merely advancing science. And as far as their role in history is concerned, a soliloquy by the novel's main narrator, the Reverend Wick Cherrycoke, gives voice to Pynchon's notion of the multiplicity that is history against attempts to appropriate it to particular interests. "History is hir'd, or coerc'd only in interests that must prove base,"[50] the Reverend states. Rather than leaving history to "anyone in power,"[51] it must be put in the hands of those with the wit not to impose a unitary facticity but to recognize multiplicity:

Facts are but the Play-things of Lawyers, — Tops and Hoops, forever a-spin. . . . Alas the Historian may indulge no such idle Rotating. History is not Chronology for that is left to lawyers,—nor is it Remembrance, for Remembrance belongs to the People [the historian, he adds, must have the "wit"]—that there may ever continue more than one life-line back into a Past we risk, each day losing our forebears in forever,—not a Chain of single links, for one broken link could lose us All,— rather, a great disorderly Tangle of Lines, long and short, weak and strong, vanishing into the Mnemonick Deep, with only their Destination in common.[52]

Throughout the novel Mason and Dixon serve as the thought ve-hicles of that multiplicity. They function, in Gilles Deleuze and Felix Guattari's terms, as "conceptual personae," performing in Pynchon's text the role that Socrates performs in Plato's. They are vehicles to en-act the author's conceptual apparatus.[53] The contrast is dramatic; while Jefferson's politics are disguised in his objectivist-style descriptive lan-guage, Pynchon's *Mason & Dixon*, a dialogic rather than monologic text, has characters who serve as the contrapuntal carriers of Pynchon's politically acute historical analysis. At one point Mason affirms his role as conceptual persona explicitly when he notes that he and his fellow astronomical observers are not mired in mere details but are "philo-sophical Frigates."[54] And once he and Dixon take up their surveying task, and have taken their philosophical commitments, as well as their technical apparatuses, on the road, Mason refers to his team as part of the European "Mobility." They are not simply sitting in a status and are not mere measurers; they are involved in "Acts that in Whitehall would merit hanging" but are not criminalized on the Euro-dominated American scene. It is a political rather than merely a scientific map-ping, as is implied when Dixon apprehends "something invisible going on," and Mason says that it is "American politics."[55]

Pynchon's novel makes evident that Mason and Dixon's enterprise is not a minor, technical task; the surveyors are involved in a world-his-torical project. As they assist in imposing the European thought-world, they liken themselves to another historically significant actor in an earlier globalizing, ecumenical caper, Mark Antony, one who would "lose the world for Cleopatra . . . not Dick his Day's Wages at the Tav-ern."[56] And one of Dixon's interlocutors attests to the global scale of the surveying enterprise. Referring first to an earlier, religious ecumene, when the globe was coded spiritually, allowing for much more enigma, he offers a brief genealogy of the forces coding the planet, noting that

where once "Forms of land, the flow of water, the occurrence of what us'd to be call'd Miracles" obtained, the present "Age sees a corruption of the ancient Magick," dominated by "Projectors, Brokers of Capital, Insurancers, Pedlars, Enterprisers and Quacks."[57]
    Articulating the politics of the survey, the novel makes clear that "[t]he surveyor . . . replicates not just the 'environment' in some abstract sense but equally the territorial imperatives of a particular political system."[58] And it emphasizes the violence associated with the Euro-American ethnogenesis that Mason and Dixon's surveying aids and abets. The surveyors "mark the Earth with geometric Scars,"[59] and, at one point, a squire refers to their task as a "Geometry of slaughter."[60] Moreover, before the novel is finished, the surveyors learn that they are in a world where slavery is the rule. Masked by the discourse of enlightenment science are practices of oppression, which Dixon especially (Mason remains relatively naive to the end) comes to acknowledge as he notes how unfriendly the world they are enacting is to alternative ones,[61] and, more specifically, that the American complaint about their treatment by the British pales in comparison with "how both of you treat the African Slaves, and the Indian Native here."[62] Ultimately, Dixon's gradually evolving awareness constitutes the novel as a challenge to the liberal democratizing narrative of America's continental expansion. Looking at the surveying process, rather than the Declaration of Independence, as the foundational nation-building enactment reveals a project that Dixon describes as the drawing of "a Line between their Slave-Keepers, and their Wage-Payers."[63] The Reverend Cherrycoke is explicit about this darker side of the American experiment, noting that "the word *Liberty*, so unreflectively sacred to us today, was taken in those Times [the period of the survey] to encompass even the darkest of Men's rights."[64] In contrast with Jefferson's optimistic attachment to enlightenment rationality, Pynchon's novel reveals the dark side of the Euro-American enactment of the enlightenment through its surveying vehicles, and, through the words of the Reverend Cherrycoke, makes a case for radical doubt.

The Method of Radical Doubt

There are two conceptual frames within which Pynchon's novel contests the enlightenment conceits animating Mason and Dixon's surveying task. One is geographic. Despite their attempt to draw a definitive, unambiguous boundary line (a total rationalizing of what they confront initially as "a realm of doubt"), the task cannot be consummated because of a "Wedge," a triangular section in Delaware that is "priz'd for its Ambiguity" and inhabited by "all whose Wish, hardly uncommon in this Era of fluid identity, is not to reside anywhere."[65] The "Wedge" contains unresolvable anomalies and cannot be unambiguously divided. While those on either side of Mason and Dixon's line are on a course to be located within clear, universalized collective identities, those within the Wedge "occupy a singular location in the emerging moral Geometry."[66] Rather than being enlisted within the new *terra cognita*, the enlightenment spatial politics organizing the rest of the surveyed domain, those residing in the Wedge occupy an "unseen World, beyond Resolution, of transactions never recorded," and they resist being drawn into the moral crotchets that pertain to the new spatial politics. Their world, which resists definitive surveying, is "[a] small geographick Anomaly, a-bustle with Appetites high and low."[67] And Dixon himself never capitulates to the Jeffersonian enlightenment program of turning all of America into an unambiguous grid. For example, when he encounters the American surveyor Isaac Shelby, he is put off by Shelby's totalizing approach to the survey—"Shelby's rabid pleasure in converting space to lines and angles"—and, more generally, to the Jeffersonian teleology of an America that "waits the surveyor."[68]

Supplementing "the realm of doubt," which Mason and Dixon's survey cannot wholly rationalize, is a second conceptual frame, to which the narrator, Reverend Cherrycoke, refers as "Christic doubt." One of his "undeliver'd sermons" reads in part:

> Doubt is the essence of Christ. Of the twelve Apostles, most true to him was ever Thomas,—indeed, in the *Acta Thomae* they are said to be twins. The final pure Christ is pure uncertainty. He is become the central subjunctive fact of a Faith, that risks ev'rything upon one bodily Resurrection. . . . Wouldn't something less doubtable have done? A prophetic dream, a communication with a dead person? Some few tatters of evidence to wrap our poor naked spirits against the coldness of the World where Mortality and its Agents may bully their way, wherever they wish to go. . . .[69]

Through his narrator, Pynchon interweaves the value of (Christic) doubt with his novelistic treatise on the threat to the subjunctive spaces of America—the depluralizing assault—that Mason and Dixon's surveying process poses. Pynchon prizes a "fluxational reality" that is being compromised by Mason and Dixon's Jeffersonian "protracted ceremony of ordinance."[70] To preserve a "subjunctive America" against the rationalization of the surveying process, Pynchon's method of radical doubt is enacted in part through the Reverend Cherrycoke's image of a re-enchanted Earth that retains the air of the mystery and doubt that one finds elaborated in Eastern religions. Cherrycoke articulates this image in a sermon-like narration throughout the novel. But *Mason & Dixon*'s critique of the way the enlightenment was visited on the Americas is political as well as epistemological. Because in one instance it refers to "the cruel sugar islands," it is appropriate to summon a contemporary voice that hails from one of them, Antigua. The voice belongs to Jamaica Kincaid, a naturalized American, who provides yet another alternative perspective on Jefferson's imperial project.[71]

Kincaid contra Jefferson

Kincaid is a descendant of the coerced labor force in the Caribbean, where slaves with no control over the conditions or pace of the work produced both cotton and sugar, the latter a product that by the mid-seventeenth century (and for one and a half centuries thereafter) was "by far the most valuable product exported from the Americas."[72] She became a writer after initially arriving in the United States as a servant (an au pair). She is now nationally and culturally divided. As she puts it, "My feet are (so to speak) in two worlds."[73] Given a heritage of coerced labor and her experience as a bonded servant, it is not surprising that Kincaid sees Jefferson et al.'s democratic experiment differently from those who unambivalently celebrate the creation of America's founding documents. For example, while viewing the famous portrait of the signers of the Declaration of Independence in Philadelphia's Liberty Hall, Kincaid ponders the occupational infrastructure of their studied ease. Evincing an imagination of those not in the picture, but whose labor has assisted in the enactment of the European thought-world in America's founding, she says: "America begins with the Declaration of Independence . . . but who really needs this document. . . . There is a painting in Philadelphia of the men who signed it. These men looked relaxed; they are enjoying the activity of thinking, the luxury of it. They have time to examine this thing called their conscience and to act on it . . . some keep their hair in an unkempt style (Jefferson, Washington), and others keep their hair well groomed (Franklin), their clothes pressed." She then speaks of those who have worked to prepare the men for the occasion, "the people who made their beds and made their clothes nicely pressed and their hair well groomed or in a state of studied dishevelment."[74]

The "disheveled" Jefferson also appears in what is arguably Kincaid's most politically perspicuous work. Written mostly in a personal, autobiographical style and innocently entitled *My Garden Book,* the work is a trenchant analysis of the botanical imperialism that Europeans visited on the Americas. She refers to Jefferson as "a great gardener in his time" and notes that he "owned slaves and strongly supported the idea of an expanded American territory, which meant the demise of the people who owned and lived on the land. At the same time, he passionately advocated ideas about freedom, ideas that the descendants of the slaves and the people who were defeated and robbed could use in defense of themselves."[75]

Although Kincaid's reflection on the contradiction that impugns Jefferson's legacy in the tradition of American democratic thought frames the analysis in her garden book, her more significant contra-Jeffersonian story is contained in her treatment of the imposition of names that European thinkers lent to the botany of the Americas. Prior to the imperial acts of naming, "in the beginning," she notes, "the vegetable kingdom was chaos, people everywhere called the same things by a name that made sense to them."[76] Subsequently, however, the imperial project of naming, which purported to impose names "arrived at by an objective standard,"[77] was part of the process of possession, imposing "a spiritual padlock with the key thrown irretrievably away . . . an erasing."[78]

While Jefferson saw the Linnaean system for classifying the botanical world as merely an aid to a universalizing knowledge project, Kincaid, noting that Linnaeus developed his views within the garden of a rich man in the Netherlands, connects the Linnaean order with the process of conquest, in which people like her, people of "the conquered class," lost control over the meanings of both their places and their bodies.[79] The imperially imposed mode of the garden exemplifies that loss of control: "The botanical garden reinforced for me how powerful were the people who had conquered me; they could bring to me the botany of the world they owned."[80] Reacting to this recognition, Kincaid notes that her construction of her garden is "an exercise in memory, a way of remembering my own immediate past, a way of getting to a past that is my own."[81] In short, Kincaid's gardening is a practice of counter-memory, a recoding and recovery of the world effaced by the botanical part of imperialism's coding practices.[82]

The politics of counter-memory that Kincaid's garden book offers derives much of its historical context from the symbolic relationship of the English garden to both Britain's and Euro-America's imperial expansion. Pynchon offers a brief hint of the connection when his version of Jeremiah Dixon refers to England as "that Garden of Fools," while pointing out to Mason that the common element in the venues in which they have worked is the institution of slavery.[83] Historically, the special valence of the English garden, an exemplar of Euro-civilizational order, arises from a juxtaposition between England and the others who experienced England's imperial ambitions. As Stephen Daniels points out, "the very regional reach of English imperialism, into alien lands, was accompanied by a countervailing sentiment for cosy home scenery, for thatched cottages and gardens in pastoral countryside."[84] Before the wildness of the Americas constituted an invidious otherness for the English, Ireland was England's ecologically and culturally uncivilized other: "It was the Irish 'wilderness' that bounded the English garden, Irish 'barbarity' that defined English civility, Irish papistry and 'superstition' that warranted English religion; it was Irish 'lawlessness' that demonstrated the superiority of English law and Irish 'wandering' that defined the settled and centered nature of English society."[85]

There is abundant evidence that Jefferson's model for Europeanizing the American landscape was greatly influenced by his admiration of the English garden, which, unlike the overly manicured French variety, seemed to allow the order of nature to articulate itself within the order of the garden. Instead of "formal lines of trees and paths," characteristic of the baroque era, the English garden of the neo-classical era, which manifested "a cultivated but naturalistic landscape," and often "invoked historical and archeological images,"[86] supplied Jefferson with a model for a symbolic order as well as a conceptual vehicle for turning nature into history. Reading widely in the literature of European gardens as well as observing many models in his travels, Jefferson's attachment to gardening, his micromanaging of his estate's garden, constituted a prototype for his subsequent attempt to shape the landscape of the continent as a whole. Just as he anglicized the landscape of his own property, he sought to anglicize the American landscape.[87]

Picking up this historical theme, Kincaid notes that in contrast with the English, who seem to be led to obsessively order and shape their landscape, "obsessive order is lacking in Antiguan people."[88] And, reversing the historical valence of the British imperial project, Kincaid enjoys the disorder of her garden, which she sees as part of her resistance to the historical domination of the English with "their love, their need to isolate, name, objectify, possess various parts, people, and things in the world."[89] Kincaid's reflections on Anglo American botanical imperialism serve to decode the process of colonial objectification both generally and specifically. At a general level, she sees the world of transplanted species in terms of their role in the creation of coerced labor—for example, offering a gloss on cotton in terms of "the tormented, malevolent role it has played in my ancestral history."[90] And commenting on the breadfruit, which was sent to the West Indies by Joseph Banks (the botanist accompanying Captain Cook) and was "meant to be a cheap food to feed slaves," she observes, "in a place like Antigua the breadfruit is not a food, it is a weapon."[91]

Ultimately, Kincaid recognizes the organization of her garden as a way to reestablish part of the Antigua that was overcoded by botanical imperialism. It is both a "map of the Caribbean and the sea that surrounds it" and "an exercise of memory; a way of remembering my own immediate past, a way of getting to a past that is my own."[92] Kincaid's garden is therefore a text that exposes the historical hold of the colonizing/naming process that has gripped her homeland and imposed a history within which she "and all who look like me"[93] cannot recognize themselves. In challenging and denaturalizing the world of names that the colonizing process imposed on the Americas, her garden book accords well with Pynchon's deconstruction of the surveying process on the American continent.

Writing as Counter-Memory

As is the case with Jamaica Kincaid's novels and commentaries, much of the politics of contemporary "ethnic" American writing reflects the counter-memories of those groups that have been victimized by a history of political economy associated with the formation of the Euro-oriented model of political order, which was largely responsible for depositing or spatially containing the diverse bodies that inhabit the system of disparate but interconnected social fields within the nation-states of the Americas. For example, in the U.S. case, many African American writers, Native American writers, and third world migrant writers do not, as much of Euro-American theorizing implies, select from extant idioms within the hierarchy of available styles that have persisted within state-dominated social orders.[94] Rather, their writing expresses profound ambivalence toward the dominant literary field within which their work is deployed, precisely because of the tendency of that field to be complicit with the state's presumption (its primary mode of "thought") that it governs a culturally singular social order.

Although there are numerous examples, here I focus on three writers with diverse and fraught relationships with the dominant American social and political imaginaries. All three express explicit ambivalences about participating in America's mainstream, commercially controlled literary culture. And they resist a simplistic identity politics that would quarantine their ethnic address. Michelle Cliff, a diasporic Jamaican, Sherman Alexie, a Native American, and Toni Morrison, an African American, enact in their writing modes of thought that challenge the conventional nation-building narrative within which every individual is an undifferentiated citizen subject, the social order is merely an ahistorical class structure, and individuals can be allocated unambiguously to racial and ethnic groupings.

Michelle Cliff.   Michelle Cliff is explicit about her desire for her writing to produce a counter-memory to the prevailing, mono-ethnic versions of an American history in which, among other things, "the history of armed and organized African American resistance has been made unimaginable." "It is through fiction," she states, "that some of us rescue the American past."[95] Moreover, her observations on languages, expressed by one of her fictional characters, serves to characterize the agenda for writers who recognize the ideational traps lurking in the familiar systems of intelligibility created by a historical trajectory of Euro-American political thought. In her novel *Free Enterprise*, the narrator refers to the historical role of each language's participation in the imperial domination of her homeland. "English," she says, "was the tongue of commerce." "Spanish was the language of categories" (by which she means the creation of a biopolitical matrix of economically and politically ineligible, miscegenated blood types), and "Latin was the language of Christian spiritual hegemony." "Against these tongues," she adds, "African of every stripe collided."[96]

Like Kincaid, Cliff stands with "her feet . . . in two worlds" and thus writes not only in an English toward which she feels ambivalent but also from disjunctive loci of enunciation.[97] Identifying with the diasporic part of social order, which cannot be comfortably assimilated as unitary national subjects, much of her writing focuses on transnational lives. For example, in her novel *No Telephone to Heaven*, a diasporic perspective is enacted both geopolitically and linguistically—geopolitically by the back and forth movement of her main character, Kitty Savage, between the United States and Jamaica (as well as back and forth from England) and linguistically in the collision of idioms, standard English and Jamaican patois, and in the novel's anti-narrative structure, a set of dissociated narrative fragments.

Cliff's novelistic contribution to diversifying America's thought-worlds reflects a significant historical change in the role of that genre, which in the nineteenth and early twentieth centuries displaced other narrative forms in the third world. Although initially the novel was primarily a nation-building genre, subsequently Cliff, like many other third world writers, diasporic and otherwise, have made the novel a site of resistance to the global, national, and social imaginaries of the "first world."[98] Yet Cliff evinces a profound ambivalence toward writing in general because she recognizes the difficulty of extracting a thought from the outside within languages that encode a dominant Anglo American thought-world.[99] As she has noted, her primary linguistic imaginary is silence, a form of resistant aphasia, which she sees as the ultimate discursive location for one who would wholly resist the colonizing forces within language.[100]

Cliff's political inflection of silence is manifested in her *No Telephone to Heaven* when her character Kitty Savage is described as breaking her silence when she discovers a shop with Jamaican foods in New York.[101] Ultimately, Cliff's "attempt to bound off a space of silence via the symptom of aphasia"[102] is never consummated. She continues to write, while her aphasic imaginary reflects her suspicion that however hybrid and resistant her cacophony of voices and assemblage of narrative fragments in her novels are to the dominant idioms and historical memories of the Euro-dominant state, she can never be wholly present to herself as a resisting body in her writing. Nevertheless, her struggle with the ambiguous achievement of an intelligibility that bridges thought-worlds is exemplary. It plays a role in articulating a subjunctive America that the familiar Euro-American narratives (for example, the melting pot story) overcode.

Sherman Alexie.   Like Michelle Cliff and Jamaica Kincaid, Sherman Alexie embodies the split consciousness of one with his feet in two different life worlds. And he shares Cliff's expressed ambivalence toward writing. In his short story "Indian Country," Alexie treats the geographic and ethnographic ambiguity of his Indianness through his character Low Man Smith, a writer and doubtless his alter ego. Low Man describes himself in one of the story's conversations as one who is "not supposed to be anywhere."[103] His Indianness, along with that of other Native American characters, is highly diluted; a "Spokane," he speaks and understands no tribal languages, was born and raised in Seattle, and has visited his own reservation only six times.

The "Indian country" for which Alexie's story provides a fragmentary mapping has resonances with Black Elk's sentiments about how the Euro-American conquest has created an Indian country that consists of "little islands [that are] always . . . becoming smaller." But Alexie adds another, more ambiguous "Indian country." The Indian landscape he maps, which, if represented pictorially, would be a few color flecks on a map of the United States' western states, is also a discursively muffled Indian country. Alexie's dialogic version of the precarious and obscure visibility and audibility of that country is reinforced throughout the story's conversations, which convey a dilemma of intelligibility for Native Americans existing in two alternative thought-worlds, articulated in different idioms. For example, at one point, Low Man asks an older Indian, Raymond, if he is an elder. Shifting to a non-Indian idiom, Raymond replies, "elder than some, not as elder as others."[104]

Reflecting Alexie's awareness of the ways in which Native American sense making is always already colonized by a Euro-American idiom, Low Man Smith manifests a profound ambivalence toward being immersed in the United States' Euro-dominated literary field. He refers to the chain bookstores that carry his books as "colonial clipper ships,"[105] and in the process of moving about an urban venue in search of a non-chain bookstore, he tries to divest himself of his laptop, first trying to trade it in a 7-Eleven convenience store and then handing it to a clerk in a Barnes & Noble bookstore, pretending he found it.

The discursive ambiguities and writer's ambivalence in Alexie's short story are reflected in the condition of his characters throughout his writing—novels, poetry, and screenplays. His Indians struggle within what M. M. Bakhtin refers to as "the framework of other people's words."[106] In several places, Alexie evokes a reversal of the captivity narrative, locating the Indian instead of the white woman as victim. When he worked in Hollywood as a screenwriter, a writing vocation subject to studio revisions, he became blocked, he says, because he "started to hear 'their' voices, those Hollywood voices whenever [he] tried to write anything."[107] And in one of his poems, addressed to Mary Rowlandson's captivity story, he articulates his struggle against captivity by the "[l]anguage of the enemy: *heavy lightness*, house insurance, *serious vanity*, safe-deposit box."[108]

Alexie's response to the perils of linguistic capture is not to retreat to a version of Indian discursive authenticity. As he puts it, he resists the "corn pollen and eagle feather school of poetry."[109] Recognizing that he writes from a colonized locus of enunciation, he articulates the dilemma of the contemporary Indian writer who stands partly within the dominant system of intelligibility (for example, he acknowledges such disparate influences as Stephen King's novels and television's *The Brady Bunch*) but seeks at the same time to disrupt the power relations inherent in conventional sense making. John Newton describes the dilemma of Alexie (and Native American writers) well: "As the subjugated 'other' of an invader discourse synonymous with global media saturation, the Native American subject finds himself spectacularized on a global scale. . . . Alexie makes his stand in the struggle for subjective agency not in some autochthonous interiority but on the flat, open ground of the invader's own image-repertoire."[110]

To figure his dilemma, Alexie invokes the concept of the treaty. Seeing the history of the Euro- and Native American relationships as a series of broken treaties, his love poems are often allegorical; they feature Indian-white romances that must manage the historical and ethnic rift with "tiny treaties."[111] And doubtless, the allegory works at another level; it refers to the treaty that his participation in a white-dominated literary culture represents. Accepting the necessity of using a language that will not allow an expression of an Indianness that escapes Euro-American hegemony, Alexie's writing nevertheless restores another dimension of subjunctive America, however buried it might be within a hybridized and overcoded landscape.

Toni Morrison.   Toni Morrison expresses the same ambivalence toward her participation in U.S. literary culture as Cliff and Alexie. She functions within what she calls "a singular landscape for a writer," inasmuch as she writes "in a nation of people who *decided* that their world view would combine agendas for individual freedom *and* mechanisms for devastating oppression."[112] Given that the extant American literary culture articulates the legacy of this duplicitous founding, there is a paradox inherent in her participation as a novelist in the culture of literacy. Although she "participates in the public sphere constituted by print literacy, . . . her fiction strains to constitute itself as anti-literature and to address a type of racial community that she herself recognizes to be unavailable to the novelist."[113] Morrison's audience/constituency takes on its coherence as a protean transnational black culture, forged as much through structures of exclusion and episodes of displacement as through practices of solidarity. And much of the cultural imaginary, which forms the implied readership of her novels, is "preliterate."[114] Yet like Cliff and Alexie, Morrison continues to write. And, most significantly, her novel *Paradise*, which addresses itself to a historical episode of racial exclusion, effectively enacts the critical posture that Pierre Bourdieu has identified as the antidote to "state thinking," the necessity of creating a "rupture" that challenges the state's "*symbolic* violence," its mobilization of and control over the mental structures that make its institutions appear "*natural*."[115] In Morrison's case, the tools for rupture are literary. They involve, as a commentary on her novel *Beloved* puts it, "the creation of a narrative text that radically opens the literary canon to counter-discursive strategies of re-memory, as well as grounding of the cultural politics of difference in the language of the contingent and the provisional."[116]

Morrison's enactment of a "tool for rupture" is especially evident in her *Paradise* because that novel involves, in Bourdieu's language, "the reconstruction of genesis," which brings "back into view the conflicts and confrontations of the early beginnings and therefore all the discarded possibilities."[117] Her *Paradise* recovers vestiges of a subjunctive America that are obliterated in the dominant version of Euro-America's national memory. Specifically, the "genesis" to which Morrison's novel is addressed is the ideology and story of American exceptionalism that fueled a major aspect of the Euro-American nationhood project. Initially, the religious, patriarchal leaders of the early New England settlers strove to inculcate the presumption that America was to be a new

Jerusalem, "a site specifically favored by God—perhaps the very place that he had chosen to initiate the millennial Kingdom of Christ."[118] Subsequently, from the early nineteenth century on, a secularized version of American exceptionalism has held sway among many American historians, who have been vehicles of "the assumption that the United States, unlike European nations, has a covenant that makes Americans a chosen people who have escaped from the terror of historical change to live in timeless harmony with nature."[119]

The idea of the covenant and the imperatives that flow from it—the need to resist change and the need to maintain the purity of the lineage that is charged with the special mission—produce the woeful consequences described at the beginning and end of Morrison's novel. The novel suggests that at best the exceptionalist narrative stifles politics and at worst it leads to violence. In addition to the closure of the political, the other consequence provides the chilling opening to the novel, whose first line is, "[t]hey kill the white girl first." Thereafter, an understanding of this opening event requires that the reader follow a complex and shifting narrative that eventually explains a deadly attack by a group of men from a covenanted, all-black community in Oklahoma on the women in a nearby women's shelter.[120]

The attackers are from Ruby, a small, western all-black community in which the older members situate themselves in a self-described historical narrative that celebrates the perseverance of their ancestors in the face of rejection and their subsequent redemption through adherence to the codes of a special mission. Descended from former slaves, the town's ancestors left post-Reconstruction discrimination in the late nineteenth-century American South only to be denied entry into both white and black communities in Oklahoma, which, as Morrison had learned, had twenty-six all-black towns at the turn of the twentieth century.[121] The Rubyites' special mission, an African American version of American exceptionalism, is engendered by their rejections, to which they refer in their narrative as the "disallowing." Having walked from Mississippi to Oklahoma, attracted by an advertisement about an all-black town, they discovered that their blackness was a threat to the lighter-skinned "Negroes," who shunned them: "The sign of racial purity they had taken for granted had become a stain."[122]

Coping with the shock of a rejection (which they had expected only from whites), they founded their own all-black community of Haven in Oklahoma and subsequently moved even farther into western

Oklahoma to found Ruby, which they regarded as the fulfilment of their ancestor's intention to construct an Eden, a paradise on earth run by a group of racially pure blacks. The town chronicler, Patricia, summarizes the "8-rocks" (descendants from the original founders) model for maintaining purity: "Unadultered and unadulteried 8-rock blood held its magic as long as it resided in Ruby. That was their recipe. That was their deal. For immortality."[123] But while "Ruby" ("Who can find a virtuous woman? For her price is far above Rubies," Proverbs 16:10, KJV) contains paradisaical signs—for example, the soil seems almost miraculously fertile, so that while Haven had only barren muddy ground, Ruby has flourishing gardens—it also turns out to be a stiflingly conservative, patriarchal, and even misogynistic community. And rather than turning self-reflectively inward to confront divisive issues when the younger Ruby generation departs from the original covenant, the patriarchs of Ruby displace their problems on a nearby community functioning with a different covenant. The assault with which the novel begins is on a shelter for women, whose inhabitants have had intimate relations with some of the town's men. The shelter is in a former convent (in a mansion that had once served as a "cathouse") outside the town.

Morrison's novel enacts Bourdieu's suggestion about the necessity for creating a rupture by returning to the founding myths that sustain violence, actual or symbolic. While identifying a racially fractured America, she contests, at once, the Puritan reading of American exceptionalism and the African American attempt to simulate that exceptionalism and to treat it as a dogma by attempting to preserve or freeze the meanings generated in founding acts. A resistance to the freezing of meanings also characterizes Morrison's approach to her writing. She seeks to avoid "oppressive language . . . [w]hether it is the obscuring state language or the faux-language of mindless media . . . [or] the calcified language of the academy or the commodity driven language of science . . . or language designed for the estrangement of minorities, hiding its racist plunder in its literary cheek."[124]

Conclusion: Redeeming Political Theory and Restoring the Subjunctive

A history of colonialist political economy haunts the writings of Michelle Cliff, Sherman Alexie, and Toni Morrison. Taken together, their texts reflect diverse life worlds that have been assembled by a history of state-directed, and largely coercive, "nation-building" and its attendant forms of political economy. Although they all write in English, "the tongue of commerce," as one of Cliff's characters puts it, rather than merely affirming the world that "English" (in all of its power-related manifestations) has made, they use language in a way that accords with Thomas Pynchon's novelistic restoration of contingency, his displacement of the declarative with the subjunctive. Their articulated ambivalence toward the language within which they write encourages recognition of the contention that the dominant thought-world, recycled in conventional approaches to American political theory, tends to obscure.

However, there is a remaining issue, one of how such a variegated socio-literary order can migrate into an effective notion of the political, one that effectively references the persistence of the "colonial divide" within the present and affords a loosening of the hold of necessity.[125] If we recognize the rifts that such a divide constitutes in what tend to be regarded as homogeneous and coherent national orders, an avenue of transition from the literary examples to a model of the political is provided in Gilles Deleuze and Felix Guattari's critique of the majoritarian emphasis in democratic theory. They argue that no majority has an unproblematic representational value because there is no homogeneous order from which it can be drawn as a quantitative solution. Rather, such "majorities" are a product of "state power and domination." Deleuze and Guattari offer as an example "the average adult-white-heterosexual-male-speaking in a standard language" and note that this "man . . . holds the majority, even if he is less numerous than mosquitos, children, women, blacks, homosexuals."[126] Such a character can constitute a majority by being a norm, or what Deleuze and Guattari call a "majoritarian 'fact'" that "constitutes a homogeneous system in which the minorities are subgroups."[127]

A conventional political response, in which one posits a multicultural solution that creates minority rights, does not address Deleuze and Guattari's critique of the commitments underlying the concept of a majoritarian democracy. The issue for them is not that "minorities" are excluded. Their point is that no majority can represent because there is no definitive unity from which it can be drawn. All such unities are imposed as norms. In the face of such norms, the political gesture that Deleuze and Guattari sponsor is not one of assigning oneself to an extant minority but of becoming minoritarian. Such a becoming is an act of de-identification, an act in which one does not add oneself to a group but rather subtracts onself from all definitive identifications. Inasmuch as essentialized identities achieve their seeming naturalness by eliding the encounters through which the identities are imposed, to "become minoritarian," in Deleuze and Guattari's sense, is to escape fixed essences and thence to be open to encounters; it is to rejoin the contingencies of time and allow new relations to be established and new experiments in life to take shape.

Such a political sensibility provides an insight into how a social order with multiple, historically engendered loci of enunciation maps onto a literary one. The writers Cliff, Alexie, and Morrison—all products of historical encounters and acts of coercion—are in effect minoritarian writers. Like Franz Kafka, Deleuze and Guattari's exemplar of one who becomes minoritarian through writing, they stage new encounters in their writing to affect both the past and present.[128] Writing in the major language but seeking to escape its historical trajectory of domination, they write to "deterritorialize" the extant grid of biopolitical and geopolitical essences. They refigure the past, creating counter-memories that challenge the narrative of an emerging, homogenous society (a definitive declarative) and, at the same time, create the imaginative conditions of possibility for a restoration of the subjunctive, a contingency-embracing order where new relations, based on de-identification with old imposed essences, can flourish.

Finally, the critical achievements of literary texts are also realized in the modern history of political philosophy/theory. In addressing the question of where such critical interventions into dominant thought-worlds sit in a trajectory of philosophico-political thought, my emphasis is on an alternative to the kind of empiricist "fact-mindedness" that was the standard for Judith Shklar's celebration of the thought-world of the founding fathers. As I noted at the outset, Jefferson's fact-mindedness consisted not in disinterested scientific observation but in an enlistment of the natural world as a history-making ally. Using his reading of nature to turn contingency into necessity, Jefferson's version of the natural world promoted a Euro-American, continental ethnogenesis. In contrast with such an approach to facticity, where norms are evoked with reference to a "nature" that is read as an entity independent of human will and as a source of norms for organizing the past, present, and future of the life world, is Miguel Vatter's evocation of the "factical," a

term he applies to a world capable of change as opposed to a world of
fixed essences (for example the world figured by the classical discipline
of natural history).[129]

To elaborate the idea of the factical, Vatter begins by contrasting
the traditional, Platonic notion of facticity, which presupposes a world
of essences, with the idea of virtú in Machiavelli, which he construes as
a form of "factical freedom." It is a freedom that derives from a "movement of transcendence of reality through which an objective or legitimate order of things can be virtualized, i.e. can have its foundation or
essence withdrawn and be reduced to mere appearance, semblance or
ideology."[130] By transcendence, Vatter does not mean a position oriented to an ideal. It is a form of realism that is to be effected in practice;
it results from "the capacity of freedom to transcend an objective state
of affairs . . . [to change] objective reality."[131] Vatter's turn to Machiavelli is thus a recognition of Machiavelli's concern with historical finitude, with "the way we live" rather than with an abstract model of the
good life. Beginning with an appreciation of Machiavelli's approach to
"goodness," which he situates in concrete historical time, Vatter conceives the factical as oriented toward the facticity of historically specific
human conditions. His Machiavellian presumption is that virtú is what
is good and right at a particular time.

Among those who have incorporated the Machiavellian presumption about the historical specificity of what constitutes political virtue
in their attempts to forge philosophies of politics are the contemporary
theorists Michel Foucault and Jacques Derrida. In Foucault's case it
has been through his rethinking of the enlightenment in the light of its
application to historical finitude, to the "historico-critical attitude" that
emerges from a focus on "who we are today" rather than on a model
of timeless, universal rationality.[132] Similarly, Jacques Derrida, edified
by a neo-Machiavellian model of virtú, has addressed himself to what
is distinctive *today* with respect to the bonds uniting political subjects.
In accord with Vatter's suggestion about transcending conventional
political constraints, Derrida, noting that the social order contains attachments that cannot be contained within a nation-state grammar,
suggests that political action can take the form of "protest against citizenship, a protest against membership of a political configuration as
such."[133] Vatter supplies an apt version of this way of construing political action: "Political life becomes dialogical by having to determine
'who ought to rule' in a situation that allows the desire for no-rule to

be voiced by those who are dominated in any given political order. As a consequence, after Machiavelli the question of political freedom in modernity ceases being the classical one of establishing and maintaining the best political form of rule, but instead becomes that of knowing how to change political forms in order to respond to the ever renewed, and never satisfied, demands for freedom as absence of oppression."[134]

Vatter's rendering of the Machiavellian legacy offers a moral geography that comports well with the model of a divided socio-literary order I have proposed. Given the rifts in the order that reflect the persistence of a colonial divide and thus the lack of a homogeneous social order, from which diverse political positions can be brought into a unifying political discourse, Vatter's model of the good and the right offers an appropriate alternative to conventional, statist models of political freedom. His concept of political freedom entertains the possibility of rejecting the dominant form of rule and has the effect of decentering "the moral point of view."[135] In accord with a politics that would loosen the institutionalized declarative and restore a subjunctive "America," Vatter's version of fact-mindedness (his evocation of the "factical") points to "the capacity to remove [the] 'conditions of necessity,'"[136] which Thomas Jefferson helped to put in place and which have since been affirmed by a conventional history of American political thought. In chapter 2, I again evoke Judith Shklar's conception of fact-mindedness in order both to extend my critique of the politics of facticity that obtains within a conventional empiricist epistemological imaginary and to set up the epistemological frame within which I adduce the implications of a non-essentialist, multiethnic, and a multigenre approach to American political thought.

2 The Micropolitics of Crime

Aesthetic Comprehension and the "Brutality of Fact"

Vocations of Political Theory

During the latter half of the twentieth century, Judith Shklar's vocational model for political theory, analyzed in chapter 1, stood in dramatic contrast with that of another notable political theorist, Sheldon Wolin. While they both evinced deep commitments to American democracy, produced influential bodies of work, and served as mentors to generations of political theory students, they diverged sharply in their views of the political theory–social science relationship.[1] Wolin viewed the development of a method-obsessed, social scientization of political science as radically incompatible with the vocation of the political theorist. In contrast, Shklar insisted that there is a fundamentally congenial relationship between political theory and social and political science because both are committed to scientific rigor. Wolin, writing during a cold war– and Vietnam War–influenced period of intense turmoil within the U.S. political culture at large as well as within academic institutions, sought to redeem the "tradition" of political theory.[2] He indicted the behaviorist trend in political science for its "methodism," for exhausting the space of political education with methodological details to the neglect of a historically informed and politically engaged knowledge. Shklar, writing more than twenty years later, during a period of the United States' post–cold war Reagan years triumphalism, sought to redeem American political theory by suggesting that its major (Euro-American) progenitors, Jefferson, Madison, and Hamilton, were as rigorous as modern social scientists, and that at its best, political theory remains "far from being demeaning and scientifically superfluous," it continues to share social science's fact-mindedness.[3]

In this chapter, I review alternative views of facticity, prompted by Wolin and Shklar's contrasting efforts at redeeming political theory, and go on to elaborate an approach to political thinking that relies on what Gilles Deleuze, in accord with his ambivalent relationship to Immanuel Kant's philosophical legacy, calls "aesthetic comprehension."[4] Then, pursuing the implications of this mode of comprehension, I offer readings of the crime stories of diverse "ethnic" Americans—brief treatments of Euro-, Latino, and Asian American versions and extended treatments of African and Native American examples—in order both to analyze the ways that facticity emerges from alternative experiential and interpretive loci and to expose the micropolitical differences that obtain across the United States' different experiential- and thought-worlds. Jacques Rancière's observation connecting aesthetics, politics, and alternative worlds is apropos here: "The aesthetic nature of politics," he notes, directs our attention not to "a specific single world," but to "a world of competing worlds."[5]

One of those competing thought-worlds, which is manifested in a novel that articulates a crime story with a philosophically oriented racial allegory, is exemplary with respect to the tensions and connections I am exploring. In *The Intuitionist*, Colson Whitehead constructs an allegorical plot that ties issues of racial inequality to contending epistemologies of elevator inspection in America's most vertical (read hierarchical) venue, the metropolis (seemingly modeled on New York City).[6] Bearing comparison with the Shklar-Wolin encounter, the tension in the novel involves two warring factions in the city's Department of Elevator Inspection: the empiricists, who operate within a data-oriented rationalism, and the intuitionists, who rely on instinct and tacit knowledge. Much of the plot is centered around the writings of the (fictional) late author James Fulton, the trajectory of whose various treatises closely matches the progression of Immanuel Kant's critiques. Fulton, revealed to be an African American who has passed for white, began his theorizing of elevators with a canonical, empiricist text, but he subsequently published one entitled *Theoretical Elevators*, a treatise that introduces an intuitionist elevator inspection philosophy to which the novel's protagonist, Lila Mae Watson, the Department's first black woman employee, is a devotee. Lila Mae's intuitionist approach, which distinguishes her both epistemically and politically, is predicated on the assumption that no account of the practice of inspection can yield a closed, final reality (as in Kant's discovery, articulated in his third critique, that the subjective faculties cannot achieve "subjective necessity" or a definitive accord with the world of things). She ultimately becomes a civically engaged "citizen of the city to come."[7]

Aside from the drama surrounding the protagonist, whose life is threatened by empiricists seeking to cover their errors and intrigues, the novel's philosophical trajectory constitutes its primary mode of thought. The Kantian-type clash of reason and imagination, which Fulton's later text exhibits, constitutes a challenge to the scientific rationality of his first text, in which he had argued that "the light of reason" alone is an adequate basis for understanding elevators. While Fulton's revisions of his position, especially his unpublished third text, which anticipates a more flexible, even utopian urban modernity, are the ultimate inspiration for Lila Mae to embrace the contingencies associated with a future city life, whose characteristics cannot be reliably anticipated, it is the novel's composition and conceptual insights that inspire me. Whitehead's inter-articulation of a crime story, an allegory of the city's racial-spatial order, and the problem of knowledge sets the stage for the philosophical, methodological, and illustrative materials in this chapter, which I inaugurate with attention to the Shklar-Wolin encounter over method, context, and, ultimately, the determination of how to approach facticity.

What is the nature of the divide between Shklar's and Wolin's approaches to facticity? For Shklar, to be fact-minded is to operate within a pre-Kantian, epistemological perspective. Her world of facts, like that of mainstream social science, exists independently of the activity of theorizing. To theorize within such an epistemological imaginary is to subject your theoretical apparatus rigorously to what can be observed in the world. In contrast, Wolin rejects the radical separation between theoretical commitments and facticity. As he puts it, "Perhaps facts are somehow molded by the logical forms of fact-stating language."[8] Heeding the Kantian epistemological revolution, Wolin rejects the simplistic model of objectivity that privileges "detachment, fidelity to fact and deference to intersubjective verification by a community of practitioners." He asserts that rather than presuming a pre-given world of objects and points of observation, knowledge judgments are predicated on a contingent context. "Method" [in the sense in which empiricists construct it], he writes, "is not a thing for all worlds. It presupposes a certain answer to a Kantian type question, what must the world be like for the methodist's knowledge to be possible?"[9]

Aesthetic Comprehension

While I accept the primary implication that Wolin derives from his critique—an injunction to the theorist to resist a fixation on method and to be alert instead to the political implications of choosing among alternative theoretical options—my focus here is on his brief evocation of "a Kantian type question," in which he recognizes that epistemological issues are not exhausted by attention to verifying one's observations. As Deleuze acutely puts it in *his* gloss on the Kantian revolution, "I do not perceive objects . . . it's my perception which presupposes the object-form."[10] If one heeds Kant's self-described Copernican Revolution in philosophy, attention to issues of knowledge requires an appreciation of the conditions of possibility for an object to emerge and thereby constitute part of what is recognized as facticity. Without going into elaborate detail on Kant's first critique, it should be noted, at a minimum, that Kant overturned traditional philosophy's focus on the extent to which what appears can be reliably observed. Substituting a productive mode of consciousness for mere passive perception, and rejecting a search for the essence or thing in itself behind the appearance, Kant introduced a subject who is no longer subjected to the object. Kant's subject retains a receptive sensibility but also has an active understanding that legislates and reflects. It is a subject responsible for constituting the conditions in which things can appear as things.[11]

Certainly there are critical limitations to Kant's reliance on a subject of consciousness. In changing a question about "what is a thing" to who we are such that things emerge for us, he neglected what Martin Heidegger identified as experiential involvement or the question of "how" subjects are situated in the world such that things emerge *as* things for them.[12] And just as certainly, there are critical limitations to Kant's attempt to have judgment create a unity of the different faculties. Jean-François Lyotard's substitution of a conflict of genres for Kant's conflict of faculties moves in the direction of a decentered aesthetics that activates the kind of radical pluralism that Kant's trajectory of critiques implies but fails fully to recognize.[13] These among other post-Kantian modifications of the Kantian epistemological revolution help me address some implications of his third critique, in which Kant develops his notion of aesthetic comprehension: the acts of imagination through which the productive results of the various faculties are brought into an encounter and create the possibility of a synthesis that would preserve "subjective necessity."[14]

To summarize the Kantian models: In his initial formulation of the synthesis through which understanding is achieved, Kant located productive consciousness in three separate acts: apprehension, reproduction, and recognition. In his first narrative of comprehension, the various parts of experience extant in a world of multiple sensation undergo a spatio-temporal synthesis (where space and time are internal to consciousness) by the apprehension and reproduction of the *parts* before the third operation, recognition, takes place to complete the synthesis by connecting to the world of objects.[15] Subsequently, however, in the *Critique of Judgment*, Kant's staging of an encounter between the faculty of reason and the work of imagination renders unstable the perspective from which understanding can occur. Although he wanted to establish consistent and universal loci from which the "higher faculties" could legislate understanding, as the world of phenomena is synthesized, Kant's aesthetic explorations deepened his commitment to the subjective action involved in comprehension. Although he failed to push his discovery very far toward its pluralistic implications, his third critique creates the conceptual basis for a mobile geography of knowledge. The ultimate implication of Kant's last approach to comprehension is that there is no one central place from which a calculus for a synthesis can occur.

It is this implication in Kant's third critique that inspires Deleuze's approach to aesthetic comprehension. Kant's question, which "was unformulated in the first critique: what counts as a part,"[16] encourages the realization to which Deleuze addresses himself. As Deleuze puts it, in *The Critique of Judgment*, Kant realized "that the synthesis of the imagination, such as it arises in knowledge, rests on a basis of a different nature, namely that the synthesis of the imagination in all its aspects assumes an aesthetic comprehension, an aesthetic comprehension *both of the thing to be measured and the unit of measure*" (my emphasis).[17] Deleuze goes on to treat the ways in which the issue of aesthetic comprehension stands outside of Kant's desired synthesis and therefore registers the contingencies and fragilities associated with the understanding that the "synthesis" is meant to effect:

> You must be clear that aesthetic comprehension is not part of the synthesis, it's the basis [*sol*] that the synthesis rests on. I

would say that it is not the ground [*fondement*] of the synthesis but that it is the foundation [*fondation*] of synthesis. At the same time that he discovers this basis, he discovers the extraordinary variability of this basis. He doesn't discover this basis without also seeing what this basis is. . . . Why? Because what the synthesis rests on is fundamentally fragile, because the aesthetic comprehension of the unit of measure, assumed by all effective measurement, can at each instant be overwhelmed, which is to say that between the synthesis and its basis there is the constant risk of the emergence of a sort of thrust coming up from underground [*sous-sol*], and this underground will break the synthesis.[18]

What is the methodological implication of the fragility of understanding that Kant's discovery implies? Here we can return to the answer Wolin supplies to his Kantian query about what the world must be like for "the methodist's knowledge to be possible." Such a world, he notes, has "regularities," so "that the methodist is in trouble when there are deformities."[19] Like Wolin, Deleuze is more concerned with the knowledge-relevance of deformities than with regularities. For example, turning to the canvasses of Francis Bacon in an elaboration of the issue of aesthetic comprehension, Deleuze notes that it is wrong to assume that the artist "works on a white surface." Rather, "everything he has in his head, or around him is already on the canvass, more or less virtually, before he begins his work."[20] To resist what Deleuze calls "psychic clichés" and "*figurative givens*," the artist must "transform" or "deform" what is "always-already on the canvass."[21]

It is especially apropos that Deleuze turns for illustration to the paintings of Francis Bacon, because Bacon's work manifests not only the explicit aim of deforming rather than reproducing figurative givens, but also the Kantian concern with the conditions under which things appear. As Bacon testifies, "what I want to do is to distort the thing far beyond the appearance, but in the distortion to bring it back to a recording of appearance."[22] However, the deformation of psychic clichés or figurative givens is but one aspect of those painters' compositions that promote critical thinking rather than merely aiding a recognition of ready-to-hand versions of facticity. In art that thinks rather than merely recognizes, there is often another important step taken, the inclusion of what Deleuze calls an "attendant."

Illustrating the attendant function, Deleuze observes the presence in some of Bacon's canvasses of a figure or figures that have no narrative relationship to the central figure. An attendant serves as "a constant or point of reference," a "spectator," but not in the ordinary sense. The attendant is a "kind of spectator" who "seems to subsist, distinct from the figure."[23] Deleuze's attendant provides the basis for determining the facticity of the scene, or, in his words, "the relation of the Figure to its isolating place," or "what takes place,"[24] for it "indicates a constant, a measure of cadence," and thereby serves to direct the (Kantian) fragile synthesis by being the basis of measurement for a scene that foregrounds the "thing to be measured."[25]

The Deleuzian attendant function is robust enough to apply to other visual media. For purposes of illustration, we can witness the operation of the attendant function in the most dramatic scene in Louis Malle's *Pretty Baby* (1978), a film whose plot involves the transition from childhood to the vocation of a prostitute of a young girl raised in a New Orleans bordello. In keeping with the bordello's tradition of an elaborate ceremony for the transition, the twelve-year-old virgin, Violet (Brooke Shields), is auctioned off in a setting that bears a startling resemblance to a slave auction. After being carried into the main sitting room on a large palette, Violet stands on a small raised platform as the bidding begins. Prior to the start of the bidding, the camera explores the grinning faces of the potential buyers, but as the bidding progresses, the camera lingers for some time on the face of Professor (Antonio Fargas), an African American piano player in the bordello, who, until the moment of the bidding, had seemed to share in the celebratory spirit of the occasion. In contrast, during the bidding, there is a series of extended framing shots of his grave, contemplative expression.

The attendant effect of the framing shot inflects the facticity of the episode. Professor's witnessing of the scene constitutes the "taking place" of the event. The Professor-Violet connection is not a story or narrative. Rather, the cut from one to the other is in keeping with Deleuze's insistence that the attendant establishes a point of view on variation. In this instance, the cut to Professor signals a meeting of two variations. The episode for Violet is one in which a generational dynamic is taking place. Violet is in the process of becoming a commodity, while Professor stands for people who bear the task of emerging from commodity status. As a result, the attendant's presence renders the scene comparable to the historical episodes associated with the slave

Professor in *Pretty Baby*. Courtesy of Paramount.

trade, in which bodies were sold to the highest bidder. Although he is a free man, Professor's look is historically situated; it conveys the point of view of one connected to a particular history of coercion in which bodies were rendered as commodities. In short, the basis for measuring the scene—for constituting its dominant facticity—is Professor's historical locus of experience as a "unit of measure."

Comprehending Crime Stories: Hard-Boiled Detection

Deleuze's attendant function is also robust enough to apply to literary texts. In the case of the crime novel, one attendant in particular, "a man named Flitcraft," in Dashiell Hammett's *The Maltese Falcon*, stands out, serving as a "unit of measure" to identify what is taking place in the story. Like the attendants to which Deleuze refers in his treatment of Francis Bacon's canvasses, Flitcraft has no current relationship with the main figures in the novel. He is a character from detective Sam Spade's investigative past, whose story is told as a parable by Spade to Brigid O'Shaughnessy, Spade's client and, ultimately, the suspect-turned-perpetrator that he turns over to the authorities as a murderess.[26]

Flitcraft is a man who jumps out of his conventional American life—a wife, two children, and a house in the suburbs—after a brush with accidental death. One day as he is walking on his way to lunch, a beam from a construction site crashes to the sidewalk and narrowly misses him. Physically, his only injury is the loss of a small piece of skin when a chunk of sidewalk flies up and hits him in the face after the beam crashes. But the event seemingly jars his consciousness, making him realize that he lives in an unsponsored, random world in which no normative order governs life. As Hammett puts it, "[h]e felt like somebody had taken the lid off life and let him look at the works."[27] Flitcraft realizes that his effort at "sensibly ordering his affairs" is not "in step with life," and, after some aimless wandering in another city, he begins another life that looks quite similar to the one he left.[28]

Hammett's Flitcraft parable in the midst of *The Maltese Falcon* should direct our attention not only to the contingencies of the order within which the crime, the murder of Spade's partner, Archer, operates but also to the shift in the genre that Hammett helped to invent. The traditional classic detective novel, developed most famously in Arthur Conan Doyle's Sherlock Holmes novels, presumed that crimes are temporary aberrations in a cohesive normative social order, a society functioning within an implicit social contract. The order is rectified and the contract renewed when the crime is solved. In contrast, in the hard-boiled version developed by Hammett and Raymond Chandler, among others, there is no presumption of a common normative order. Dean McCann offers a useful summary of the difference: "Traditionally the classic detective story celebrated the victory of public knowledge and civic solidarity over the dangers of private desire. . . . Hard-boiled crime fiction transformed that story by radicalizing its tensions . . . civil society can no longer contain private desire, public knowledge rarely trumps specialized expertise, and the idea of a common culture seems both profoundly appealing and ultimately unbelievable."[29]

Raymond Chandler's social world is not unlike Dashiell Hammett's. There is no stable normative order presumed. But whereas Hammett, seemingly an anti-populist, created characters such as Sam Spade, who are self-interested, unsentimental, and utterly lacking in redeeming qualities, Chandler's detective, Philip Marlowe, and even such violent characters as Moose Molloy in his *Farewell My Lovely*, evoke sympathy as they participate in exchanges of recognition and concern rather than being wholly self-interested, even though they articulate the radically different vernacular idioms and ways of perceiving that inspired Chandler's writing.[30] While both Hammett and Chandler help to illuminate some of the more dystopic aspects of twentieth-century urban politics, Chandler's novels reflect a redemptive vision of the contributions of vernacular culture to modern life.

Some of the contemporary ethnic crime novels to which I now turn draw on the contributions of both Hammett and Chandler in varying degrees. In the case of the modern African American crime story, those of Chester Himes, written during the mid-twentieth century, exhibit Hammett's cynicism, while Walter Mosley's late twentieth- and early twenty-first-century Easy Rawlins detective novels are more Chandleresque. Nevertheless, both Himes and Mosley, as well as others who write from alternative ethnic loci of enunciation, articulate different versions of the history and structure of America's ethnoscape while, at the same time, providing alternative implications of the relationship between aesthetic comprehension and political thought.

Mosley's *Devil in a Blue Dress* and the African American Crime Story

In his *Discipline and Punish*, Michel Foucault charts the emergence of a productive relationship between modern policing and what he calls "the delinquent milieu." Many of the consequences of that emergence, in which policing authorities suborn criminal informants to make use of their insider knowledge, are elaborated in twentieth-century, hard-boiled detective fiction and in its cinematic, film noir, realizations. However the law-delinquency relationship requires a different political sensibility when one takes account of the historical trajectory of America's racial-spatial order. For example, both in terms of its narrative and its imagistic (often dysnarrative) moments, Walter Mosley's *Devil in a Blue Dress*, which incorporates much of the hard-boiled detective genre, supplements the familiar detective story with a politically inflected emphasis on the connection between the administration of legalities and America's black-white relations.

Specifically, while mapping Los Angeles's mid-twentieth-century racial geography, *Devil* affirms, and gives substance to, Foucault's argument that the penalties administrated by the law give "free reign to some [while] putting pressure on others" and that rather than checking illegalities, penalties "differentiate them, [providing] them with a general 'economy.'"[31] *Devil* treats a variety of economies: monetary, symbolic, and penal. And while the classic, nineteenth-century crime novel "*belongs* to the disciplinary field that it portrays," because it reproduces the identities generated by the penal system (juridical authorities on the one hand, and the distribution of criminal types on the other), Mosley's novel resists what D. A. Miller calls the traditional "micropolitics of novelistic convention."[32] Instead of a single social order, with the identities of a class hierarchy produced within a single discursive frame, Mosley's *Devil* articulates the politics of an "urban frontier" in which separate, racialized "microcultures" operate with different epistemic purchases on the social order, which they express within different discursive idioms and with alternative sentiments about authority, legality, and civic responsibility.[33]

If we read novelistic form from M. M. Bakhtin's perspective, instead of the policing-complicit representational practice that Miller attributes to nineteenth-century crime novels, we are able to discern the centrifugal ideological commitments that the novel, as a many-voiced (heteroglossic) genre, offers. Given its "verbal-ideological decentering," which articulates its recognition of multiple cultures and linguistic styles, the novelistic form, of which Mosley's *Devil* is an exemplar, generates alternative and frequently clashing micropolitical segments.[34] Moreover, given the persistence of the racial divide foregrounded in the novel, *Devil*'s protagonist, Easy Rawlins, does not restore a coherent and quiescent order by solving a crime. Like the white detectives in the hard-boiled detective novels of Dashiell Hammett and Raymond Chandler, the "hero" does not achieve a definitive closure. Indeed, as Bakhtin notes, the novel distinguishes itself from the epic precisely because of the hero's "inadequacy to his fate or his situation."[35] He or she functions within "a highly unstable 'field' of representation."[36]

Thus, like Hammett's Sam Spade and Chandler's Philip Marlow, Easy Rawlins operates within a social domain that lacks the liberal contractual accord that provides the presumptive political context in classic detective fiction. And given the instability of the "field of representation" that *Devil* maps, Mosley's novel, like the other texts analyzed thus far, requires an attendant to orient its facticity, to guide an interpretation of what is taking place. Easy's friend Odell plays that role because, although he maintains a friendship with Easy, he is the kind of spectator who exists outside of the main action. However, to recognize Odell's role, which offers a "unit of measure" to assess what is taking place, one needs to appreciate how the novel implicates Easy in a complex crime story.

Devil begins with a powerful evocation of the spatio-temporality of post–World War II black-white relations. The year is 1948. Ezekial (Easy) Rawlins, having just lost his job in an airplane assembly plant, is sitting in Joppy's bar in a black section of Los Angeles, reading the employment pages of the newspaper's classified section. While at the individual level, the scene introduces Easy's personal problem, at a collective level, Mosley's opening indicates the extent to which LA's social order is color-coded. Racial segregation in mid-twentieth-century America remains unaffected by the war service of African American GIs. As Easy looks up from his newspaper, his first-person narration says: "I WAS SURPRISED TO SEE A WHITE MAN WALK INTO JOPPY'S bar. It's not just that he was white but he wore an off white linen suit and shirt with a panama straw hat and bone shoes over the flashing white silk socks. His skin was smooth and pale with just a few freckles. One lick of strawberry-blond hair escaped the band of his hat."[37]

With the creation of the novel's primary villain, Albright, Mosley's *Devil* exhibits a significant deformation of the hard-boiled detective novel and its film noir ("black film") realization. The hyper-white chromatics with which Albright is introduced reverses the morally oriented coding that lightness versus darkness has had in both genres. As Manthia Diawara puts it, in the case of cinema versions, a film achieves its noir designation because "it puts into play light and dark in order to exhibit a people who become 'black' because of their shady moral behavior."[38] And as Eric Lott points out, in affirming the racial coding to which Diawara refers, some characters in the hard-boiled detective story and its realization in the film noir genre exhibit whiteness as a marker of their moral purity. For example, Raymond Chandler's detective, Philip Marlowe, is shown to resist corruption by the shady company he keeps by "remain[ing] true to a racial physiognomy, that of whiteness, which indexes his pristine soul."[39]

Albright's whiteness in a black venue serves other important functions. Its most obvious role is its indication of the constraints of the mixing of black and white presences in the mid-twentieth century. Moreover, there is a historicity to the aberration intrinsic to Albright's startling appearance. Beyond the significance of 1948 as a postwar period, there is a longer time period, that of the institutionalization of

Jim Crow laws and the persisting racial divide they have effected. As is the case with all critical interpretation, to "transcode" the novel from a simple action story about an individual to a critical reflection on race, crime, and politics, one must lend what is an individual story collective, historical depth.[40]

Accordingly, two significant aspects of this opening scene require elaboration. First, Albright undoubtedly hails from Foucault's "delinquent milieu," a domain that is "separate and manipulable," a form of "controlled illegality."[41] Although Albright describes his vocation (in response to an Easy query) as doing "favors for friends, and for friends of friends,"[42] the more systemic perspective on his role, elaborated by Foucault, locates him as a product of the historic policing-initiated mode of useful delinquency, which developed along with modern penal systems. Albright's mode of illegality consists in "a diversion of illegality for the illicit circuits of profit and power of the dominant class."[43] He alleges that he has been hired by a wealthy mayoral candidate to find his female partner, who is thought to be a white woman who frequents black venues. In fact, however, Albright is working for the other candidate.

This revelation articulates with the second historically freighted aspect of the scene, not only the way it reflects on the still-extant racial-spatial order of Los Angeles, but also the way it speaks to the interpretive and behavioral demands that Los Angeles's racialized geography imposes. Albright's trip to Joppy's reveals that however dominant white LA is, economically, politically, and administratively, it needs blackness to function. Like the police who need black informants to police or exploit black areas, Albright cannot pursue his extralegal work without a black investigator who can visit African American venues without causing alarm. Black mobility is of course even more constrained, as becomes evident when Easy is justifiably reluctant to meet Albright at Santa Monica Pier after dark, where he is ordered to go to report on his initial findings.

As the story unfolds and Easy takes up his assignment and begins negotiating the spaces within and around Los Angeles, it becomes evident that he has learned what Ralph Ellison testified to after he moved from Alabama to New York, earlier in the same century, the "thou shalt-nots" governing the movements of differently raced bodies. Faced with the demands on one's performances imposed by spaces of welcome, spaces of indifference, and spaces of disparagement and exclusion, Ellison had to become alert to "the arcane rules of New York's racial arrangements."[44] Similarly, although Easy cannot wholly avoid disdainful, coercive, and violent treatment—by his former employer, by the police, by Albright and his minions, and by the employees of political candidates—he survives, thanks in part to his spatial canniness and in part to his violent friend Mouse, who comes to LA after a summons Easy conveys through Mouse's estranged wife, Etta-May. At the same time, Easy's spatial odyssey makes much of a segregated and racially coercive Los Angeles intelligible to the reader.

Making cities intelligible has been a primary feature of crime fiction since the nineteenth century: during the first half in the crime fiction of Edgar Allen Poe, and later in the century in Sir Arthur Conan Doyle's Sherlock Holmes stories. In his "The Man of the Crowd," Poe invents a new urban spectator who serves as a prototype for his detective stories. His character roams the city, seeking to impose a coherence on what he observes, while narrating the story.[45] The avatar of this new urban spectator is Poe's detective, Auguste Dupin, who solves mysteries and, at the same time, acts as "a meta reader of urban languages."[46] Doyle's Sherlock Holmes is similar to Poe's Dupin, insofar as the city for both is a geography of clues. But instead of a general reading of urban space, Holmes's London is portrayed as a class order. The "epicenter" of crime in the Holmes stories "from 1891 onwards" is London's West End, where Doyle's fictional crime centers around London's fashionable set.[47] London's criminal world (for example, that described as the venue of the "dangerous classes" in Charles Booth's 1889 "Descriptive Map of London Poverty") is a place that Holmes eschews, in part because it lacks mystery. As Franco Moretti suggests, Doyle's detective fiction focuses on enigma rather than visible crime. The "fictional crime in the London of wealth," rather than "real crime, in the London of poverty."[48]

It is evident, then, that the literary version of crime fiction articulates a spatial map. This is the case in nineteenth-century novels (for example, in Charles Dickens's *Our Mutual Friend*, where one encounters a middle class caught between "the fraudulent arrogance of the West End and the physical violence of the docks"[49]) and in the twentieth-century ones (for example, in the way Hammett's and Chandler's books map the class and ethnic domains of San Francisco and Los Angeles, respectively). But while spatial canniness is central to how Easy, as an informal, coerced investigator in this first Easy Rawlins novel,

Odell and Easy in *Devil in a Blue Dress*. Courtesy of TriStar Pictures, Inc.

manages his role, telling friend from enemy is also something he must ultimately learn in order to survive. It is with respect to this latter problem that his friend Odell serves as an attendant.

In the novel version of the story, it is noted simply that Odell is a relatively silent presence at "John's" illegal club over a store, where Easy begins his search for Daphne, the woman Albright has hired him to find. However, Carl Franklin's film version of the novel is imagistically attuned to Odell's attendant role. At the point at which a heavy flirtation begins between Easy (Denzel Washington) and Coretta, the spouse of Dupree, who is another of Easy's friends, the camera lingers on Odell's (Albert Hall) worried expression. It is the first instance in which the story explores the vagaries of friendship betrayal. Odell's positioning with respect to the micropolitics of friendship surfaces again at the end of the novel. But before treating the politics of friendship, which becomes evident late in the story, it is important to recognize the distinctive identity issues that *Devil* explores, because there is a sharp contrast between the identity disturbances confronted by such classic detectives as Doyle's Sherlock Holmes and Mosley's Easy Rawlins, a contrast in the difference in character between the "black sleuth" (or "blues detective") and the classic white detective.[50]

Identity Disturbances

A complex articulation of identity, space, and politics drives the narrative in *Devil*. What must be understood first is the historical heritage of African American creativity. As Houston A. Baker Jr. summarizes it: "All African American creativity is conditioned by (and part of) a historical discourse that privileges certain economic terms. The creative individual (the *black subject*) must perforce come to terms with 'commercial deportation' and the 'economics of slavery.'"[51] As a result, Baker observes, African American writing invariably involves "an encounter with economic signs,"[52] as the characters in their stories seek to effect the historical transition from having been, or having descended from, people who *were* commodities to being economically effective actors who can *manage* commodities. The fraught relationship of the African American to economic signs becomes especially evident when contrasted with white characters in classic (white) fiction—for example, the comfortable relationship with economy that Charles Dickens attributes to a white gentlemen, Alfred Lammle, whose very identity as a gentlemen consists in his economic *savoir faire*: "The mature young gentleman is a person of property. He invests his property. He goes in a condescending and amateurish way into the City, attends meetings of Directors, and has to do with a traffic in Shares."[53]

In contrast, Easy Rawlins is not positioned to dabble in shares. His acceptance of Albright's contract is a result of his need to pay his mortgage. Indicating that his home is an economically unstable *pied a terre*, Easy says, "I was a man of property and I wanted to leave my wild days behind."[54] Those "wild days" are rendered in Easy's recalling of an event from his days in Houston, where his friend Mouse killed a man involved in an altercation with both Easy and Mouse. Yet as it turns out, Easy's wild days return. Ironically, he ends up having to summon the violent Mouse to help extricate him from the threat of a murder rap and from violence at the hands of Albright and his minions.

In juxtaposing Easy's earlier association with a criminal act with his current effort to achieve economic security, *Devil* enters a thought-

world that precedes Easy's immediate dilemma. In addition to its affirmation of Baker's insights about the centrality of the "encounter with
economic signs" in African American writing, Easy's remark about
property has strong historical resonances, especially if we note that in
1705 the state of Virginia passed legislation that designated slaves *as*
real estate (people *as* rather than *of* property).[55] But even though the
white-controlled factory in which Easy had worked represents an extension of the southern plantation—"A job in a factory is an awful lot
like working on a plantation in the South," Easy's narration says[56]—his
story takes place during Jim Crow rather than in the slave era. He is
afflicted by the post-Reconstruction forces that have emerged to shape
the identity spaces within which he strives to shape himself. And Easy's
struggle in a world whose identity spaces are produced primarily by
white dominance is shared by the woman he is hired to find, Daphne
Monet, a "Negro" (so designated by the Jim Crow "one drop of blood"
criterion), who is fair-complected enough to pass as white. Her lover,
a wealthy white aristocrat running for mayor, ends their relationship
because the exposure of her "racial" origins would compromise his
election bid.

   Daphne, who ends the story as a tragic figure—she cannot fit comfortably in either black or white worlds—harks back to a character in
one of the first crime stories written by an African American. Pauline
Hopkins's "Hagar's Daughter," situated in 1860, is a manifestly political
crime story that begins with a reflection on the rift between the ideals of
the Declaration of Independence and the existence of a nation whose
economy incorporates slavery in its southern section, while witnessing
a vast gulf between the free Negroes of the North and the slaves of the
South. The story, originally serialized in *Colored American Magazine*
in 1901, treats the disruption of Hagar's life after the discovery of her
African American heritage. The devoutly religious Hopkins puts it this
way: "Here was a woman raised as one of a superior race, refined, cul-
tured, possessed of all the Christian virtues, who would have remained
in this social sphere all her life, beloved and respected by her descendants, her blood mingling with the best blood of the country if unto-
ward circumstances had not exposed her ancestry. But the one drop of
black blood neutralized all her virtues, and she became, from the moment of exposure, an unclean thing."[57] Although Hopkins's Hagar story
is framed as detective fiction, its most important thematic, in this as in
her other stories, treats the paradoxical issues surrounding the cultural,

social, and political dimensions of racial separation. Typically, when her characters' disguises are breached, the interdependencies of identities becomes apparent—for example, the importance of racial segregation for status within the world of white society in "Hagar's Daughter" and the complex interaction of identity and inheritance in "Of One Blood."[58]

The historical vicissitudes of African American identity indicate a more general phenomenon: Identity is relational, not self-contained; it has both symbolic and material debts to alterity. Moreover, the intersubjective, symbolic economy, which parallels the material economy, is influenced by some of the same antagonisms that afflict socially situated monetary exchanges, primarily because individuals are loathe to acknowledge their debts to otherness, just as the social order as a whole seeks to impose a unitary identity coherence on the social topology and ignore "its heavy burden of debt to [the] space of otherness."[59] A telling example at a collective level is the way in which the so-called advanced western nations require for their distinctiveness the gaze of others who have not achieved their democratic institutional structure, while denying that identity dependence by producing national narratives that emphasize autonomous histories of institutional invention.[60]

At an individual level, we encounter the character Easy Rawlins, who is afflicted with a complex identity paradox. In seeking economic independence or freedom from reliance on white structures of domination, he must negotiate an effective, economically situated self within the same white world that impedes that achievement. His dilemma is exemplified in two juxtaposed episodes, one in which he has to stifle his desire for self-assertion and beseech a hostile white foreman to give him back his job, and one in which he has to take on work from a dangerous white man, who is undoubtedly connected to the city's white power structure.

Similarly, as I have noted, Albright and the police detectives, both in roles that represent and reinforce a white power structure, need a representative of black Los Angeles to accomplish their work. Hired initially by Albright to find Daphne Monet, who, as Albright puts it, has a "predilection for the company of Negroes," Easy is subsequently pressured because he is treated as a suspect by the police in two murders that are connected to the search for Daphne. As is the case for Easy, neither Albright nor the police can move effectively in all spaces. Their Los Angeles, like Easy's, is a racial-spatial order that restricts the movement and performances of raced bodies. Doubtless, the extraordinary aggressivity of both Albright and the police can be understood, at least in part, as a reaction to their identity dependence. To promote the power of whiteness, which is already symbolically dependent on what it is not, they must depend on blackness, materially as well to be able to effectively conduct their investigations. This identity dependence of the powerful—treated by Hegel in one way, in terms of the paradoxes of the way the dominant and dominated are locked into a structure of mutual recognition, and by Lacan in another, in terms of the complex interdependencies of the law and desire—yields an extraordinary aggressivity, which, according to Lacan, is heightened when space is constricted.[61]

The Politics of Space

There is a nodal point at the center of *Devil*'s spatial story, Easy's home, primarily because the story is focused on Easy's hard-won economic efficacy, which is bound up with his desire for home-ownership. At the same time, an individual's drama is framed by a treatment of the more general difference between white election politics and the black micropolitics of survival in a white-dominated city, where elections and the other political processes and ceremonies that distinguish the American political imaginary from the national to the local level are not vehicles that benefit African American communities.

To treat critically the novel's individually inflected spatial story, it is necessary to treat the political frame within which the politics of *Devil* can be made intelligible. For this purpose, we can heed the ways in which *Devil* reproduces much of the political perspective articulated in the hard-boiled detective fiction of such writers as Hammett and Chandler. Fredric Jameson captures that politics succinctly in his commentary on Chandler's stories: "Chandler's picture of America has an intellectual content . . . the darker concrete reality, of an abstract intellectual illusion about the United States. . . . On the one hand, a glamourous national politics whose distant leading figures are invested with charisma, an unreal, distinguished quality adhering to their foreign policy activities, their economic programs given the appearance of intellectual content by the appropriation of ideologies of liberalism or conservatism. On the other hand, local politics, with its odium, its ever-present corruption, its deals and perpetual preoccupation with undramatic, materialistic questions such as sewage disposal, zoning regulations, property taxes, and so forth."[62]

How can one account for the persistence of the imaginary, given such a disjuncture between the national symbolic and the on-the-ground realities? For this, Jameson offers a corollary: "As in certain types of mental obsession and disassociation, the American is able to observe local injustice, racism, corruption, educational incompetence, with a practiced eye, while he continues to entertain boundless optimism as to the greatness of the country, taken as a whole."[63] Certainly Mosley's story is concerned with illuminating the hypocrisy of America's celebration of its democratic imaginary. Accordingly, Carl Franklin's film version of the story has Easy remark about the irrelevance of the mayoral election for black Los Angeles in one of the film's first voice-overs, as he is going through the employment section of the newspaper: "The newspapers was goin' on and on about the city election . . . like they were really going to change someone's life. My life had changed when I lost my job three weeks before."

Subsequently, Easy's spatial odyssey at the center of the novel is driven by his attempt to remain an economically viable actor in a racially discriminating job market and to hold on to his home, a drama that reflects the difference between election politics and the African American micropolitics of survival. The novel implies that while elections are part of white politics, an assessment of African American micropolitics requires a focus on the social uses of the neighborhood and the drive to overcome impediments to property ownership: legal manipulation, discriminatory criminalization, and exclusion from mortgage funds and grants. As Stephen Haymes has noted, "the territorial maintenance and integrity of black settlements [has been a] form of civic association."[64] Given the centrality of this aspect of African American micropolitics, the novel's tracking of Easy's spatial odyssey has his home as the central nexus. Both the initiating condition for the drama of the crime story and the story's subsequent mobile organization are based on his need to secure his home.

Because Easy must traverse many hostile (effectively foreign) spaces and because time is of the essence — the police give him twenty-four hours to solve the murders or else they will pin them on him — Easy's actions can be recruited into the frame suggested by Michel de Certeau. Lacking strategic control over space, Easy must rely on tactics rather than strategy in order, ultimately, to maintain some control over one small space, his home. As de Certeau notes, whereas a "strategy . . . postulates a *place* that can be delimited as its *own* and serve as a base from which the relationships of an *exteriority* composed of targets or threats . . . can be managed," a "tactic . . . is the space of the other; it must play on and with a terrain imposed on it and organized by the law of a foreign power."[65]

Ultimately, Easy's ability to survive in a situation in which policing is a threat rather than a basis of security requires him to become a man of knowledge as well as a "man of property." Two dimensions of this knowledge stand out: one involves the blues, and the other friendship. In the case of the former, he employs "blues epistemology," which, as Clyde Woods has described it, emerged first as a regional political reaction against the post-slavery depredations of the "plantation bloc." It involved a "constant reestablishment of collective sensibility in the face of constant attacks by the plantation bloc and its allies" and "the historic commitment to social and personal investigation, description, and criticism present in the blues."[66] In practice, blues epistemology involves collective methods of survival in the face of diverse forms of white oppression. In *Devil*, that oppression is mobilized in the forms of a discriminatory job environment and policing, along with its delinquent supplement.

Once Easy shifts from informant to detective, he becomes, effectively, a "blues detective." Unlike his early counterparts in classic and hard-boiled detective genres, Easy, like other blues detectives (for example, Chester Himes's Coffin Ed Johnson and Grave Digger Jones in his Harlem novels), manifests an added dimension to his sleuthing; rather than having the abstract and sketchy life of classic detectives, such as Poe's Dupin and Conan Doyle's Holmes, and hard-boiled detectives such as Hammett's Spade and Chandler's Marlowe, Mosley's Easy Rawlins disports a "blackness [that] is an integral ingredient in the success of his investigation," and more importantly, Easy has an awareness of his "place within the fabric of [his] black society," of his embeddedness within a "cultural community."[67] Easy's first-person narrative in *Devil* delivers a pedagogy about the special difficulties associated with African American physical and economic survival. In the African American detective story, detection therefore has a double resonance. Because the black detective is "intimately connected to [his or her] surroundings," the story involves the detective's growing awareness of what blackness means both to the self and to the other black characters.[68]

The Politics of Friendship

The second epistemic dimension of Easy's investigation, the problem of friendship, surfaces early in the novel. Crucial to an appreciation of the politics of *Devil* is a comparison of two of Easy's queries, one to Albright at the beginning of the novel and one to Easy's friend, Odell, at the end. After his initial meeting with Albright in Joppy's bar, when Albright describes his vocation as doing favors for friends in response to an Easy query, the issue of friendship comes up again, when a friendship query is directed to Odell. Easy asks him if it is alright to retain the friendship of someone you know does "bad things." Odell's response, "All you've got is your friends Easy," is one of the story's most significant lines. Throughout his odyssey, Easy is thrust into situations in which he must test the value of friendship and distinguish between true and false friends. This aspect of Easy's process of detection is more relevant to the novel's disclosure of black micropolitics than his solving of the murders.

In a meditation on Aristotle's approach to the politics of friendship, Jacques Derrida provides a sketch that excludes people like Albright from the pool of possible friends: "Why are the mean, the malevolent, the ill-intentioned (*phauloi*) not, by definition, good friends? Because they prefer things (*pragmata*) to friends. They stock friends among things, they class friends at best among possessions, among good things. In the same stroke, they thus inscribe friends in a field of relativity and calculable hypotheses, in a hierarchical multiplicity of possessions and things."[69]

Albright fits especially well in Derrida's profile of the malevolent, non-friend because, beyond being ill-intentioned and ruthlessly pragmatic, Albright explicitly regards Easy as a temporary possession, which he tells him when Easy tries to end his contract. And Joppy, who works for Albright, also turns out to be a false friend, even protesting (in the film version) at one point: "Easy, look at me; I'm your friend." In contrast, Mouse fulfills one of Derrida's criteria for the friend—he is someone whose friendship has endured the test of time: "Primary friendship does not work without time . . . it never presents itself outside of time: there is no friend without time . . . and no confidence which does not measure up to some *chronology*, to the trial of a sensible duration of time."[70]

While time is integral to the friendship phronesis that becomes a parallel investigation for Easy, its spatial aspect also plays an important role. Easy exists in a friendship network that extends to Houston (a place that, as I have noted, appears once in a flashback). Mouse's timely arrival from Houston to rescue his friend from having his throat cut, and ultimately from having two murders pinned on him, derives its political significance from a juxtaposition of two networks—the network of law enforcement personnel and its supplement constituting the criminal justice system, a racialized police-delinquency mapping of LA, and the friendship network that ultimately provides relief for Easy, who is victimized by the criminal justice network.

To understand these networks it is necessary to recognize that from the mid-twentieth century onward, LA has been increasingly an "urban landscape made up" (as one comprehensive interpretive mapping would have it) "of layers of premium network spaces, constructed for socio-economically affluent and corporate users, which are increasingly separated and partitioned from surrounding spaces of intensifying marginality—spaces where even basic connections with elsewhere, and basic rights to access spaces and networks, are increasingly problematic."[71]

As is made clear in *Devil*, it is the administration of the criminal justice system that connects the various partitioned spaces in a racially splintered LA, in ways that disadvantage the African American community. Effectively, *Devil* tells us, through form as well as story line, that those who are unable to anticipate relief from either the electoral process or law enforcement must rely on friendship. Certainly Mouse does "bad things," as Easy recognizes. But, as Odell reminds him, for African Americans friends are your only resort. We can locate Odell's insight in a political context that transcends the politics of the race-crime-politics relationship within Los Angeles. Once we recognize the fault lines in America's urban land- and ethnoscapes, in which the geometry of the city must be seen as a historically effected collage of diverse life worlds, which have been coercively assembled by (among other things) the trajectory of Jim Crow laws and practices, we are positioned to offer a challenge to the dominant political narrative of nation-building shared by the legitimation stories of many states and canonical political theory texts. *Devil*'s larger contribution to political theory consists in its repudiation of the Hegelian narrative of modernity, in which (in the case of the European-inaugurated nation-state model) a state-managed political order effectively supercedes other modes of affiliation.

As Derrida notes at the beginning of his treatment of the politics of friendship, "no dialectic of the state ever breaks with what it supercedes . . . and from which it arises."[72] Accordingly, if we turn our attention to such racialized micropolitical orders as Los Angeles's African American community, we encounter an extra-state network, based on historical grievance, on the history of a crime that has been constitutive of "the American political tradition." Mosley's crime story is embedded in a more venerable (and continuing) crime story, the story of the historical trajectory of America's racial-spatial order as it is understood within a politically attuned segment of the contemporary African American thought-world. However, the crimes constituting that order are conceived differently in the crime stories of other ethnic groups, to which I now turn.

Another Ethnicity, Other Crimes: Native America

Given the forces that have determined Native American habitation—forcible removal to the Southwest, the invention of a reservation system, and the subsequent destruction of their tribal identity through the Dawes Act (1887), which broke up the Indian territories—their crime stories tend to be territorial rather than urban. Exemplary in this respect are novels by Louise Erdrich, Linda Hogan, Louis Owens, and James Welch, all of which involve parallel pursuits: the investigation of murders and the recovery of the worlds of Native American thought and experience, which have been inflected by assaults on their territorial integrity and their cultural attachments. But describing landscapes as "territory" hardly achieves the meaning of place for Native American peoples. Their landscapes are treated as living things that are teeming with history. For example, as James Welch's exemplary novel *Fools Crow* opens, a mountain range is referred to as "the backbone of the world," and its main peak, Chief Mountain, is invested with historical significance; it is the place where the notable warrior/leaders "Eagle Head and Iron Beast had dreamed their visions in the long-ago, and animal helpers made them strong in spirit and fortunate in war."[73]

Not surprisingly, when Andrea Opitz had the task of translating the novel into German, she found that a focus on words would not suffice. The novel portrays an otherness that word-for-word translation could not capture: "*Fools Crow* does not simply offer an alternative vision but an alternative space in which the reader dwells."[74] Seeking to come to terms with the novel's "foreignness," even though it is written in English, Opitz discovered the articulation of a precolonial world within a colonized one: "In the novel, culture is imagined from inside. . . . The points of reference exist mainly in the Blackfeet universe. The Blackfeet in this novel are not seen or portrayed with a colonial mind-set, as neither the noble nor the displaced silent minority. They inhabit their world with a confidence, relying on themselves rather than whites for their sense of self, of belonging."[75] Accepting her alienation from the world created in *Fools Crow*, Opitz tried to capture the ways in which the novel's "language speaks directly from the land Welch's ancestors inhabited and exemplifies the relation between the Blackfeet and the world around them."[76] Transcending "existing territorial boundaries," the novel "imagines a 'Native textuality' that reclaims the land and its lost culture within it."[77]

Although there is a large and growing corpus of Native American crime novels that articulate the singularity of their landscape practices and culture habitus as a whole, I am restricting my analysis to Linda Hogan's *Mean Spirit* because of the way it distinguishes itself from the typical Euro-American (and even African American) crime story, not only with respect to the kind of world it renders, but also because of its narrative inversion of the knowledge process involved in its featured murder investigation. In Hogan's story, facticity becomes more fugitive instead of more present.

Hogan's approach to a crime story exemplifies the resistance to the psychic clichés and figurative givens to which Deleuze refers in his suggestion that the artist is faced not with a white surface but instead a surface on which "everything in his head or around him is already on the canvass." The beginning of Hogan's *Mean Spirit* fulfills the standard expectation of the crime novel genre. When a wealthy Osage woman, Grace Blanket, is murdered and her daughter and heir to her oil-rich property, Nola Blanket, has her life threatened, an investigation is begun by a Native American, Stace Red Hawk, a Sioux from South Dakota who has become a Washington-based federal official. His official task is to solve not only this crime but also a pattern of tribal deaths. As one commentator astutely puts it: "After the first fifty pages, 'mainstream' readers familiar with detective fiction can expect the novel to conform with the genre's 'rules of configuration' . . . [which convey the expectation] that the crimes will be solved and the mysteries surrounding them explained . . . that in the working out of the plot, readers will acquire an understanding of historical conflicts in the Oklahoma oil fields and of the Indian community around which those conflicts revolve; and . . . that Stace Red Hawk is the agent who will accomplish both of those tasks—that Red Hawk, as detective, will serve as mentor and guide."[78]

However, Hogan's *Mean Spirit* does not ultimately conform to the genre's "rules of configuration." Rather, like the critical painter, who deforms what is "always-already on the canvass," Hogan deforms the typical crime story, especially by reversing the narrative sequence. Instead of beginning with a mystery and ending with knowledge, *Mean Spirit* begins by evoking normal expectations of investigative closure only to end by deepening enigma. Hogan's detective novel is therefore unlike the typical detective story whose epistemological trajectory fulfills positivist epistemological assumptions. As William Spanos has noted in his treatment of the typical version, there is a remarkable parallel between the detective genre and mainstream empiricist epistemology, because "the form of the detective story has its source in the comforting certainty that an acute 'eye,' private or otherwise, can solve the crime with resounding finality by inferring causal relationships between clues."[79]

Although the drama of *Mean Spirit* involves a process of investigation, leading to a murder trial, the novel's political significance derives from two historical frames. The more proximate historical context involves the development of the oil-rich lands of Oklahoma. After the story is initiated in Watona, Oklahoma, in 1922 by the murder of landowner Grace Blanket, Stace Red Hawk, locates the murder in its contemporary set of forces: "He knew exactly what was happening. He'd seen it before. Large number of murders in the Badlands. All Indians, all with something the settlers wanted."[80] But there is a prior and more enduring historical context, which involves the destruction of Indianness, not only the Indian Removal Act of 1830, which led to the creation of the Indian Territory of Oklahoma, constituted as a mosaic of tribal holdings, and the Dawes Act of 1887, which dissolved those holdings and replaced them with individual allotments of 160 acres, but also other mechanisms—for example, the teaching at the famed Carlyle School of Indians, "where the founding father General Pratt's slogan was 'kill the Indian and save the man.'"[81] The murders to which Stace Red Hawk refers are therefore smaller predatory acts against individuals within a larger historical predation that was aimed at collectives, at destroying Indian nations.

Nevertheless, the doubleness of *Mean Spirit*, which is enacted through alternative ways of reading signs, reflects the persistence of Indianness throughout the period of collective destruction. The Osage of Watona, whose "double lives . . . grew more obvious"[82] over time, express that doubleness not only through their personal preferences — wearing braids and moccasins and turning away from white doctors — but also through their interpretive practices. In particular, as the novel explores an encounter between two different worlds, two different levels of facticity are excavated by two of the novel's different characters, each of whom have radically different ways of reading signs. For one, Stace Red Hawk, the signs to be read are the clues in the individual murder story. For the other, the water diviner named Michael Horse, the signs are part of the forces of destruction unleashed by Euro-Americans on Native Americans. But it takes Michael Horse some time to recognize the signs. Years of violent encounter ultimately alert Horse to the Indian predicament and encourage him to heed the earth's troubled signs and, moreover, to recognize the way worldly signs speak of subjects.

Such recognition often requires the experience of encounter, for as Deleuze puts it, "to be sensitive to signs, to consider the world as an object to be deciphered, is doubtless a gift. But this gift risks remaining buried in us if we do not make the necessary encounters, and these encounters would remain ineffective if we failed to overcome certain stock notions. The first of these is to attribute to the object the signs it bears."[83] Perhaps even more to the point of how alternative worlds clash in *Mean Spirit* are Bakhtin's observations about Dostoevsky's poetics, where he argues that in the kind of novel Dostoevsky inaugurated, there is "a plurality of equally-valid consciousnesses, each with its own world."[84]

The encounter between the two different worlds is remarked upon early on in the novel when the "the young Reverend Joe Billy" says to Michael Horse, "The Indian World is on a collision course with the white world."[85] And rather than reading interpersonal signs to discern the role of individuals in the murders, the Indians of Watona heed the signs of nature, such as the dead bees that the character Belle finds near their hive. It is not until the end of the novel that Michael Horse puts the various signs emitted by nature together and recognizes, as his thoughts are developed in the "Book of Horse" he has been writing, that "we did not know the ends to which the others would go to destroy us."[86]

It is ultimately Michael Horse, who has no official relationship with the investigation of the murders, who plays an attendant role in the story. If the events are viewed from his perspective, the small crime fails to command the "taking place" of events. Instead, the novel's primary facticity surrounds the destruction of Indianness. Michael Horse's rendering of an understanding from the various parts or events is articulated in his journal, undertaken to "keep track of everything."[87] Contrasting the kind of facticity that applies to the genre of a murder trial with the larger issue of the survival of his Indian community, he offers the observation that the genre of the trial prevents an accounting of the crucial facts: "Right or wrong. For us, it is such a simple thing, only a matter of whether a wrong has been done, or someone harmed. But they have books filled with words, with rules about how the story can and cannot be spoken. There is not room enough, nor time, to search for the real story that lies beneath the rest."[88]

As was the case with Mosley's *Devil*, Hogan's *Mean Spirit* adduces a survival ethos. But the ethos of *Devil*, an injunction to heed genuine friendship, is already an ongoing practice of survival for African Americans. Instead, the ethical injunctions in Hogan's novel, addressed to Native Americans, whose survival has always been in doubt, are utopian. While witnessing the trial, Michael Horse enacts an imagination of a just accord between the white and Indian worlds by adding pages to the Christian Bible. As he tells one of the older women, who asks what he has written: "First I have to tell you about the book they call the Bible. It is a holy book for the European people, like those who live in the towns. It carries visions, commandments and songs. I've added what I think is missing from its pages."[89] What Horse adds is the Osage respect for the earth and all living things: "Honor father sky and mother earth . . . life resides in all things, even motionless stones. Take care of the insects for they feed the people. . . . Treat all people in creation with respect; all is sacred, especially the bats. Live gently with the land. . . ."[90]

In its deformation of the crime story genre, Hogan's *Mean Spirit* therefore makes critical contributions at two levels. Philosophically, its restructuring of the knowledge problem displaces the search for clues to a murder with a meditation on historical crimes, showing that there is no privileged locus of enunciation with respect to knowing. Politically, the novel stages an encounter between two different thought-worlds and registers the persistence of the injustices that stem from Euro-America's reluctance to acknowledge its historical debts.

Conclusion: Other Histories, Debts, and Voices

Alexis de Tocqueville famously stated, "I can conceive of a society in which all men would feel an equal love and respect for the laws of which they consider themselves the authors; in which the authority of the government would be respected as necessary and not divine; and in which the loyalty of the subject to the chief magistrate would not be a passion, but a quiet and rational persuasion."[91]

Leaving aside the (male-dominant) gender politics of the social imaginary Tocqueville articulates as an ideal, it becomes clear by the end of the first volume of his *Democracy in America* that he viewed the continent's racial politics as a threat to his social ideal. Although he lamented the injustices of slavery and the encroachments on Native American territories, Tocqueville's attention to the "three races that inhabit the territory of the United States" (black, red, and white) convinced him that Anglo American dominance was both inevitable and desirable. Oddly, however, Tocqueville excluded the "brown race" from his fears about the impact of racial conflict on America's democratic future. While apparently uninformed about the Hispanic-Anglo struggles in California, he was at least aware that Texas was a contested territory. But he read the conflict geopolitically rather than culturally, foreseeing the outcome as militarily definitive. Noting that "the province of Texas is still part of the Mexican dominions," he added, this "'province' . . . will soon contain no Mexicans,"[92] and he goes on to remark favorably about the "British race's" civilizational superiority, as though its imposition on the United States can be expected to be unmediated by the encounters in a vast territorial and cultural Spanish America.

Without going into an elaborate recovery of the thought-world of Spanish America, it is worth noting one of its representatives, Mariano Vallejo, because he played an important role in the governance of Spanish America and articulated a largely ignored, binational perspective on America's democratic future. His legacy hovers in the background of the exemplary Latino American crime stories of Lucha Corpi, which I address briefly here. Coincident with Tocqueville's American tour, Vallejo was commandant of the San Francisco Presidio and, subsequently, the military governor of Sonoma, after having had a major hand in the secularization of Mexico-ruled California, which at the time of Tocqueville's writing was populated by six to seven thousand Hispanics and people belonging to nearly four hundred other nationalities.[93] A republican and cosmopolitan who envisioned a multicultural California, even if annexation to the United States was inevitable, Vallejo's hold on power and his vision fell victim to the American conquest, led by Captain John Charles Fremont. Vallejo's model of annexation was one that would have permitted equality between Hispanic and Anglo Californians: "When we join our fortunes to hers [the United States], we shall not become subjects, but fellow citizens possessing all the rights of the people of the United States and choosing our own federal and local leaders."[94]

Historically, however, those "rights" have been fugitive for Latino Americans. Now Vallejo's Sonoma stronghold is better known for its wineries than for its Hispanic cultural and political history. Nevertheless, although mainstream American history texts tend to gloss over the historical significance and still-active memories of Spanish America, it remains alive for many contemporary Chicana/o writers, particularly those concerned with issues of rights for Latinos. In the case of Lucha Corpi's most notable crime stories, *Eulogy for a Brown Angel* and *Cactus Blood*, the Vallejo legacy emerges as part of the historical framing of the contemporary politics of Chicano-Anglo contention in her plots. As her Chicana detective, Gloria Damasco, says in *Cactus Blood*, "I had never been in Sonoma, the heart of the wine country and the site of historical events that changed the fate of Mexicans in California forever."[95]

The tendency of Corpi's crime stories to transcend the immediacy of their murder plots is a more general tendency of Chicana/o literature. As Ramon Saldivar notes, "history cannot be seen as the mere 'background' or 'context' of [Chicana/o] literature; rather history turns out to be the decisive determinant of the form and content of literature."[96] More generally, it is a tendency evident in many "ethnic American authors [who] inherit . . . two syncretic histories in which to place themselves and their characters: the 'official' history of America, with its discoveries, wars, social and cultural movements, and the particularities of ethnic histories in America that include, if not silenced events, ones that have been subsumed into larger stories of America."[97]

In the case of Mexican Americans during the period in which Anglo conquerors took over California, Texas, and the rest of Spanish America, "those who had been Mexican suddenly found themselves inside the United States [as] foreigners on their own land."[98] General Vallejo's hoped-for equal citizen became instead a national and cultural exile, a part of a people subjected to economic and political discrimination. And the forces of that discrimination were both political and economic. While mainstream U.S. histories have tended to ignore the fate of the Californios (the California Mexicans) after the 1848 Treaty of Guadalupe Hildago, Spanish American literature testifies to it. For example, in *The Squatter and the Don* (1885), a romantic novel at one level, Maria Amparo Ruiz de Burton "writes against the grain of dominant U.S. historiography and represents the cultures of U.S. imperialism not only as territorial and economic fact but also inevitably as a subject-constituting project."[99] While much of the novel involves a romantic quest, it follows "two tracks," for it is also "marked by its historicity." In the novel, the Californio characters are initially displaced by squatters, who are aided by governmental acts, but are subsequently oppressed by the manipulations of powerful economic monopolies.[100] Thus a drama about a main character, the rancher Don Mariano Alamar, is also a commentary on a history of encounter in the Southwest. As Don Mariano, referring to himself and the other Californios as "the conquered people," complains at one point in the novel, "We have no one to speak for us. By the Treaty of Guadalupe Hildago the American Nation pledged its honor to respect our land titles."[101]

Lucha Corpi's detective fiction also follows two tracks, one a set of personal dramas and the other historical reflections. In her contemporary Gloria Damasco detective fiction, which in *Eulogy* treats the murder of a child during the 1970 Moratorium March, and in *Cactus Blood* treats serial killings in which Native American artifacts are left around the corpses, both nineteenth-century Spanish American and contemporary Chicana/o historical events surround the murder mysteries. In both novels, the Chicana/o political movements of the 1970s are foregrounded. In *Eulogy*, the story begins with the murder of a small boy, Michael Visneros, found after the march is over, and in *Cactus Blood*, which focuses more on the United Farm Worker's strike of 1973, the 1970 march is mentioned with reference to the "repressive actions of police against us at the 1970 National Chicano Moratorium March."[102] But both novels also reach back to California's Hispanic past. In *Eulogy*, while perusing the Oakland History Archives, Detective Damasco discovers information about the Peraltas, a former land-owning family who held significant power during California's Mexican period.[103] And in *Cactus Blood*, reference is made to the end of Mexico's control of California, when "the Mexican army, led by General Vallejo laid down their arms . . . [and] California became a U.S. territory and every gold-digger's rainbow's end."[104] The novels are therefore enactments of "Chicano mestizaje," which "represents the trace of a historical material process, a violent racial/colonial encounter."[105]

Other ethnic groups who are aggrieved as a result of oppression and exclusion, or are simply ungrammatical within the dominant languages of America's ethnic imaginary, also tend to emphasize a historical counter-memory to the one that articulates a narrative of democratic inclusion. For example, contemporary Asian American crime fiction tends to reference alternative American histories, screened through voices that articulate the tensions experienced by ethnic Americans who exist in divided historical imaginaries. While there are many examples, in this brief conclusion I treat one, Japanese American Dale Furutani's *Death in Little Tokyo*, which features Ken Tanaka, a member of a crime club who begins by playing a game of detection but ultimately becomes an involuntary detective and gets caught up in an actual murder story.[106]

As the crime story unfolds, two different levels of politics are articulated. First, the story treats LA's city politics, as Tanaka learns about the LA that Raymond Chandler maps in his crime novels: "a local politics with its odium, its ever-present corruption, its deals and perpetual preoccupation with undramatic, materialistic questions such as sewage disposal, zoning regulations, property taxes, and so forth."[107] Specifically, Tanaka becomes aware of the corruption and racketeering that surround LA's water politics and the distribution of fraudulent claim tickets.[108] Second, whereas the main crime drama is a contemporary murder in a typically corrupt local political context, Tanaka, while helping the police solve the murder, discovers a older murder case connected to a unique, Japanese American experience. The pursuit of the older case reveals some details about the lives of individuals who experienced the racist internment of the Japanese during WWII, a historical episode that haunts generations of Japanese Americans, compromising the sense of citizen attachment for many. Moreover, Tanaka discovers that racial discrimination persists. As his investigation maps the contemporary racial-spatial order of Los Angeles, he realizes that growing up in Hawaii, where he thought the world was more color blind, he was unaware of the hostility that many Asian Americans experience.

As Tanaka becomes aware that California's Asian American ethnoscape is a legacy of violent historical encounters—for example, Filipinos from a war with Spain and Koreans from a war on the Korean peninsula—he comes to "the frightening conclusion that race is becoming the defining factor of our lives."[109] As a result, he surmises that there is a gap between what he was taught about American justice and democracy and what have been democracy's notable failures.[110] Ultimately, Tanaka's role in solving a murder pales in comparison with what he discovers about the micropolitical struggle of Japanese Americans, some of whom seek to maintain some of their singular cultural values while coming to terms with past injustices, and some of whom forsake that singularity to participate in the more predatory aspects of American economy, particularly real estate transactions.[111]

Finally, what is discernible with a focus on diverse ethnic crime stories is a heteroglossic, polyvalent, diverse set of micropolitical cultures. Although there are no obvious attendants *within* Corpi's and Furutani's texts, the authors themselves can be construed as attendants. Like other crime story writers, they offer alternative facticities, alternative angles of vision with respect to what is and has been taking place in American politics. Taken as a whole, the alternative thought-worlds they articulate display the radical pluralism that Kant's ultimate investigation of aesthetic judgment implies and Deleuze's subsequent elaboration encourages. The political imaginaries resident in their aesthetic productions involve complex interarticulations of social space, angles of vision, alternative voices, and diverse modes of historical time and memory—all resulting largely from the different trajectories of arrival and subsequent modes of experience they represent. It is appropriate at this juncture to revisit Jacques Rancière's remarks on aesthetics and politics, where he says that "the aesthetic nature of politics" directs our attention not to "a specific single world," but to "a world of competing worlds."[112]

3 Deforming America's Western Imaginary

Westerns

One of the legacies of the western political theory canon is the myth that the modern state emerged as a historically evolving contract in which individuals, seeking to avoid getting caught up in a war of "every man against every man," assent to a centralized authority. For security reasons, or so the story goes, they participate in a collective sensibility that assembles and legitimates the body politic as a centrally governed, sovereign entity.[1] Among the more articulate and strenuous challenges to this enduring fable of the social contract is Michel Foucault's *Lectures at the Collège de France, 1975–1976*. In them he challenges those legendary histories, embedded in the political theory canon, that presume that the state is founded by the motivation to avoid war. Contrary to the familiar social contract theories of the origin of states, Foucault argues that state-initiated legalities or jurisdictions cannot be attributed to social consensus; instead, he insists, they have followed in the wake of battles.[2] While Foucault's historical field of reference is the European continent, a similar and compelling case has been made for the United States, whose realization as a nation-state on the North American continent is attributed by Richard Slotkin to "the rule of the gun." Specifically, Slotkin locates America's national consolidation in its Indian wars rather than in the deliberations leading to its foundational charters. And he turns to western films as the genre in which the westward-moving frontier of violence has been mythologized to legitimate Euro-America's acts of violent (dis)possession.[3]

However, even classic westerns provide an ambiguous support for the legitimation to which Slotkin refers. For example, John Ford's westerns, which created the most familiar Hollywood version of the West, portray a heroic nation-building resolve on the one hand, but also depict a nation-destroying cruelty that threatens the national mythology in which his films participate on the other. Robert Burgoyne's observations about westerns and America's self-actualizing narratives disclose that threat. Drawing on a remark by the Cherokee artist and writer Jimmie Durham, who writes, "America's narrative about itself centers upon [and] has its operational center in a hidden text concerning its relationship with American Indians . . . the part involving conquest and genocide, [which] remains sacred and consequently obscured," Burgoyne adds, "one of the most durable and effective masks for the disguised operational center of the nation-state has been the western, a genre that has furnished the basic repertoire of national mythology."[4] Although for the most part the classic western film genre represents Indians as a temporary impediment to the Euro-American nation-building project, they nevertheless call attention to a historical epoch in which there is undeniable evidence of an encounter of nationhoods, a period in which, prior to white dominance, there was a process involving Euro-Native American international relations.[5]

Effectively, before Euro-America turned Native Americans into a "race," their encounters with native peoples constituted a period of extended "foreign policy."[6] During the period of European colonization of the North American continent, "the constructed category 'Indian' occupied the space of the quintessentially 'foreign.'"[7] This was also the case from the Native American point of view, as a notable encounter in the American Southwest in 1847 indicates. A Comanche chief, Janamata (Red Buffalo), tried unsuccessfully to instruct a U.S. Army major, John C. Cremony, about the difference between Euro-American reasons of state and his Comanche nation's politics of grievance, which had just been activated as an attack on a Mexican town across the Rio Grande, near where Cremony and his soldiers were protecting a mining operation on the American side.

When Cremony asked Janamata to end his raids, the conversation, in their only shared language, Spanish, was as follows: Cremony insists that Janamata recross the river and leave the Mexicans in peace. Janamata replies, "I hear your words and they are not pleasant. These Mexicans are our natural enemies," and, inasmuch as he is familiar with the history of the U.S.-Mexican War, he adds, "they are also your enemies." Cremony rejoins to the effect that the Mexicans are no longer U.S. enemies and explains that the friend-enemy relationship must be understood in the context of reasons of state, not tradition or historical grievance. To this Janamata responds that "your revenge is for yourself. It does not satisfy us for the blood of Comanches slain by Mexicans." Cremony, backed by superior force of arms, refuses to accept a bi-national jurisdiction and thus a pluralistic model of war making/peace keeping.[8] This paradigmatic encounter between two different imperatives vis-à-vis enemies was one among many inter-nation issues that arose before the U.S. government effectively disarmed and displaced the remaining Native American nations and imposed a political model in the form of a fixed and sovereign territorial state with no space for the more fluid territorial organization characteristic of many of the Native American nations.

In their construction of Indian territories, the classic westerns tend to bypass the historical trajectory of the Indians' relocation from nations with treaty-making rights and territorial integrity to races under the aegis of the U.S. government. And they rarely touch upon Native America's perspectives and unheeded protests during the refiguration and relocation process. Instead, they focus on Euro-American national expansion and the dramas accompanying the tensions during the period of white settlement. Nevertheless, although the era of the classic western is now decades in the past, some contemporary films, which return to the same western landscapes, deserve recognition as critical engagements with both the history of Euro-American expansion and the film-nationhood projects involved in the classic westerns. Accordingly, analyses of two such films are the bookends of this investigation, whose middle section treats the way classic westerns, particularly those directed by John Ford, supply insights into the Euro-American geo- and biopolitical ethnogenesis, their privileging of the Euro-American presence on the North American continent. I juxtapose Ford's westerns (the last of which was produced in the mid-1960s) with two of Robert Altman's films of the 1970s that deform the classic western, which Ford himself had already significantly modified, and challenge America's dominant expansionist imaginary.[9]

While the Ford and Altman films with which I deal can be easily recruited into the category of westerns, the film with which I begin my analysis, Sean Penn's *The Pledge* (2001), and the one with which I conclude it, Wim Wenders's *Paris, Texas* (1984) are more difficult to assign to genre classifications. Neither of these films were identified in their promotions or by reviewers as westerns. *The Pledge* seems to be primarily a story about a man losing his mind, while *Paris, Texas* seems to be a story about a man who regains his. However the settings and much of the imagery in both contain subtle references to the western film genre and testify to the violence attending Euro-American "nation-building" (to repeat the euphemism that remains central to the discourse of American political science).

Temporally the two films remain in the present. Their testimony to events from a violent past is achieved through portrayals of the traces that remain on the landscape. In this respect their approach to the genocidal assault on Native America is comparable to Claude Lanzmann's monumental documentary on the Holocaust, *Shoah* (1985), which contains no historical footage but rather documents what remains on the landscape and in the memories of survivors and witnesses. Deliberately excluding archival materials, Lanzmann's recording of the extant traces of a violent, genocidal past in the present is conveyed by such images as "the overgrown siding at Sibibor [where concentration camp inmates were off-loaded] pecked at by chickens or the scrubby copse that now grows on the site of [the extermination camp] Treblinka's so-called 'hospital.'"[10]

The Pledge

The Pledge, like Lanzmann's *Shoah*, is set well after the genocidal period. It is filmed in a West whose violent past also retains few visible markers, either on the landscape or in the daily lives of its residents. The Far West, Reno area venue of *The Pledge* is now a well-established region of the contemporary United States. It is a "region" in the sense that the former "boundaries on the land," particularly that most dramatic and fluid one—between Euro-American settlers and "Indians"—have disappeared. The inter-nation "frontier," in which self-other identity relationships were once subject to contention and negotiation, has been displaced by a more stabilized form of possession and set of identity relations. Whereas in the frontier moment people were inventing a world, with regionalization "[p]eople felt that they were no longer inventing a world but inheriting one."[11] The discourses associated with the management of the United States' geopolitical prerogatives have left little discursive space for the violent biopolitical and spatial dynamic that preceded national consolidation.

In short, once that inherited world became established, an implementation of the dominant geopolitical imaginary, which is articulated on the maps of the contemporary nation-states system and in prevailing, state-oriented political discourses, displaced alternative modes of political and social life, rendering them invisible. As John Agnew points out, the prevailing geopolitical imagination, which was inaugurated in sixteenth-century Europe, remains the primary mode of global visualization. And, inasmuch as this geopolitical imagination provides but one vision and effaces history by turning time into a singular model of space, the overcoded life worlds of Native American nations, victimized by Euro-American "nation-building," are difficult to recover.[12] In analyzing Sean Penn's *The Pledge* and other films, my focus is on imagery in some cases and alternative loci of enunciation in others in order to recover what the modern geopolitical imaginary hides. At the same time, I am concerned with showing how a state-centric, macro-level politics fails to register the continuing micropolitical struggles of Native American peoples.

Historically, the relationship between cinema and nationhood has been intimate. In most cases, and in many national venues, film has been supportive of state cultural governance—the practice in which state-oriented cinema constructs homogeneous and coherent national cultures. Elsewhere, I have referred to this phenomenon as "cinematic nationhood," where film has been involved in the cultural articulation of the nation-building and -sustaining projects of states.[13] However, as I also note, pointing in particular to "post-westerns," film is an increasingly critical medium that has tended to challenge the hegemony of the modern state system. In subtle ways, *The Pledge* participates in that challenge.

In *The Pledge*, the legacy of Native America in the area of Reno is not immediately evident. Throughout the film, social relations within the Euro-American settlement, and in the few Anglo-Indian interactions, take place in the well-articulated and settled normative order of Reno and its mountain and lake surroundings (although the filming actually took place in British Columbia, Canada). Apart from a main Indian character who is falsely accused of a murder, Indian presence is sparse, existing for the most part as part as a behaviorally indistinguishable clientele for small businesses, a gas station in one scene and a diner in another.

Briefly, as a plot about an individual character, *The Pledge* treats the events surrounding longtime Reno police detective Jerry Black's (Jack Nicholson) retirement, which is compromised by a promise he makes to the mother of a murder victim, after the eight-year-old girl's mutilated body is discovered by a teenage snowmobiler in a snow field outside of Reno.[14] The discovery is reported to the police. Its reception interrupts Jerry's retirement dinner party and ultimately his retirement. Resisting his department's position that the case is closed, and driven by his promise and his belief that the Indian (Benicio Del Toro) on whom the police pin the murder is not the perpetrator, Jerry works at solving the crime as a freelance investigator. His mapping of a pattern of similar crimes leads him to take up residence in the vicinity where they occurred. Although that vicinity seems merely to be the setting of contemporary, Euro-American daily life, it contains signs of the international encounters whose resolution has integrated the region into a seemingly culturally unified, sovereign United States.

Eventually, as a result of local encounters and contingent circumstances, Jerry ends up living with Lori (Robin Wright Penn) and her daughter, Chrissy (Pauline Roberts), who fits the victim profile. After wrongly suspecting a local part-time clergyman, Jerry focuses convincingly on a likely suspect, who has arranged a meeting with Chrissy. But after Jerry and his former colleagues set up a surveillance post adjacent to the spot of the meeting, the suspect fails to show up (seemingly because he is killed in a traffic accident). The film ends as it begins, with a flashback. Jerry is seen wandering around in a daze, muttering to himself. He has become a man broken by a combination of desires and contingencies that provoke his investigation, disrupt its consummation, and leave the viewers without a clear answer as to whether he is destroyed by self-absorbed delusions or by contingent circumstances.

The film's dramatic tension is maintained by the ambiguities in what drives Jerry's investigation. Although the evidence of a serial killer, and thus the Indian's innocence, becomes increasingly plausible (the murder victim had drawn a picture of a man who gave her gifts shortly before the murder, and his body and car in her drawing do not fit the Indian-suspect), it also sometimes seems that Jerry's interpretations of his evidence are obsession-driven. In particular, the camera shots that focus on Jerry's facial expressions encourage a psychological reading of his quest. Such shots constitute what Gilles Deleuze calls "affection-images." They are primarily close-ups of faces at intervals of "indetermination," moments between what the subject perceives and an action, moments, moreover, when the subject "feels itself 'from the inside.'"[15] These shots, which are the primary vehicles for conveying the psychological register of a cinematic narrative, occur often in the later scenes of *The Pledge*, as Jerry Black becomes increasingly obsessed with his investigation and increasingly attentive to ambiguous clues.

A key scene in the psychological drama takes place in the office of a counseling psychologist (Helen Mirren). After Jerry asks her to help him interpret the victim's drawing of "a porcupine giant" (a tall stranger who gives the child small, carved, wooden porcupines), she shifts the interview to an interrogation of Jerry, asking him if he has always been a chain smoker, if he is recently retired, and whether he is still sexually active. As this later part of the session progresses, the camera offers frequent affection-images. Yet while the frequency of af-fection-images may foreground the psychological level of meaning in the narrative, its mode of presentation has an additional significance. To the extent that the face close-up is "abstracted from spatio-tempo-ral coordinates," it has the effect of "undoing space,"[16] which in the case of *The Pledge* is a pervasive part of the film's supplemental and largely disjunctive story. On the one hand, there is one man's personal drama, conveyed in shots of his demeanor and personal interactions, but on the other, there is an exploration of the landscape, conveyed with wide-angle framing and panning shots, which are interspersed throughout the film. And because the cuts and juxtapositions often take place at moments that encourage one to see the landscape scenes in the context of the scenes containing signs that the West retains a mixed ethnoscape, the landscape shots have resonances with earlier international encounters.

Thus, although interiors—primarily offices and small business-es—contain much of the dramatic interaction of the film, time is ever present, for *The Pledge* never abandons its spatio-temporal thematic. Certainly the film is concerned with a character, Jerry Black, who is situated in time, first as an aging retiree, then as one partially stymied by the temporal rhythms of police investigations (once a suspect is se-lected, there is enormous pressure to close the case), and finally as one whose investigative opportunities are affected by seasonal changes (there are several seasonal tableaux that are interspersed in the imagis-tic mechanisms of the story line). But surrounding one man's drama is an institutionalized space, a western venue with a significant temporal trajectory. Reno and its surroundings exist in both ethnic and geopo-litical time. The area is not only a consolidated and recently white-dominated region of the West, but is also a part of the larger national picture.[17] That Reno is a city in a state in a nation, and is therefore subject to a dense normative hierarchy, is made evident by, among other things, a parade scene in which many national flags and other symbols of a national story (for example, disabled war veterans) are in evidence. And most significantly, the signs of the process of whitening (the process of Anglo dominance of what were formerly Indian nation places) are presented abundantly, not only in the few scenes that include Native Americans and in some of the landscape scenes (which include both panoramas and depth-of-focus shots), but also in the way Anglos are depicted.

With respect to the spatial narrative of the film (or dysnarrative insofar as it is disarticulated with the individual drama), the opening scene is telling. We encounter Jerry Black, initially ice fishing on a lake outside of town. After a distance shot of a lake and mountain snow-scape, interrupted only by a small fishing shack, the camera takes us inside the shack and focuses on Jerry's almost empty bottle of scotch. The sequence of shots portrays a historical rather than individual story. A virtually timeless landscape is juxtaposed with a sign of the Euro-American arrival; a European brand of scotch, Glenfiddich, testifies to the origin of part of white America. And lest the viewer forget the place of alcohol in the story of the western encounter, the film continues to dwell on alcoholic beverages. Several shots of the revelers at Jerry's retirement party at a downtown ersatz Hawaiian bar-restaurant, "The Luau," foreground whiskey. One is a tracking shot of a tray carrying a cocktail, and one is of a police detective dancing with a drink in his hand. The juxtaposition of Euro- and Native America that the focus on alcohol implies is deepened by a series of cuts between scenes during the retirement party. There is a cut from the party to a scene in which an overweight and awkward young boy, whose complexion is ultra white (so white that pink blush marks show, emphasized with several close-up face shots), appears in the deep snow field near the crime scene on his snowmobile. As the camera shifts from the affection-image to a "perception-image" (where the images are delivered from the boy's perspective),[18] the viewer sees an Indian running through the snow toward his truck. He is carrying the traps with which he catches game (beaver, we later learn).

While the crime story part of the narrative locates the boy as a witness who places the Indian at the murder scene, another more venerable story is being juxtaposed. Shortly after the Indian, Toby Jay Wadenah, is arrested and brought in for an interrogation, a framing shot shows a drawing of an Indian caricature made by a police artist, who is viewing the interrogation room on a closed-circuit screen. The caricature, an Indian's head with a single feather, which looks nothing like the suspect, articulates with the dismissive perspective of the police, one of whom, the interrogator, derisively calls the Indian "chief." And the interrogation scene itself, after which the Indian grabs an officer's gun and kills himself, is arguably an allegory of white America's ambivalent view of Native Americans. In the process of cajoling a confession from the Indian, the interrogating detective rubs him, hugs him, and speaks to him in a soothing, almost lascivious tone. The homoerotic tenor of the interaction is commented on by Jerry, who, after watching the interrogation on the closed-circuit monitor, says, "he practically blew him."

Since the initial, extended contact in the seventeenth century, Euro-Americans have located Native Americans in an ambiguous place, at times romanticizing them for their alleged qualities of grace, beauty, bravery, and natural genius, and at times abhorring them for their alleged primitiveness, savagery, cruelty, and guile. For the Reno police, as for the dominant history of Indian-white relations, the abhorrence codes are ultimately privileged, even as the former ones are allegorically played out. Once the pseudo confession is extracted, and the Indian is nearly faint from the pressure, the interrogator, while holding him from falling, says, "I gotcha, I gotcha," the first gotcha referring to the support and the second to having achieved a confession. But, of course, there is a third resonance, the historical one in which whiteness has contained Native America, and settlement has dominated the more nomadic habitus of Native America. And within the crime story, the legacy of the containment and disparagement of Native Americans is so well assimilated into the policing habitus (in which both whiteness and closed cases are valued above justice) that Jerry's former colleagues strenuously resist his attempts to seek an alternate perpetrator.

The Indian suspect's lifestyle receives relatively little coverage. During the interrogation, he mentions that he hunts beaver. And in the earlier scene, in which he is seen running to his truck by the fat, teenage, pink and white snowmobiler, who appears to be too corpulent to run through the snow, his animal traps are visible, dangling from his side. But the white-Indian lifestyle (and habituation to moving in a snow field) juxtaposition is also made evident by the role that fishing plays for Jerry Black. His fishing is represented primarily as a leisure

Jerry Black's Native American customer in *The Pledge*. Courtesy of Warner Home Video.

sport (especially for retirees) rather than food gathering, a representation that is underscored when his retirement gift from the police department is a fishing trip to Baja, California. The other Indians that appear, once Toby is out of the picture, are simply customers, whose lifestyles have been assimilated to the white habitus. Some are shown briefly as part of the clientele of the diner where Jerry meets his temporary family.

However, an especially telling (and doubtless allegorical) Indian-white interaction takes place at Jerry's gas station shop, which he has purchased to be near the pattern of murders he has uncovered. After Jerry fills the tank of an Indian customer's car, he has difficulty getting the credit card machine to record the Indian's American Express card. As he botches the transaction several times, having difficulty making the slide mechanism on the recording machine work, the two men stare awkwardly at each other. An ex-policeman on unfamiliar commercial ground is failing to process smoothly the credit card of a person whose people have been historically discredited (on their former ground). Doubtless it is not incidental that it is an *American* Express card, which lends additional resonance to the allegorical aspect of the transaction, calling to mind a history of fraught Anglo-Indian transactions and negotiations. Ultimately, despite the intensity of its foregrounded, psychological drama and the suspense it generates around its crime story, the haunted land- and ethnoscape that *The Pledge* presents, primarily with images that are often disjunctive with the psychological and crime narratives, reflects a historical crime, the violence attending the Euro-American continental ethnogenesis.

Although North America experienced an undeniable Euro-American ethnogenesis, minutely recorded in mainstream histories of the West and in other genres, there are alternative Wests. While, for example, the Broadway musical *Oklahoma!* (1948) portrays an almost exclusively white ethnoscape, the Oklahoma territory existing at the time referenced in the musical, which is situated at the beginning of the twentieth century prior to statehood, contained many displaced Native American tribes, a considerable number of "Negro cowboys," and twenty-six all-black towns.[19] But the most familiar genre participating in the effacement of alternative Wests remains the classic Hollywood western, among which John Ford's are the most notable and enduring.

John Ford's Cinematic West

Arguably, no one has been more influential than director John Ford in locating the Anglo-Indian encounters in the West within the dominant American imaginary. But although some of Ford's westerns seem to celebrate the displacement of a Native American "wilderness" with Euro-American settlements (symbolized, for example, by the evocation of gardens in both *My Darling Clementine* (1949) and *The Man Who Shot Liberty Valance* (1962), others offer critical perspectives on the heroic versions of Euro-America's continental expansion. While some of his best-known films unambiguously portray, and seemingly approve, a whitening of the American continent, others resist an unambiguous endorsement of Euro-American expansion; they *think*, not always by virtue of the main story line but often through the image sequence, which is at times disjunctive with a heroic, Euro-American nation-building narrative.

Among Ford's less critical versions of an increasingly Anglo-dominated West is *Stagecoach* (1939), his first film featuring John Wayne (as the Ringo Kid). Although the film does not display the clashes among alternative meaning systems, Euro versus Native American and eastern versus western Euro culture, the former of which is featured starkly in *Cheyenne Autumn* (1964) and the latter in *The Man Who Shot Liberty Valance*, *Stagecoach* is nevertheless where Ford first makes the landscape itself effectively one of his major characters.[20] As Gilles Deleuze

puts it, in this film, as subsequently, Ford stages "intense collective moments" that reflect a historical social dynamic in a setting where "the
milieu encompasses the people."[21] The moments involved in *Stagecoach* are those that Ford creates to select which character types are
to become part of the dominant national culture. He tracks the social
changes involved in the shaping of a nation in the context of a landscape that appears to invite those changes. As Deleuze insightfully puts
it: "For Ford . . . society changes, and does not stop changing, but the
changes take place in an encompasser which covers them and blesses
them with a healthy illusion as continuity of the nation."[22]

A cinematic version of a story he found in the magazine *Colliers*,
Ernest Haycock's "Stage to Lourdsburgh," Ford's *Stagecoach* is more
or less complicit with the view of the West favored in *Colliers*, which
is typified by Owen Wister's *Colliers* stories and is depicted in Frederick Remington's accompanying illustrations (influences that Ford,
among other directors of classic westerns, acknowledged). The West
is presented as an evolving social order that is to become assimilated
into the Euro-American geopolitical and social space.[23] In *Stagecoach*
this evolving order is manifested during the long stagecoach journey
that occupies the primary narrative and image spaces of the film. The
occupants of the stagecoach, a disparate and often feuding group of
types, are a microcosm of that evolving social order. While constituting
a tribute to the historic expansion of a tolerant social democracy, the
film's Anglo characters—a southern gentleman gambler, a prostitute, a
soldier's pregnant wife, an outlaw, an alcoholic doctor, a liquor salesman,
and a banker—despite their lack of social cohesion, are a group of types
represented for all their flaws as part of a Euro-American-dominated
future. They are represented as destined to displace unreliable Hispanics and dangerous "savages," who are depicted, during the stagecoach's
various stops, as characterologically unfit to negotiate a shared political
order.

While the romantic part of the story, in which the Ringo Kid and
the ex-prostitute, Dallas, become a couple, is one dimension of the
film's resolution, the film's more general historical resolution involves
the successful incursion of white society into Indian country. Nevertheless, the film conveys some ambivalence about that success, primarily
through its use of irony—for example, the exaggerated fright reactions
of the travelers when they encounter an Indian woman, who is the wife
of a Mexican managing one of the stagecoach stations. For the most

part, however, the Indians are simply a menace in the western land-scape. Their attack on the stagecoach is repulsed, thanks to the heroics of the Ringo Kid and the last-minute arrival of the cavalry, which is depicted as an effective arm of white governance.

The imagery of the landscape and the tendency of Ford's camera to view Indians from a distance accords with Theodore Roosevelt's in-fluential rendering of the western landscape in his monumental *The Winning of the West,* which simultaneously celebrates Euro-American cultural and territorial expansion and evacuates the Native American presence.[24] As the nineteenth-century anthropologist Lewis H. Morgan noted, to make "Indian life" intelligible, "their house life and domestic institutions must furnish the key."[25] In contrast, Ford's Indians, shot for the most part outside, are represented only as threats to white domes-ticity (especially in *The Searchers* [1956]). At a minium, they achieve no ethnographic depth in *Stagecoach* and very little in his subsequent films. However, as Ford's filmic corpus develops, the injustice of the white dispossession of Native American provenances surfaces. In one of his later westerns, *The Man Who Shot Liberty Valance,* Ford's celebra-tion of Euro-American nation-building takes a dark turn. A soliloquy by the town's newspaper man, Dutton Peabody, when he nominates Ransom Stoddard (the man whose main claim to fame is his alleged shooting of the outlaw Liberty Valance) for the post of territorial rep-resentative, emphasizes the film's nation-building narrative. However that narrative is compromised by the fact that Tom Doniphon (John Wayne), who lives by the gun, actually shot Valance, not the book-toting lawyer, Ransom Stoddard (James Stewart). Peabody begins with a gloss on the West's past, which dismisses its prior Native American inhabitants as lawless and violent savages. That West contained, he says, "The vast herd of buffalo and savage redskins roaming our terri-tory with no law to trammel them except the law of survival, the law of the tomahawk and the bow and arrow." He then refers to the first wave of representatives of white America, who replaced one form of violence with another, more heroic (albeit now outmoded) variety: "And then with the westward march of our nation came the pioneer and the buf-falo hunter . . . and the boldest of these the cattlemen who seized the wide open range as their personal domain . . . and their law was the law of the hired gun." And, finally, he addresses himself to the present need for statehood in order to incorporate the territory into a populist, demo-cratic nation: "Now today have come the railroad and the people, the citizen, the homesteader, the shopkeeper, the builder of cities . . . and we need statehood to protect the rights of every man and woman however humble." Peabody's genealogy of the characters whose presence has dominated the West at different historical junctures sets up the conclusion he seeks, the appropriateness of electing Ransom Stoddard, whom he identifies as one who "came to us not packing a gun but a bag of law books . . . a lawyer and a teacher" and became subsequently "a man who has become known in the last few weeks as a great champion of law and order."

But the misrepresentation that is central to Stoddard's identity impeaches the patriotic, nation-building tenor of Peabody's soliloquy. The "what kind of man" query that Stoddard aims at Liberty Valance early in the film effectively haunts Stoddard's misleading heroic existence and, by implication, America's nationhood as a whole. Alan Nadel puts it well when he refers to Stoddard's "chronic inability to give authority to his assertions until be becomes the man who shot Liberty Valance . . . until he becomes the person he's not."[26] Ultimately the reverence for words and books, for which Stoddard is an avatar, is undermined by the moral ambiguities afflicting his identity.

The issue of words and the West arises again in what is Ford's most sympathetic treatment of Native Americans, his *Cheyenne Autumn*, based on a historic, futile trek by what was left of a branch of the Cheyenne nation as they attempted to defy the U.S. government and leave their arid southwestern reservation to return to their homeland in the Dakotas. In his earlier *Fort Apache* (1948), Ford also treats white injustice toward the Indians, but there, as Tag Gallagher points out, the dramatis personae are white, never red; Ford's focus is on "the traditions and community values that render otherwise decent individuals into willing agents of imperialism and genocide."[27] But in treating the Indian with more ethnographic depth in *Cheyenne Autumn*, Ford emphasizes the Cheyenne's inability to have their words count and includes scenes in which they have decisive, within-nation conversations about their options. The film foregrounds the disjuncture between white and red systems of intelligibility and ultimately represents the Euro-American victory as not simply an example of superior firepower but also as a discursive one. As it is put in the film, "It is white words, white language that have been our potent weapon against Indians."

Ford's ambivalence toward the victory of white words in the West in *Cheyenne Autumn* articulates with his more general ambivalence toward the white American continental ethnogenesis, which is most evident in what is arguably one of the most significant twentieth-century films, Ford's *The Searchers*. In *The Searchers*, Ford's West becomes more complicated than it was in his earlier films. Here the main character, Ethan Edwards, played by John Wayne, who is unambiguously heroic in *Stagecoach* as the Ringo Kid, becomes both hero and anti-hero. On the one hand, he is an exemplar of heroic masculinity, wise in the ways of his adversaries and protective of those with whom he is associated. But on the other, he is an Indian-hating racist, unfit to participate in the West's multiethnic future.

Certainly *The Searchers* partakes of the traditional Euro-American patriotism, inaugurated in the silent westerns and continued in the classic ones. Virginia Wright Wexman describes well the patriotic sentiments conveyed in the historical trajectory of westerns that feature Euro-American settlers encroaching on Indians, and who in turn are menaced by Indian attacks and saved by the U.S. cavalry: "Patriotic motifs overwhelm the sense of violence and exclusion implicit in such scenarios by appealing to a mythology of American national origin centered on the sanctity of the image of the family farm."[28] *The Searchers* opens with a shot from inside the family farm out toward a vast, open landscape, from which Ethan Edwards is approaching. However, the details of the family drama in the film—it is implied that Ethan has had a romantic attachment to his brother's wife—are less important than the historical context and social setting. Ford's film maps the expanding world of post–Civil War America and reenacts the encounters among white settlers, Spanish aristocrats, and Indian nations shortly after Texas had become independent.

The film's historical moment is right after Texas had violently extracted itself from Mexican control and was in a period of ongoing war with Comanches (who were not defeated until the Red River War of 1874–1875). In the film, a Comanche war party led by Scarface kills Ethan's brother and wife, rapes, mutilates, and kills their eldest daughter, Lucy, and carries off Debbie, the younger daughter. The episode precipitates a captivity narrative (one of the oldest modes of American literature). The main searchers are Ethan and young Martin Pawley, a part Cherokee, whose Indianness is constantly disparaged by Ethan during their quest to find Debbie and exact revenge for the massacre. The search proceeds for five years, allowing Ford to present the articulation of generational and historical time. Ethan's paternal relationship with Martin (which he resists until making his will near the end of the film) sets a background for his anti-miscegenation fixation. Although Ethan ultimately resists the impulse, he has sworn to kill Debbie when he finds her, because she has become an intimate of a Comanche and, in his words, is "no longer white." Although Ford's film is somewhat more ambivalent about the ethnogenesis of the Euro-American state than, for example, James Fenimore Cooper's novels, he offers a similar resolution, put into the mouth of Mrs. Jorgensen, the mother of Martin Pawley's "intended," Laurie. She remarks at one point that the West will have a white future, but perhaps not until "all their bones are in the ground."

Nevertheless, Ford's film is not simply a narrative of white civilization displacing savage Indianness in the West. As is the case with Ford's films in general, a strictly narrative account misses the play of opposing forces and world views that clash in the film. Indeed, Ford's film anticipates the "dysnarrative" aspect of later, so-called experimental cinema,[29] for *The Searchers* contains a resolution-inhibiting encounter between two different orders of coherence, the narrative and the structural. While in the narrative register a resolution occurs because Ethan decides to bring Debbie home rather than killing her, structurally much of the imagery—stark juxtapositions between dark domestic interiors and a wide, seemingly untamable landscape—suggests that the space is too large to afford easy incorporation into the cultural habitus of any one group. Moreover, there is no clear dividing line between Euro- and Native Americans. Certainly Euro-American practices of exchange are juxtaposed to Native American trading practices, most notably the difference between the Double Eagle coins that Ethan throws around and the trade that Martin effects for a blanket (while he is unaware that he is also acquiring a wife). But Ethan and his adversary, Scarface, operate with similar revenge motifs. And Ethan, despite his articulated contempt for Indians, displays many instances of Indianness—for example, speaking Comanche, desecrating a corpse to compromise its spiritual future, and scalping the dead Scarface. And the different groups are also similar in their violence. The scene of Ethan's brother's burned farmhouse and dead bodies is parallel to a scene of a burned Indian village with dead bodies, courtesy of the Seventh Cavalry.

Most significantly, the antagonisms and boundary protection exhibited by Ethan Edwards are juxtaposed to that of a searcher who is seemingly peripheral to the main search, old Mose Harper, the man who without even trying actually finds the missing Debbie (and whose various appearances constitute a dysnarrative). Although the humorous antics of Mose tend to be treated by viewers as mere comic relief (for example, while he and the other Texas Rangers are under fire during a ferocious Indian attack, he exclaims, "thank thee Lord for what we are about to receive"), Mose can be seen instead as one who operates outside of the racial-spatial order and its attendant antagonisms. While controlling territory, seeking revenge, and, in general, having one's eth-nos dominate the landscape is what drives Ethan and Scarface, Mose is unimpressed with boundaries and enemies.

In one scene, when chasing Indians is on the agenda, Mose begins an Indian dance rather than grabbing a weapon. And when he appears at each key juncture in the story, first at the farmhouse when the Rang-ers form a posse in search of stolen cattle, then as he returns to see the farmhouse burned, and toward the end when he is asked to report on Debbie's whereabouts, a rocking chair is central to the scene. In the first, he sits in a rocker inside the house and, on taking his leave, thanks his hostess for the chair (while the others mention only the coffee). In the second, he finds the rocker outside the burned-out farmhouse, and while the others are dealing with their anger and grief, he sits down to rock. Finally, in the third, he offers the information to Ethan about how

Mose grabbing a rocking chair in *The Searchers*. Courtesy of Warner Home Video.

to find Debbie in exchange for a promise of his very own rocking chair. Rather than merely exhibiting a demented and lazy loafer, through the character Mose, Ford's film offers a different kind of life world, one in which the main desire is to abide without ethnic enmity and territorial displacement. For this reason among others, the film cannot be easily enlisted along with those texts that warrant or celebrate the nineteenth-century version of Euro-American imperial expansion.

The exceptional ambiguity evinced in *The Searchers* and the criticism of Euro-American imperialism implied in *Cheyenne Autumn* are important for subsequent critical treatments of the Euro-American ethnogenesis, particularly the latter film's emphasis on the dominance of white words in winning the West. The scenes of a vast expanse in *The Searchers* and the insight about a linguistic/cognitive form of imperialism in *Cheyenne Autumn* have a phantom presence in Wim Wenders's *Paris, Texas*, which contains numerous filmic references to both. Despite how oblique those references are, *Paris, Texas* articulates Burgoyne's above noted insight about "the disguised operational center of the nation-state . . . [its] hidden text concerning its relationship with American Indians." However, before treating Wenders's western palimpsest, I subject Ford's West to the version provided by Altman, which confronts the classic western more directly.

Despite Ford's more critical turn in his later films, a refiguring of Euro-America's continental ethnogenesis in order to achieve a more powerful critique requires a different mode of cinematic thinking, one that articulates itself in Robert Altman's two westerns, *McCabe and Mrs. Miller* (1971) and *Buffalo Bill and the Indians: Or Sitting Bull's History Lesson* (1976). In what follows, I treat the way Altman structures his films to dislodge the imagistic and narrative clichés with which the West has been produced in classic westerns. In these two films, Altman exercises his exemplary politics, a subversion of "set ideas, fixed theses, platitudes, things that say this is this."[30] In the process he offers a cinematic politics of history that restages and thus rethinks America's western experience.

Resisting the Cliché: *McCabe and Mrs. Miller*

What has been the dominant figuration and story of the American West? From the three aesthetic genres of legendary history, painting, and fiction—of Theodore Roosevelt, Frederick Remington, and Owen

Wister, respectively—to the classic western films of at least part of John Ford's film corpus, the West, as it was narrated and figured throughout much of the twentieth century, has been primarily a heroic story about Euro-American cultural and political expansion on a large panoramic frontier, under a big sky. The movie screen to which Altman addressed his work was thus not blank; it was already filled symbolically with figures, spaces, and narratives. The conceptual implications of the already-saturated historical West with which Altman was faced when he decided to do a western are effectively addressed in Gilles Deleuze's already noted treatment of the painter Francis Bacon (in chapter 2), who faced a similar historical plenitude. To repeat Deleuze's important insight: it is wrong to assume that the artist "works on a white surface." Rather, "everything he has in his head, or around him is already on the canvass, more or less virtually, before he begins his work."[31] To resist what Deleuze calls "psychic clichés" and *figurative givens,*" the artist must "transform" or "deform" what is "always-already on the canvass."[32] This is as much the case with the silver screen as it is with the painter's canvass. Given, for example, John Ford's West, the vast open prairie located in Monument Valley, where he filmed eight of his westerns, Altman needed to find a different kind of landscape, filled with characters other than the heroic types, in order both to deform the classic western and to achieve a different, more complicated and politically perspicuous West in his *McCabe and Mrs. Miller.* He called his film an "'anti-Western' because the film turns a number of Western conventions on their sides, including male dominance and the heroic standoff; gunplay is a solution only after reputation, wit, and nonviolent coercion fail; and law and order do not always prevail."[33]

Altman's resistance to the clichés of the classic western is pervasive in *McCabe,* beginning with the opening scene, whose deformation of the earlier westerns becomes apparent if we contrast it with the opening scene in Ford's *The Searchers,* which depicts the slow arrival from a large, open prairie of Ethan Edwards (John Wayne), viewed by his sister-in-law from the interior of her cabin. This shot, repeated at the end of the film, with a different figure in the doorway, as Ethan's departure is viewed from within a domestic venue, is a moment of referential montage reflecting the nation-building theme that lends coherence to most of Ford's westerns. The "Anglo couple" or "family on the land" thematic is part of a "nationalist ideology" in Ford (as in the prior D. W. Griffith silent westerns). Although, as I indicated, Ford eventually evinced ambivalence about the advance of Euro-American civilization westward (in his *The Man Who Shot Liberty Valance* and *Cheyenne Autumn*), most of his films have participated—but not without ironic qualifying moments—in the figuring of the Euro-family as a bastion against the threat of interracial marriage and against a competing model of familial attachment, the Indians' clan- or lineage-based system of intimacy and attachment.[34]

In *The Searchers*, the theme of domesticity and belonging versus migrancy and separation is reinforced by the soundtrack. As the credits are run against a playbill-style font face on an adobe brick wall, we hear the Sons of the Pioneers singing the Stan Jones ballad "What Makes a Man to Wander?":

> What makes a man to wander?
> What makes a man to roam?
> What makes a man leave bed and board
> And turn his back on home?
> Ride away, ride away.

In contrast, as the credits are run in the opening scene in *McCabe and Mrs. Miller*, it becomes apparent that Altman's film is not a story about the importance of establishing a stable, Euro-American domesticity in the West. The difference between McCabe's opening ride and Ethan Edwards's overturns the Ford clichés in various modalities. As John McCabe (Warren Beatty) rides toward the town of Presbyterian Church, the soundtrack begins with a ballad, in this case Leonard Cohen's "The Stranger Song." While the ballads by the Sons of the Pioneers in *The Searchers* and Leonard Cohen in *McCabe* manifest the typical ballad style—they are narrative poems with repeated refrains—Cohen's portrays a very different kind of character. Rather than a heroic wanderer, Cohen's "stranger" is an anti-hero, a hustler looking for shelter rather than the typical western hero, a tough loner who is unfit for domesticity even though he helps those who are weaker to achieve it[35]:

> It's true that all the men you knew were dealers
> Who said they were through with dealing
> Every time you gave them shelter
> I know that kind of man
> It's hard to hold the hand of anyone

who is reaching for the sky just to surrender
who is reaching for the sky just to surrender . . .
He was just some Joseph looking for a manger,
He was just some Joseph looking for a manger . . .

It should be recalled, however, that Ford's Ethan Edwards is not entirely the stereotypic western hero. Although Edwards is the rugged loner who saves those less tough and wily from destruction, his departure is not simply that of one too individualistic to accommodate a social or domestic existence. Because of his racism he cannot accommodate himself to a multiracial society. In deforming Ford's approach to the hero, Altman is thus deforming something already to some extent deformed. Ford had already complicated the traditional hero of the classic western.

However, Ford's landscapes remain unaltered clichés. As the Joseph line is sung in Leonard Cohen's first ballad in the *McCabe* soundtrack, the outskirts of the town of Presbyterian Church come into view, with a church in the center background. It is evident that Presbyterian Church contrasts dramatically with John Ford's frontier. As the story unfolds, what is presented is not the displacement of a wilderness with a garden, as the wild west becomes civilized (imagery both shown and verbalized in Ford's *My Darling Clementine* and *The Man Who Shot Liberty Valance*), but rather a chaotic and violent mélange of unenviable characters. And rather than a vast frontier, Presbyterian Church is a muddy town in a rainy mountain venue that is far from the exemplar of an outpost for building national community in the wide open West. Filled, as the story progresses, with hustlers, derelicts, profiteers, and predatory corporate advance men, Presbyterian Church's anti-western tenor is marked not only by the difference in landscape and character but also by cinematically evinced moods—cinematographer Vilmos Zsigmond's dark tones and washed-out, almost colorless landscapes and Leonard Cohen's melancholy ballads.

Cohen's "The Stranger Song" complements the moody, unsure, and blustering McCabe; his "Winter Song" articulates with an emotionless, opium-distracted, managerial Mrs. Miller (Julie Christie); and his "Sisters of Mercy" song accompanies (while playing into the pervasive religious idiom) the arrival of the homely, disheveled "chippies" (in McCabe's unbusinesslike, sexist idiom), prostitutes McCabe plans to employ in his under-construction saloon-bathhouse-bordello. The

McCabe in *McCabe and Mrs. Miller.* Courtesy of Warner Home Video.

somber cinematic mood evoked by sound, light, and color is of a piece with the "somber mood of the new western history," which in recent decades has lent complexity to a West that had been represented as a beckoning destiny. In the new western histories, the West becomes instead a site of imperial expansion, involving, alternately, negotiation and violence, trading and exploitation, among Euro-, Native, and Spanish Americans.[36]

The color tones play an especially important role in Altman's attempt to code the West. As Altman implies, the washed-out tones are intended to give the audience a historical sense of the West: "I was trying to give a sense of antiquity, of vagueness, and to make this not a life that you're living but a life that you're looking through."[37] And he had to invert his characters as well in his cinematic coding because of the way the West already existed in the audience's received stock of signs. Given what is always already on the screen as one attempts to write and direct a western—the platitudes and clichés of the advance of civilization, of the heroic gun fighter taming a lawless wilderness, and of women who are vehicles for expanding a stable domesticity westward—Altman's *McCabe* is thoroughly subversive. McCabe is a dressed up dandy and low-level card shark who achieves undeserved charisma after his arrival because of the character vacuum that precedes him and because of the false rumor that he has "a big rep," spread by a saloon owner, Mr. Sheehan, who claims that McCabe shot the dangerous Bill Roundtree. And in contrast with the canniness of Ethan Edwards in *The Search-*

ers, a man who anticipates dangers and survives while rescuing others with his daring and deep knowledge of the land- and ethnoscape of the West, McCabe is a not-very-bright bumbler. He cannot control his "chippies" (one of whom is shown attacking a client with a knife); he proves unable to do the math when he and Mrs. Miller go into business together; and fatally, he fails to discern the consequences of rejecting an offer from the large and predatory mining company to buy out his business. Unable to convince him to take their generous offer, they send a hired killer to get him out of the way.

Yet it is not simply a lack of intelligence that ultimately dooms McCabe, who dies in a snowdrift after being fatally wounded by the company's hired gun, Butler (Hugh Millais), whom McCabe dispatches as well with his derringer before he dies. McCabe is done in by his stubborn adherence to the myth of the small independent entrepreneur. He rejects Sheehan's early offer of a partnership aimed at excluding outsiders with the words, "partners is what I came here to get away from." And he is a prey to the naive, moral economy code mouthed by the lawyer he consults, Clement Samuels, who, full of pomposities and clichés, says, "when a man goes into the wilderness and builds something with his own hands, no one is going to take it away from him." Referring to "the very values that make this country what it is today," Samuels adds that "til people start dying for freedom, they aint goin' to be free." Ultimately, Samuels encourages McCabe to "strike a blow for the little man." Clearly the reversed name of Samuel Clemens (Mark Twain), a writer whose tongue was always planted firmly in his cheek, Samuels helps to convey Altman's disdain for self-destructive and unrealistic platitudes. By the time McCabe realizes that pious platitudes will not save him, it is too late. Unable to make a deal with the hired gunman, who says he does not make deals, McCabe flees to an assortment of buildings that represent other architecturally materialized pieties—the church, from which he is flushed out by a gun-wielding parson, and a "house of fortune" run by a local entrepreneur.

However, the overturning of verbal and visual clichés does not exhaust Altman's cinematic strategy in presenting a critical version of western history. The perspective on the facticity or the nature of what is taking place that the film invites the viewer to adopt is assisted by characters who have little relationship to the film's dramatic narrative, the catastrophe that befalls the McCabe-Miller enterprise. A young African American, Sumner Washington (Rodney Gage), shows up in a wagon with some of Mrs. Miller's sex workers, whose wagon had broken down. He introduces his wife to Mrs. Miller and says that he's a barber by profession. Thereafter, he and his wife are present to the action at various moments, offering by dint of shot/reverse shot sequences a perspective from their points of view.

To understand the Washingtons' role in the film's aesthetic strategy we can return to Deleuze's treatment of Francis Bacon, to the place where he points to the presence in some of Bacon's canvasses of a figure or figures that have no narrative relationship to the central figure, the "attendant," who (as noted in chapter 2) is a "spectator," but not in the ordinary sense. It is a "kind of spectator" who "seems to subsist, distinct from the figure."[38] As I have pointed out, this spectator plays an epistemic role, according to Deleuze, and provides the basis for determining the facticity of the scene, "the relation of the Figure to its isolating place," or "what takes place."[39]

Invariably, the look the viewer gets from the Washingtons' point of view, each time the camera cuts from a group of men to the observing couple, reveals childish, self-centered behavior associated with interactions among crude, uncivil men. While the Washingtons always appear well dressed and dignified, the disheveled men they watch, at times cavorting and at times brutalizing each other, are the opposite. The point of view and contrast offered by these cuts to the Washingtons-as-attendants establishes a mode of facticity in the West that was largely fugitive in the classic westerns. What the Washingtons' comportment and gaze tend to emphasize is the unreliability of a culture, shaped by the interactions among men, to establish a mode of communal intimacy. And what we see (as we see them and with them) is reinforced in numerous scenes as well as in Altman's multi-aural soundtrack. From an early scene in Sheehan's saloon, through the other male gatherings, the peripheral conversations taking place outside of the main camera shots are audible. They often involve the exchange of unreliable and/or mythic information. In contrast, the scenes among women reveal a playful, caring, and supportive communal harmony.

A telling moment of parallel editing emphasizes the difference: while a group of Mrs. Miller's sex workers, which includes a Chinese woman, are sharing a bath and engaging in playful exchanges, the scene cuts to the men playing cards in another room. As the scene cuts back to the nude women, one of the men's voices can be heard as he passes on a rumor about the distinctive physical attributes of Asian women, a rumor that is belied by what the viewer can see. Throughout the film, once the contrast between the bumbling McCabe and the canny Mrs. Miller is established, inept, violent, and uncivil men are contrasted with what appears to be an orderly and civil women's society within the brothel. In scene after scene, the viability of the civility among women trumps that of the (un)civil culture among men as a basis for community.

Certainly John Ford, in his early *Stagecoach*, displays a generosity toward the former prostitute Dallas, who turns out to be a promising prototype character for the West-to-come. But the value of her character for such a role is inextricably connected to her coming marriage (an identity shift from prostitute to wife) to the hero, the Ringo Kid, who also emerges from a damaged identity, a change from "outlaw" to inchoate rancher/settler. And doubtless even the classic westerns sought to note the importance of strong women in the emerging Euro-dominated West—for example, "extraordinary heroines from Mae West's Klondike Annie and Doris Day's Calamity Jane, to Joan Crawford's Vienna and Barbara Stanwick's Jessica Drummond."[40] But Mrs. Miller is a different type. Her toughness is entrepreneurial. Having the knowledge and experience needed to develop and manage a sex work force, she has to convince the town's only innovator, McCabe, to develop a larger vision because he has the only building that would make a viable space for her business. And although McCabe becomes her occasional (paying) sex partner, it is through canny economic talk and a no-nonsense approach to all areas of the business that she breaks down McCabe's initial resistance and makes him her business partner.

When they first meet and Mrs. Miller asks to be taken to a place for breakfast, McCabe's face registers amazement as he watches her attack her meal without the least hint of a stereotypic feminine delicacy. Here again, Altman's camera work carries the burden of mapping the encounter of the characters. In particular, the face shots of McCabe— subsequently repeated in other scenes in which Mrs. Miller displays an unladylike manner—convey what McCabe's agency is about in the film: a puzzlement stemming from an inability to evade stereotypical thinking. Face shots, or what Deleuze calls the "affection-images" (noted earlier in the chapter), locate the intentionality of the self. The face, Delenze suggests, is the place where the meaning of all the bodily movements, as an ensemble of the agency of the self, is registered. It is responsive to the questions "What are you thinking about?" and "How do you feel?"[41] In contrast, except for the dreamy moments when Mrs. Miller is high on opium, the face shots of her demeanor register the determination of someone in control of her surroundings.

Ultimately a structural dynamic overpowers whatever effects issue from the force of the personalities that constitute the McCabe-Mrs. Miller enterprise. Here it is apropos to refer to what Noël Burch has famously called two kinds of filmic space, that within the frame and that outside of it.[42] Two visits, one by the mining company's advance men and one by their hit man, take place within the frame. In confrontation with the advance men, who try to buy him out, we witness a cocksure McCabe who rejects their offer. When the hit man arrives, riding in like all strangers in westerns, we witness a different McCabe, a fearful, ingratiating version whose attempts at mollifying these new representatives go for naught. But the two sets of visitors, whose interactions with McCabe reveal McCabe-the-anti-hero's instability, are connected to a powerful force outside the frame, the force of capital.

Altman's attention to the way that corporate capital displaces the efforts of the small entrepreneur impugns the clichés that attend settlement in the classic westerns and, most significantly, challenges various narratives of "the winning of the west," especially those based on notions of civilizational superiority. At a minimum, the heroic cowboys are displaced by bumbling maladroits, who appear as mere children compared to the women, whose civic skills create the only communal stability. But even the more perspicuous narratives that emerge from Ford's films—that the law book has displaced the gun (in his *The Man Who Shot Liberty Valance*) and that "words won the West" (in his *Cheyenne Autumn*)—are overturned by the lesson in political economy offered by *McCabe*. All that was missing from *McCabe* by way of an important political pedagogy was the fate of the "Indian." But Altman turned to this pedagogy explicitly five years later in his *Buffalo Bill and the Indians: Or Sitting Bull's History Lesson*. In this film, Altman turns his attention not simply to the unjust immiseration of Native America, but also to an issue that preoccupied John Ford, the distinction between history and legend.

History as Counter-Memory: *Buffalo Bill and the Indians . . .*

For Altman, his *Buffalo Bill* draws on elements from both *Nashville* (1975) and *McCabe—Nashville* because the film is "about show business" and *McCabe* because it is aimed at sweeping away mythic or legendary forms of history. He wanted, he said, "to take a more honest look . . . at some of our myths . . . to see what they are. It's no accident that the picture is subtitled *Sitting Bull's History Lesson*."[43] Yet, as Altman puts it, "It's going the opposite way from *McCabe*—it's saying that this idea of the West is all show business."[44] Moreover, while, as I have noted, Altman's *McCabe* becomes intelligible as a critical intervention in the symbolic production of the American West when viewed *against* some of John Ford's cinematic clichés, his *Buffalo Bill* articulates the Ford inspiration constitutive of the narrative in his *The Man Who Shot Liberty Valance*; Altman's *Buffalo Bill*, like Ford's *Valance*, renders the heroic story of the West as mythic. Although competence with the gun (a feature of the heroic cowboy) remains very much in the moral center of *Valance*, the gunplay is mythical rather than heroic, and the typical narrative of the classic western—the taming of the West by the spread of eastern culture, and the territorial extension of the white American imaginary—is undercut by the paradoxes the film explores.[45] And most significantly for purposes of comparison with Altman's *Buffalo Bill*, publicists are some of *Valance*'s major characters.

Ford's *Valance* begins with Ransom Stoddard's account of his experiences from the time he arrives in the town of Shinbone (shown as an extended flashback), told to the editorial staff of the local paper. During the nomination process, Dutton Peabody stands up and lists Stoddard's accomplishments, which include his besting of Liberty Valance in a gunfight. However, in a subsequent scene, Stoddard learns that Tom Doniphon had in fact fired the fatal shot. What seemed like a simple, heroic, nation-building narrative, a man from the East bringing law and order to a violent West and subsequently incorporating his region into the nation as a state, turns out to be a commentary on the role of myth in the nation-building process. When the narrative returns to the present, the film's most famous line is uttered by the newsman, who having learned that Stoddard is not the man who shot Liberty Valance, and having been asked if he will print this revelation, says, "This is the West, sir. When the legend becomes fact, print the legend."

In *Buffalo Bill*, Altman takes up Ford's concern with the mythic West, not to debunk myths but, in his words, to have "another look at them," to move "to a place where I can look at them from a different angle."[46] The "look" that Altman provides is distinctive, for his *Buffalo Bill* is shot almost entirely with a telephoto lens. While the history tropes in Ford's *Valance* are largely a function of the black and white tone, Altman's in *Buffalo Bill* are a function of the tableaux produced through telephoto zooming effects. Although there are some panoramas in the film, Altman uses the telephoto "even [in] those big wide shots, in order to compress images [because] . . . Long lenses change the image and evoke antiquity."[47] Thus, while he uses color tones to connote antiquity in *McCabe*, it is the telephoto lens that achieves the time image in *Buffalo Bill*. But the time at the center of *Buffalo Bill* is not ethno-historical time—not the events involved in the white-Indian encounters in the West—but media historical time. This temporality is signaled early in the film. As the credits are run the soundtrack plays a tinny version of the music associated with cavalry charges in classic westerns, and later, when Sitting Bull enters the combat ring during the show, the soundtrack replays a Hollywood version of Indian drum music.

Who is looking and listening, and what are they/we hearing and seeing in *Buffalo Bill*? The time images achieved with Altman's telephoto lens and soundtrack articulate the film's primary trope of history as entertainment. With the telephoto effect, which situates the film as arena and/or museum for remote spectators, Altman's *Buffalo Bill* is constructed as a show, a meta-commentary on the kind of West that Buffalo Bill's Wild West Show produced, the West as entertainment. As one treatment of *Buffalo Bill* puts it, "In this film, the subjects are merged in the word 'show,' which represents both The Wild West *Show* of Buffalo Bill and the movie *show* about Buffalo Bill."[48] The sequence of events in the film is more or less homologous with the performance sequence in a Wild West show, especially in the way the key characters appear in succession, Buffalo Bill (Paul Newman), Sitting Bull (Frank Kaquitts), and President Grover Cleveland (Pat McCormick).

How then does the subtitle *"Or Sitting Bull's History Lesson"* play into the show-framing of the film? Once again, the answer is supplied by the form of the film. Despite acknowledging that his "Wild West" is a show, Buffalo Bill, his publicist, John Burk, and his emcee, Nate Salisbury, represent their reproductions as accurate portrayals of history. As a voice-over announcement at the outset of the show states, "What you are about to experience is not a show for entertainment, it is a review of the down-to-earth events that made the American frontier." And to enhance that history, which is conveyed as the heroic victory of settlers over blood-thirsty savages, they decide to enlist a historical "Indian"

Sitting Bull in *Buffalo Bill and the Indians*. Courtesy of MGM.

character and fit him into the most violent scenario that white America had been willing to acknowledge, the defeat of General Custer at Little Big Horn. Accordingly, Sitting Bull is represented (fraudulently) as the killer by the emcee, Salisbury, who, at the beginning of the show, introduces Sitting Bull as "the wicked warrior of the western plains, the cold-blooded killer of Custer . . . the untamed scavenger whose chilling and cowardly deeds created nightmares throughout the West and made him the most feared, the most murderous, the most colorful redskin alive . . . the battling chief of the Hunkpapa Sioux . . . Sitting Bull."

Yet a silent Sitting Bull's body undermines Salisbury's introduction, just as he had undermined earlier expectations when he first appeared. If we heed the "cinematographic body,"[49] realized in *Buffalo Bill* with the shots of Sitting Bull's bodily comportment, we see a different relationship between narrative and body from its familiar portrayal in classic cinema. Vincent Amiel refers to the subversive filmic body, pointing to those films in which "the cinematographic body is no longer an object of film or knowledge; rather it is a model of knowledge via editing. . . . [It is] simultaneously that which is filmed and that which (re)organizes the film in the mind/body of the spectator . . . [becoming the] source rather than the object of cinema,"[50] there is a clear application to Altman's *Buffalo Bill*.

Sitting Bull's body supplies a history lesson by effectively subverting the image that the show is trying to construct (exemplified in Salisbury's opening soliloquy). The Wild West Show's attempt to turn history into both entertainment and a Euro-American vindication, through the construction of a blood-thirsty savage to be bested by Buffalo Bill in the ring, is belied by the dignified body of Sitting Bull. First, Sitting Bull's inflated reputation as a savage killer is supposed to be reflected in his size. As he and his entourage ride in when he first joins the entertainment company, his very large associate, William Halsey, is mistaken for him. Sitting Bull turns out to be quite diminutive. Then he rides into the ring for his appearance in the drama of Little Big Horn as a silent and simply adorned old man, with a dignity and wisdom in his carriage that radically transcends the "show" in which he is displayed. His dignified entrance wins over the audience, whose initial jeers turn to applause, for he has managed to move out of the antagonistic role to which the show has assigned him.

On another level, silence is the historical role to which Native Americans have been consigned in Euro-America's dominant Indian imaginary. The stoic and inarticulate Indian, an image perpetuated in novels, paintings, and films, was part of a construction of the civilizational superiority that helped justify encroachment into Indian territories. In contrast, in Altman's *Buffalo Bill* the "silence of the Indians" is portrayed as a function of white inattention to their words. While Sitting Bull's silent dignity during the staged invention of an alter-Little Big Horn engagement in the show subverts one narrative, that of the violent, blood-thirsty savage, his silence in another scene is imposed. As the film progresses, it becomes clear that Sitting Bull was willing to subject himself to the indignity of false representations because he had hoped to meet President Cleveland in order to air his people's grievances. However, when President Cleveland visits Buffalo Bill's Wild West Show and appears at an evening gathering, he refuses to hear the case Sitting Bull has come to plead.

While the "Sitting Bull" expected by the Wild West production company is a product of the fraudulent media publicity that emerged from Custer's defeat at Little Big Horn, Buffalo Bill himself is also a constructed identity, shown in part through the many scenes in which his look is a function of the wig, makeup, and buckskin he puts on to appear in the show. But well before his Wild West Show, the historical Buffalo Bill was an invention of Ned Buntline's stories in dime novels, which turned a minor scout into a frontier hero. And the mythologizing that constructed "the West" is emphasized by the nature of the main personae involved in making Buffalo Bill a media creation, first in the dime novels and then in his role in the narratives dramatized in his traveling show. In the film, there is a producer, a publicist (representing Buntline), a journalist, an interpreter, and an old soldier who verbalizes false legends. And as is the case with Altman's *McCabe*, much of the mythology is simply overheard in peripheral conversations. For example, early in the film someone off camera can be heard saying that "Sitting Bull is famous for scalping folks in their beds."

As was the case with his *McCabe*, in his *Buffalo Bill* Altman makes use of attendants, in this case characters who have no relationship with the main narrative about the show—its exploitation of Sitting Bull, its fraudulent version of the Battle of Little Big Horn, and its failed attempt to separate image from fact. In *Buffalo Bill*, one of the attendants is an old soldier who delivers nothing but clichés about Buffalo Bill's heroism, and another is a bartender who articulates the myths surrounding both Sitting Bull and Buffalo Bill, thereby serving as a vehicle for the primary facticity that the film delivers, the western hero as invention.

In an early scene, as Sitting Bull's party appears, the bartender states that Sitting Bull is seven feet tall. And subsequently, when Buffalo Bill forms a posse that fails to track and apprehend Sitting Bull's party, under the mistaken assumption that they were fleeing (they had in fact left temporarily to perform a ritual celebration of the first moon in the mountains), the bartender expresses amazement as he looks at the forlorn hunting party that has returned empty-handed: "that's the greatest Indian Hunter of them all!" The bartender/attendant, a peripheral character, thus has some of the most important lines. But then, in film after film, bringing the periphery—both visual and aural—into the mix that constitutes a story's intelligibility is what Altman does.

"What Kind of a Man?": None of the Above

The question that Ransom Stoddard poses to the outlaw Liberty Valance after he robs a stagecoach and brutalizes a female passenger, "What kind of a man are you?" is central to the issue of the making of the West for Ford. Will it be the hero of the gun, the hero of the law, an ambiguous mixture of the two, or what? If Ford seemed to remain ambivalent about the answer to that question, he showed little ambivalence about the role of gender. If community rather than anomie was to win in the West, it would be a result of some kind of masculine agency, whoever those male agents might turn out to be. His films, through both their story lines and their forms, are centered by male heroes, however flawed those heroes might be (as is the case with his Ethan Edwards [John Wayne] in *The Searchers* and his Ransom Stoddard [James Stewart] and Tom Doniphon [John Wayne] in *Valance*).

In Altman's West, the men are anti-heroes. In *McCabe*, as it is put in Leonard Cohen's lyrics, we encounter a different kind of man from those who dominate in the classic westerns; it is "that kind of man . . . who is reaching for the sky just to surrender . . . just a Joseph looking for a manger." And in *Buffalo Bill* we encounter a thin media invention with a poor grasp of history and reality. In contrast, Mrs. Miller and her sex workers/employees in *McCabe* display the strength and social sensitivity that is almost totally absent in the men of Presbyterian Church. If community is at all possible, it will rest with their initiatives. And in Buffalo Bill, Annie Oakley, who threatens to quit if Sitting Bull is fired and forced to return to custody, is the only character who displays a respect for history and for Native American alterity. Altman implies that if a negotiated, non-exploitative sharing of the West would have been at all possible, it would have had to rest with a woman like Annie. Ultimately, Altman, as was his intention, gave us another look. That look has to be assessed in terms of the challenge it offers to the heroic Euro-American nation-building narratives it deforms.

Paris, Texas

There is a remarkable parallel between the openings in Ford's *The Searchers* and Wenders's *Paris, Texas*. Recalling the opening scene in *The Searchers*, when, after the song about what makes a man wander, which accompanies the opening credits, the first images are of a man riding in from a vast panorama in Monument Valley, Wenders's film begins with a man, Travis (Harry Dean Stanton), wandering over a large western landscape, close to the Mexican border. But unlike Ethan Edwards, who has a lot to say, Travis is silent; he says nothing after being treated by a doctor, who revives him after he collapses while trying to find something to drink at a remote gas station/convenience store. And seemingly having wandered "beyond the frontiers of language,"[51] he remains speechless for some time after his brother, Walt (Dean Stockwell), is summoned from California to fetch him.

Although some of the film's narrative can be contained within a Freudian family story, particularly one oriented around patriarchal violence, the implied historical narrative of the plot, along with the dysnarrative and disjunctive effects of the landscape images, tells a political rather than a psychological story.[52] Travis and his brother begin their journey to California without dialogue and with significantly different relationships to language. That Walt is the one who summons Travis back into the world of language is paradoxical. A prototypical middle-class man, Walt's speech consists of unremarkable platitudes, and his company makes roadside billboards. Apart from the banality of the language, both oral and visual, with which Walt is associated, the West to which he belongs evokes Ford's above noted insight into the words that have won the West, but with a decidedly Wenders inflection.

Wenders's West is "*the* place [in America] where things fall apart."[53] His West has been abandoned; "civilization," Wenders states, "simply passed through." Instead of a lot of people, "in the middle of a desert you come across a road sign reading: 375th Street."[54] Ultimately, as Wenders puts it, the West holds "names and writing . . . a lot of signboards, cinema facades, billboards half worn away by the elements, already falling apart."[55] Within such a version of the West, *Paris, Texas*'s Walt is an exemplar of Euro-America's contemporary habitus. Instead of the settlers' homes, around which the action in Ford's films take place, there are signs and billboards: "a man will paint a big sign first of all, and then the sign counts for more than the building."[56] And Los Angeles, where Walt lives and works, and which is the destination of Travis and Walt's journey, represents the ultimate in an ersatz relationship with place (where representations trump built structures). When Wenders's own western journey (prior to his film) ended in Los Angeles, he noted, "I was walking around in downtown Los Angeles, and all of a sudden down this dead end I saw a painted wall with its make believe windows and a dainty awning."[57]

Much of the imagery caught by Wenders's still camera in his western journey is central to his cinematic West in *Paris, Texas*, in which many of the shots exhibit America's contemporary name-dominated habitus. The dominating imagistic aspect of the film's focus on signs is reflected in the location scouting stills, taken before the filming began. There are motel signs, road signs, abandoned café buildings with names in large lettering, and, most tellingly, a small, almost effaced sign in the midst of an empty desert tract, which reads, "Western World Development Tract 6271."[58] Rather than seeing America's "world of names" as merely a commentary on a contemporary rift between person and place, *Paris, Texas* offers hints of a history of violent displacement that the naming-dominated, white American settlements overcode. The words that won the West no longer seem to need those who vocalize them.

The naming preoccupation in Wenders and Shepard's screenplay is influenced by the Austrian novelist Peter Handke; the expressions "world of names" and "places of names" appear often in Handke's novelette *The Long Way Around,* which features a contrast between the Native American mode of dwelling in Alaska and the Euro-American mode of dwelling in cities such as Berkeley (where apartment buildings have "colonized woods"), Denver, and New York. In the novelette, the Northern Lights, which for Native Americans have cosmological significance, are reduced to the name of a street, "Northern Lights Boulevard" in a California city.[59] Foregrounding the "violence of representation"[60] inherent in such naming practices, the film narrative in *Paris, Texas* is concerned with two different levels of violence.

At an individual level, Travis, once he is summoned back into language, recovers the memory of his violence toward his estranged wife, Jane. At the end of his personal search, which is consummated when he restores the relationship between Jane and their son, Hunter, he is able to verbalize his past violent acts and take responsibility for them. At another level, however, the film ponders Euro-America's collective violence, primarily through images rather than through Travis's personal drama, which constitutes the film's major narrative thread. In a scene in which Travis returns to his son, Hunter, after a long encounter with his wife, the film cuts to an alley where the words "RACE, BLOOD, LAND" are written on a wall. At roughly the same time, the camera shows the large head of a Native American woman as part of a mural on the wall, and an African American version of the Statue of Liberty is briefly shown on a wall nearby. And yet another aspect of the history of imperial violence is thematized. When Travis finally converses with his brother, Walt, we learn that they are Hispanic on their mother's side:

TRAVIS: Do you remember how Momma's very first names were?
WALT: Mary.
TRAVIS: No, I mean her . . . before she found Daddy.
WALT: Oh, her maiden name.
TRAVIS: Yes
WALT: You don't remember her maiden name?

TRAVIS: No.
WALT: Sequin.
TRAVIS: Sequin, Spanish?

At one level, the exchange is about Travis's faulty memory, which accords with his other, temporary language and memory deficits. But at another level it can be connected to America's forgetfulness of its considerable Spanish heritage. It becomes evident that the contemporary American geopolitical imaginary is as forgetful of the demise of Spanish America as it is of Native America. The geopolitical map of the United States fails to record the fate of Mexican Americans, who, during the period in which Anglo conquerors took over California, Texas, and the rest of Spanish America (as noted in chapter 2), "found themselves inside the United States [as] foreigners on their own land."[61] America's western palimpsest, now a world of signs, is written over its erased Hispanic as well as its Native American markings.

Subsequent to the conversation that restores his recollection of his Mexican heritage, Travis sings a melancholy Spanish song while in Walt's home, and later he renews his familiarity with this part of his heritage in a conversation with his brother and sister-in-law's Mexican maid, Carmelita, who asks him identity questions to help him select a mode of dress and a body language. She encourages him to adopt a more macho image. One ready-to-hand interpretation of the mixture

Landscape with sign in *Paris, Texas.* Courtesy of 20th Century Fox.

of cultural and national codes—including the disjunctive Paris-Texas, a German doctor who treats Travis after he collapses, Walt's wife, who is French, and the Spanish maid, Carmelita—is to evoke the idea of cultural conflict,[62] which, over the course of his career, has been one of Wenders's cinematic signatures (for example, it is central to his *The American Friend*). From a critically oriented, political perspective, however, it is more apposite to invoke the concept of critical *translation*. Recalling Walter Benjamin's insight that the translator is coming to terms with her/his own national-cultural-linguistic self-understanding while making sense of a foreign text, one can read Wenders's approach to Euro-America's violent past not only as a recovery of American history but also as a reflection on Germany's Nazi past as well as on the arbitrariness of geopolitical boundaries.

Wenders's film can therefore be seen as evoking the comparison (treated earlier in the chapter) between the genocidal assault on Native America and the *Shoah*. Again, Handke's *The Long Way Around* provides a proto-text. His main character, the Austrian geologist Valentin Sorger, discovers the violence of names on the American continent, while at the same time seeking to come to terms with the violence of the Nazi period in Germany and Austria. Attempting, through his simultaneous reading of America and Europe to evince a "science of peace" in the present, Handke's Sorger discovers that he must first free himself from being an unreflective part of his national patrimony, from being "the faithful replica of death-cult masters."[63] Like Handke, Wenders effects a simultaneous treatment of Nazi Germany's and Euro-America's racial violence—dramatically through the above noted slogans and figures on the wall, but also through one of the film's characters. *Paris, Texas* evokes the violence of Germany's past through the German-accented doctor who treats Travis before the point where he recovers from his collapse and "falls literally into the world of language."[64] The doctor turns out to be corrupt and greedy; his demand of a large payment from Walt as a ransom for Travis is another aspect of Wenders's critical look backward at the biopolitics of Germany during the Nazi period.

Ultimately, Wenders's *Paris, Texas* contains a strong narrative similarity to Ford's *The Searchers* inasmuch as both searchers, Ethan and Travis, remain loners at the ends of the stories. But as I have indicated, in *The Searchers* Ford, as in his other westerns, displays an ambivalent position on myth, seeing it as both destructive and necessary. Nevertheless, his films have continued to produce a West that remains the most familiar and which, by 1893, as Slotkin notes, had been historically "closed" as "a geographical place and a set of facts requiring historical explanation." Instead, it is ready-to-hand for people to use as an unproblematic mythic West, "a set of symbols that *constituted* an explanation of history."[65] By contrast, Wenders is unambivalently hostile to national myth, both Germany's and America's. And, unlike Ford, he is unambivalently hostile to violence, which for Wenders has no heroes. As a result, in *Paris, Texas* he restores the West as a place whose history must be reopened, as a set of symbols requiring critical explanation.

The implications of Wenders's (and Sean Penn's and Robert Altman's) cinematic reopening of the West to critical reinterpretation can be reinforced with a consideration of a politically pregnant episode of resistance by remnants of the Oglala Sioux nation at what came to be known as "Wounded Knee II," a resistance that, among other things, rendered unstable the geopolitical map of South Dakota, which still contains an extensive Native American, albeit tribalized, presence. In turning to recent social movements and a reading of Mount Rushmore, as it was initially conceived and as it was subsequently reinflected in film by a Native American director, I am introducing a challenging spatial practice and a critical locus of enunciation that together reveal a history of wrong within the dominant geopolitical imaginary. A treatment of the recent social movements, which resists the discourse on law enforcement through which they were portrayed in official and mainstream media discourses, substitutes a critical historicizing perspective for the juridical one that has reinforced Euro-America's geopolitical prerogatives.

Conclusion: Contested Sites in "The Mount Rushmore State"

The map of South Dakota retains stark aspects of both Euro-American imperialism and Native American presence. Arguably, no national monument is more thoughtlessly intrusive and forgetful about the history of imperial violence in the West than Mount Rushmore, which stands as an icon to what Joseph Conrad called "geography triumphant" in his gloss on the geography-imperialism nexus.[66] Cecilia Tichi's commentary, evinced upon viewing the monument, is especially apropos: "In August 1965, Mt. Rushmore viewed through binoculars was not a contested site, at least not to a mainstream white. Those lenses did not show a sculptural ideological message of white male authority over minority groups or women. Nor did the huge heads show the extent to which Mt. Rushmore could be considered an imperialist project, since white mainstream America knew nothing of the monument's violation of the sacred ground of the Oglala Sioux (and might well have been indifferent had it known, since the Native American rights movement had not yet organized its civil rights initiatives)."[67]

However, subsequent to the time Tichi recalls, the "civil rights initiatives" *had* developed and had even escalated well beyond the issue of rights. Native American activists began to recode the landscape, seeking to recover their coherence as a territorially based nation in South Dakota. Specifically, on February 27, 1973, roughly two hundred members of AIM, the American Indian Movement, began an occupation of the village of Wounded Knee, South Dakota, that was to last almost three months. Rather than merely a rights initiative, the occupation was an attempt to reestablish Native American sovereignty and thereby challenge the racial identity model within which their territorial and historical nationhood is denied. The occupiers declared themselves an independent state at the historical site of the 1890 massacre of approximately three hundred Indian men, women, and children by U.S. soldiers under the command of General George Crook.

The political force of the occupation was therefore both temporal and spatial. Temporally, the choice of the historical landscape of massacre, which has since had powerful collective resonances for Native Americans, constitutes an exemplary case of a political "subjectification,"[68] an action or movement through which a group that has had no legitimate place within the political order has, in Jacques Rancière's terms, "made themselves of some account" by "placing in common a wrong."[69] But while the political impact of selecting Wounded Knee operates within a temporal or historical register, the actual tactics employed during the extended occupation functioned spatially: On March 10, "the Wounded Knee occupiers declared a new state: The Independent Oglala Nation (ION)," and this refiguring of the Native American geopolitical status changed the significance of Wounded Knee's boundaries: "The boundaries that defined this contested site were now declared 'borders,' whose status was to be aggressively maintained by a 'border patrol.'"[70]

The sudden reconfiguration of the meaning of the Indian-white boundary—in B. D'Arcus's terms, "a quite concrete reconfiguration of space"[71]—is a form of political resistance at a material, territorial level. The whitening of the South Dakota landscape, dramatically registered by the Rushmore faces, has also been challenged cinematically; among those challenges is an early, oblique one articulated in Alfred Hitchcock's *North by Northwest* (1959), which ends with a dramatic fight between the protagonist, Roger Thornhill (Cary Grant), and his attacker on the faces of the Rushmore sculptures. To appreciate the implicit critique one must recall the way Hitchcock treats landscapes (quoted in chapter 1): "Hitchcock's camera typically only begins by enacting a survey of a seemingly natural scene. Eventually, as the filming proceeds, it becomes evident that there is a perverse element in the landscape . . . [t]he film's movement invariably proceeds from landscape to stain, from overall shot to close-up, and this movement invariably prepares the spectator for the event."[72] Certainly in the final scene, the Rushmore faces clearly disrupt an otherwise natural setting.

If we keep the idea of the stain on the landscape in mind, we can heed the symbolic challenge evinced in Scott Eyre's film *Skins* (2002), a more direct treatment of Indian displacement. The film's primary narrative is a familial story about Oglala Sioux who live on a squalid reservation in the shadow of Mount Rushmore. But the story contains a more collective, historical level; it ends with a gesture that interarticulates Native America's reaction to their diminished presence

Rushmore's Washington with stained nose in *Skins*. Courtesy of First Look Pictures.

with a Hitchcockian cinematic demonstration of the perversities and stains on the landscape. An Oglala policeman, Rudy (Eric Schweig), in mourning for his deceased brother, Mogy, fulfills his promise to his brother, who wants him to attack the Rushmore statue of George Washington. He mounts the attack by heaving an open five-gallon can of red paint over Washington's head. One of the film's last images shows the promise fulfilled, while at the same time expressing enduring Oglala sentiments about their displacement and the whitening of their landscape. It shows a red stain running from the bridge of Washington's nose to his chin.

To return to one of the inaugurating themes in this chapter, while it is unlikely that the "international relations" that characterized the American continent will be restored, contemporary Native America is asserting itself. Through its writing, music, and cinema, among other genres of expression, it is becoming increasingly visible and voluble. Competing with the historical regionalization of the West, which, as I noted, substituted fixed geopolitical boundaries for a more fluid, negotiated, multinational spatial encounter, is a respatialization and a reintroduction to the consequences of what was an institutionalized silence.

4 Constructing America

Architectural Thought-Worlds

An Attack on the Architecture of Hegemony

When operatives of the Al Qaeda network crashed planes into the twin towers of the World Trade Center in lower Manhattan on September 11, 2001, they were attacking what they regarded as the quintessential architectural expression of American global hegemony. From their perspective, the attack was one battle in a prolonged war between incommensurate thought-worlds, a strike against an evil that expresses itself in both thought and material culture. Whatever resonances the episode has had in various parts of the globe since the attack—antagonistic, neutral, or friendly—it has created an intense process of domestic reflection on what America is about. While the more applied effects of that reflection are evident in many aspects of public policy, especially those involving militarization and securitization, much of the continuing significance of the event will be effected in the design and construction of the new World Trade Center. Architecture served as the material target of the antagonists, and it will materialize the subsequent processes of healing and remembrance. And, inasmuch as (in a Bergsonian sense) the past always "is"—it continually changes as it remains subject to endless, experience-shaping reinterpretation—it is propitious that Daniel Libeskind, many of whose designs are aimed at historical remembrance, is the architect who won the competition to oversee the design of much of the rebuilt World Trade Center.[1]

Although Libeskind's control of the design process has been significantly attenuated,[2] his participation in the design process constitutes a challenge to the tradition of memorial architecture. As one art historian puts it, "[t]he typical commemorative monument is supposed to create closure. . . . That's the ruling assumption—that there's a kind of definitive past interpretation."[3] In contrast, Libeskind's vision for the "pit" (a sunken part of the reconstruction, which will bear most of the memorial aspect of the project) is designed to resist narrative closure. Opposing a simplistic model of the adequation of architecture to history, in Libeskind's design preference "visitors to the pit probably will not be given a map to follow to find the place of magic. Instead they will be allowed to choose their own paths . . . with no authority dictating, as would have been the case in ages past, which direction is correct."[4] Moreover, Libeskind's initially proposed plan does not provide for a definitive boundary: "The memorial park's western boundary, the so-called slurry wall that held back the Hudson River from flooding in after the 9/11 attack, will continue to restrain the river. . . . There will be . . . no firm demarcation of what was and what became. Where the wall was, it still is, and in such a place memory is a live event. History plays out in real time."[5]

At a minimum, whatever is the resulting design, after the culture war within which the plan has been contested, Libeskind's design orientation is not meant to redeem a version of America's pre-9/11 sense of itself.[6] Here, as elsewhere—for example, in his design of the extension of the Jewish Museum in Berlin—his memorial architecture is anti-redemptive. As James Young points out, in Libeskind's memorial designs, "memory of historical events, which never domesticates such events, never makes us at home with them, never brings them into the reassuring house of redemptory meaning."[7] Put positively, Libeskind's memorial structures privilege renewal rather than redemption. In his words, addressing one of his European projects, "[t]o continue the Jewish tradition across the desert of assimilation and annihilation is to return to living sources of Jewish space and symbolism so that a community can be renewed." Adopting a radical strain of Talmudic textual practice, and articulating it through architectural design, Libeskind's Jewish community center and synagogue in Duisberg, Germany, is shaped like a book: "The building stands with the vertical hinge of the book facing the river and the main entrance to the complex facing the promenade, which is the one focal point of the new city development."[8] But given the absence of a definitive textual closure in this building/book (it is an "open book"[9]), the museum's plan articulates the part of the Jewish thought-world that resists "the various measures [of conservative Jewish scholars] aimed at petrifying Jewish tradition."[10]

The building reflects that strain of Talmudic textuality that celebrates change. One progenitor of such a change orientation in the Talmudic tradition is the eighteenth-century scholar Rabbi Nahman of Bratislav, who burnt one of his books as a gesture of moving beyond fixed interpretive tradition. Accordingly, the Talmudic text for those who follow Nahman's lead is treated not as an original and sacrosanct monument but as a changing script, which departs from its origin as it experiences ongoing interpretation. Rather than a fixed object, the "book" should attract active contention. In Nahman's view, "the Book has/is a 'mouth'"; it can serve as "the course of the opening of a mouth, if it creates, generates speech."[11]

Architecture and Thought: The Mediaeval European Scene

Daniel Libeskind's architectural realizations of the history-memory relationship stand in stark contrast with a long tradition in which buildings have been designed to express fixed forms of authority, to warrant particular models of political legitimacy. Accordingly, his approach to American renewal, with his design for the pit at the new World Trade Center, can be contrasted with an earlier architecture, aimed at inventing America, Thomas Jefferson's use of the designs of his Monticello estate and his University of Virginia to create a Euro-dominated American nation. However, before turning to the specifics of the way Jeffersonian architecture articulates a romantic nationalism on behalf of a Euro-American continental ethnogenesis, I want to conceptualize, with reference to Erwin Panofsky's treatise on Gothic cathedrals, the way architectural design in general constitutes an expression of thinking. Just as Libeskind's design for a synagogue and Jewish community center in Duisberg articulates one strain of Jewish thought, Panofsky shows how the Gothic cathedral's departure from the earlier, Romanesque design constituted what was then a radical shift in Christian thought, associated with the emergence of Scholasticism. With close attention to detail, Panofsky demonstrates the homologies between two different thought-worlds and their material realizations in cathedral architecture. His discussion is attentive both to the nuances of thought and to design.

Specifically, in his elaboration of the thinking materialized in Gothic architecture, Panofsky reads Scholasticism through a Kantian epistemological lens. Just as Kant transferred the conditions of possibility for intelligible experience from the thing in itself to the structure of human apprehension, Panofsky describes Scholasticism's philosophical position as one that sees intelligibility as an achievement of higher sensory powers; it is a historically superceding "mental habit" that transfers the aesthetic sensibility from the object itself to human reason and experience.[12] What was the old "mental habit"? Panofsky begins his analysis by pointing to "pre-Scholasticism," a thought-world in which faith is insulated from reason by an impenetrable barrier. The material realization of pre-Scholasticism is the Romanesque cathedral, which, Panofsky states, "conveys the impression of a space determinate and impenetrable, whether we find ourselves inside or outside the edifice."[13]

Effectively, the Romanesque cathedral materializes an enigmatic objectness; it enacts in stone an ontological divide between reasoning/experiencing faculties and the architectural realization of the spiritual-as-enigmatic-mystique. In contrast, Gothic architecture is a realization of "aesthetic subjectivism"[14]; it creates a series of homologous spaces within which the subject can experience (and gain demystifying clarity about) the totality of the Scholastic thought-world. As Panofsky puts it, "the High Gothic cathedral sought to embody the whole of Christian knowledge, theological, moral, natural and historical, with everything in its place and that which no longer found its place, suppressed."[15] Unlike the Romanesque design, therefore, the Gothic makes a space for a subject with a "perspective." Embodying "a perspective interpretation of space," the Gothic cathedral is designed "with reference to the very process of sight," so the viewing subject can achieve "a comprehensive 'picture of space,'" rather than being confronted, as in the Romanesque design, with "isolated solids."[16]

To make his case, Panofsky shows how the various requirements of Scholastic writing, for example, "arrangement according to a system of homologous parts," are embodied in the Gothic cathedral's design: "Instead of the Romanesque variety of western and eastern vaulting forms, often appearing in one and the same building (groin vaults, rib vaults, barrels, domes, and half-domes), we have the newly developed rib vault exclusively so that the vaults of even the apse, the chapels and the ambulatory no longer differ in kind from those of the nave and transept."[17] Panofsky goes on to connect the other tenets of Scholastic thought with other architectural details of the Gothic cathedral: its separations, its interrelated spaces, its hierarchized levels, and the "progressive divisibility" one experiences in moving through the edifice: "According to classic High Gothic standards the individual elements, while forming an indiscernible whole, yet must proclaim their identity by remaining clearly separated from each other—the shafts from the wall or the core from the pier, the ribs from their neighbors, all vertical members from their arches; and there must be unequivocal correlation between them."[18]

Because of the proto-enlightenment cast of Scholastic thought, realized in Gothic architecture, Panofsky's treatise on the High Gothic cathedral supplies a threshold for treating the architectural designs of Thomas Jefferson. As Panofsky notes, Scholasticism's "mental habit" professes a commitment to a disputatious reasoning in the face of incommensurate forms of historical authority and to an "all-embracing" . . . "unconditional clarification."[19] Hence, "the builders of the High Gothic cathedrals" had to work "through to the limit . . . two apparently contradictory motifs, both sanctioned by authority," and accordingly produced an "erratic yet stubbornly consistent evolution of Early and High Gothic architecture."[20]

Jefferson's American Designs

Like the builders of the Gothic cathedral, Jefferson was committed to having his buildings displace one form of authority with another. Seeing the future of America as a realization of enlightenment imperatives and a Euro-oriented, ethnocentric rationalization of continental space, he sought to render his buildings as articulations of anti-colonial, neo-enlightenment, and uniquely American political idioms. His design for his plantation house, Monticello (in both its original and extended versions—Monticello I and II), in his home state of Virginia was a deliberate departure from England's Georgian architecture. It favored a Roman, neo-Palladian architectural idiom, an architectural reinflection of classic republicanism. However, to appreciate the political significance of Jefferson's design of Monticello, one must understand the social and political forces materialized in vernacular domestic architecture in pre-revolutionary, eighteenth-century Virginia, which utilized aspects of Georgian architecture but modified them within the local context to accord with a particular political sensibility.

Virginia's eighteenth-century builders, like the builders of the High Gothic cathedral, were involved in reconciling conflicting demands.

While working within a tradition inspired by English architecture, they sought at the same time to accommodate to local social and political pressures. As one investigation of the homes of Virginia's planter elite concludes, "the predominant house plan was a traditional British one, the stand-alone Georgian inspired design."[21] But the shaping forces went beyond this inherited tradition. Social arrangements, as Gilles Deleuze suggests, are embodiments of solutions to particular historical problems; they are reified "problematic fields."[22] This insight applies well to the planter elite's homes, which constituted a (reified) "architectural response to a specific social requirement."[23]

As both a residence and a public building, the planter's house was a solution generated at a particular historical juncture. Dell Upton's rendering of the politics of the eighteenth-century Virginia planter's house architecture maps that solution: On the one hand, the planters were concerned with "defining their right to dominate their neighbors for political and economic advantages," but, on the other, the extent of their domination was inhibited "by the need of English politics for American posts as rewards for its faithful."[24] Ultimately, by the mid-eighteenth century, the planter's house design "embodied social formality as an assertion of local social and political control where Virginia's elite could hope for little more." And "[t]he social forms of control were encapsulated in a variety of houses [that articulated] the vocabulary of European classical architecture."[25]

Specifically, Virginia planters approached their acknowledged political tensions—those between local versus colonial control—through the design of their individual house plan, which had a hall that served as a space of sociality and a structure of circulation that separated private from public space. Their homes had a "developed social structure [with] a hall, a formal, public room set off from direct access to any other room, a semipublic space that mediated between outside and inside."[26] But within a larger political frame, one can see the plantation as a whole as a coercive community, "a fairly large village," which emulated a "hierarchy, with the planter at its pinnacle."[27] While the main house had a convivial mode of circulation and separation, the plantation village's design was one of domination and servitude. For example, there were separate buildings for "Christian slaves" and "Negro slaves."[28] And those slaves that served the household were located in nearby buildings, while those who worked in fields could be "a quarter mile or more away from the main house."[29]

As Upton notes, the planter saw his house as "semi-public," and as "an emblem of himself and his order,"[30] but, in contrast with the way Jefferson saw himself and his role, that order was strictly local. As a result, the Virginia planter paid little heed to the vista from the house. His social reach was expressed in the public and semi-public rooms of the main house. In contrast with this political self-understanding is Jefferson's decision to place his Monticello on a hilltop, which allowed for long views from all parts of the house. What is the significance of the long view? If we go back to one of the precursors of the Virginia plantation, the English landed estate, we discover a relevant controversy, played out in the genre of landscape painting in the late eighteenth century. Ann Bermingham points out that the tradition of painting enclosed estates with short vistas was consonant with the idea of a politically privileged few. As a result, when landscape painters departed from this tradition by painting longer vistas, some critics associated the long vistas, which connected property with the rest of the landscape, as "equivalent to the levelling tendencies of democratic governments and revolutions."[31]

Thomas Jefferson's departure, in his design of Monticello, from the architecture of the eighteenth-century planter's house constitutes a similar political disruption. Rather than merely an emblem of privilege, his house was meant to be an architectural statement about America's rejection of English domination and about the evolving institutionalization and continental expansion of a democratic ethos. One aspect of Jefferson's democratic imaginary is evident in his having given "the highest priority to the spectacular view in all directions *from* the house, and to the practical, all weather service wings whose lower-level arcades opened outward on the natural slope screened from the house."[32] The privileging of a long view from Monticello also accords with Jefferson's imperial vision, his notion (noted earlier) that nature itself was summoning a Euro-American, continental ethnogenesis: "[W]e have an immensity of land courting the industry of the husbandmen."[33]

In a telling moment (noted in chapter 1), while Jefferson is enjoying the long view afforded by Monticello's hilltop purchase and the outward orientation of its structure, he "constructs a visible scene as an icon of historical change," as a symbolic narrative of the movement from chaos to pacified order.[34] After he remarks on the "disruption" that nature creates, he has nature promise a pacified locus of possession, asserting that what nature "presents to your eye" is a "smooth" vista "at an infinite distance in the plain country inviting you, as it were from the riot and tumult roaring around, to pass through the breach and participate in the calm below."[35] Of course, once Jefferson's expansionist policies are in place, the summons of nature has to be accompanied by a "race" struggle. America's indigenous nations, toward whom Jefferson expressed admiration, were nevertheless ineligible to stand against a Euro-American future. As is pointed out in chapter 1, a different kind of Jeffersonian design contributed to the effacement of their provenances: the survey, which, along with the legal technologies that supplemented it (for example the Land Ordinance of 1785), turned nature into property, in the form of a grid that made "American geography into a single semiotic system."[36]

But another kind of race struggle is embodied in the design of Monticello. The house and surrounding plantation village embodies what Michel Foucault has identified as the "two great morphologies, two main centers, and two political functions" of historical discourse.[37] One is the familiar sovereignty discourse which Foucault locates in Rome. It is a discourse concerned with the right to rule and the limitations on the authority of the sovereign. The other is a discourse that articulates a "counterhistory"[38]; it focuses on race struggle. Rather than a recounting of the history of kings and the developing inhibitions on their prerogatives, this historical discourse, initially centered in Jerusalem, treats violence. As Foucault puts it, there is "on the one hand, the Roman history of sovereignty; on the other, the biblical history of servitude and exiles."[39] In short, one discourse treats the evolving legitimacy of institutions of governance, while the other treats a history of violence, usurpation, dominance, and enslavement.

These two different morphologies of historical discourse are evident in the case of England, where, as Foucault points out, there has been a discourse treating invasions (centering on the race struggle between Normans and Saxons) and a parallel discourse on "the history of the power of the kings."[40] But while in the middle ages the discourse on race struggle is not a form of racism, inasmuch as it is not accompanied by a discourse on biological characteristics, there is a historical point at which what was once a discourse on race war or race struggle turns into a "biological racism."[41] The intersection between the two historical narratives, the Roman, sovereignty version and the race struggle version are also evident in Thomas Jefferson's perspective. But his articulation of the latter occurs at a point at which a race struggle perspective has turned into a racism. In addition to seeing history in both ways—as a deployment of sovereignty problematics and as a clash of races—Jefferson summons the discourse of natural history to identify politically qualified versus unqualified bodies (excluding African Americans from America's political future and locating Native Americans in a diminishing capacity for participation as well). Articulating the point of view of the race struggle discourse, Jefferson worries that a race war might be precipitated by emancipation.[42] In his writings, "black slaves became a kind of Hobbesian threat posed to an otherwise harmonious natural republic."[43] But he also generates a biological racism, expressing the opinion (about which he was subsequently less certain), that blacks "are inferior to the whites in the endowments both of body and mind."[44]

Wherever Jefferson's emphasis lay with respect to the trajectory of the race struggle/racism discourse (some of his letters seem to rethink his biological racism), his design of Monticello manifests the intersection to which Foucault refers in his analysis of the two discursive morphologies that co-occur in the English case. "Monticello," as Malcolm Kelsall correctly observes, "is an ideological rather than a practical plantation house."[45] It is ideological in two senses. In one explicitly designed sense, Monticello is an icon of democracy. Certainly the "open quality" of the house, with its "geometrical shapes imbued with a sense of open space" (manifested especially in Monticello II with its extended vestibule), was a practical departure from England's closed, Georgian style, given Virginia's milder climate. But at the same time, "[t]his open quality . . . is at once the architectural symbol of hospitality and of democracy."[46]

As I have noted, Jefferson's rejection of the Georgian style was also an anti-colonial gesture. To achieve his departure from the Georgian forms, which had remained popular in Virginia plantations and country houses, he employed a modified Palladian style, which, inspired by the Roman Pantheon that Jefferson (like Andrea Palladio) so much admired, consisted of domes and geometric shapes. Although some historians of architecture have seen this architectural emphasis in Monticello as "revivalist" (most notably Fiske Kimball),[47] Buford Picken's argument, based on textual as well as architectural evidence, is more compelling. He insists that Jefferson's choices are "Roman" in the sense of articulating a republicanism.[48] The house thus exemplifies a favored model of a political past. William Howard Adams summarizes Jefferson's turn to a Roman architectural idiom succinctly: "In the architecture of Rome, Jefferson detected symbolically those simple republican virtues and rationality he hoped to see embodied in the new American experiment of government. He believed that this antique vocabulary could redeem a formless world through its translation into a house that would serve as a public symbol and at the same time express his innermost need for a private existence, uniting within its peculiar composition the life of the mind and the life of the senses."[49]

The second sense in which Monticello is an ideological plantation consists in the structure of domination that its design conveys, along with the pretension that it contradicts. In addition to its affinity with the Roman, sovereignty-oriented historical discourse, Monticello embodies the race struggle/racism morphology, both in the layout of the house itself and in the Monticello plantation village as a whole. The values that Monticello purports to represent, associated with Jefferson's democratic republicanism, are belied by the contradiction between facade and interior. As Kelsall puts it, "[t]he external facade presented to the visitor . . . is a form of mystification. It makes an ideal statement about the republican nation, but it conceals the order of class, gender and race within."[50] In addition, while Monticello is intended as "a *locus* of inherited culture for a new nation, that culture is disrupted. The ostensibly equal community is divided by the reimposition of a hierarchical order that is strictly patriarchal and exclusive,"[51] an order made evident by a floor plan whose main east-west axis leads inward and upward toward Jefferson's study/library/bedroom. The interior sequesters private quarters, dividing them from public visiting spaces as well as from the sections reserved for servants.[52] And, of course, the enactment of the spatial order was dominated by the temporal rhythms of Jefferson's work, leisure, and entertainment schedules, the details of which loomed large in Jefferson's attention to detail. For example, as I note in the preface, one of the slaves at Monticello, Isaac Jefferson, reports, "Mr. Jefferson had a clock in his kitchen at Monticello; never went into the kitchen except to wind up the clock."[53]

As for the separation between the main house and the outbuildings for slaves, the contrast is stark. Jefferson's frequent visitor Margaret Smith, observing the squalid conditions in which the slaves were living so near a grand house, remarked that "to an eye unaccustomed to such sights, they appear poor and their cabins form a most unpleasant contrast with the place that rises so near them."[54] Jefferson's slaves are thus out-of-the-picture, architecturally as well as ideologically (in his future-oriented American imaginary). The servant/slave quarters were in "Mulberry Row," both physically and ideationally outside the "landscape scheme throughout Jefferson's lifetime."[55] To some extent, Native Americans remained *in* the picture. There was a room, effectively a shrine, with the icons of the American Revolution, Washington and Franklin, among others. Their busts were displayed along with those of Jefferson's favorite thinkers (Bacon, Newton, and Locke). Jefferson also created a museum in Monticello, which was designed to record an earlier part of American history. It contained "Indian artifacts . . . [representing Native Americans as] the *Urvolk* . . . part of what is . . . shown to be a superceded past."[56]

Jefferson's Monticello was therefore designed to articulate a partly open and partly closed narrative. Departing from the conception of the Virginia "country house," built as a "retreat," its hilltop location and open vistas looked toward a national future to come.[57] But within the interior, the past is closed; it is fixed in the form of artifacts of a superceded past. It is appropriate, therefore, to once again summon the designs of Daniel Libeskind, for whom the past is figured as an open book rather than a series of artifacts to display and lock into a fixed narrative. For example, commenting on the design of his Jewish Museum in Berlin, Libeskind states that "[t]he spaces inside the museum are to be construed as open narratives." Rather than serving as a container for relics of an objectified past, or in Libeskind's words, "instead of housing a collection [his design] seeks to estrange it from viewers' preconceptions . . . to defamiliarize the all-too-familiar ritual objects and historical chronologies."[58]

In contrast with Libeskind's memorial architecture, which is designed to produce an ongoing, contentious, and ambiguously bounded interpretive culture, Jefferson's was aimed at inventing a unified national culture. Hence, his design for his University of Virginia was another step toward the invention of a homogeneous cultural nation. The university's design was conceived as a microcosm of a Euro-American nation; it was to be a harmonious village, "an agglomeration of houses of a variety of appearance with no two alike but grouped harmoniously."[59] As Jefferson put it, rather than "making one large expensive building . . . [i]t is infinitely better to erect a small separate lodge for each separate professorship, with only a hall below for his class, and two chambers above for himself; joining these ledges by barracks for a certain portion of the students. . . . The whole of these arranged around an open square of grass and trees, would make it, what it should be in fact, an academical village."[60] Architecturally, the main building is a Monticello clone in that it favors a Palladian style. It is dominated by a large dome and rotunda, and its wings are geometrically shaped. At the same time, however, the wings embody Jefferson's complex democratic imaginary. As "a physical expression of [his] intellectual activity,"[61] they articulate both harmony and individuality; each pavilion is symmetric with respect to the rest but contains a design variation as well, producing what Garry Wills notes as a "paradoxical effect [immanent in Jefferson's perspective] of regimentation and individual expression, of hierarchical order and relaxed improvising."[62]

Among what makes Jefferson's academical village harmonious is its exclusivity. Apart from its assumed gender domination (Jefferson anticipates only male professors), its student body is to be all white males, primarily from aristocratic families. Moreover, like Monticello (an "ideological plantation"), the Palladian cast of its architecture makes Jefferson's university an ideological "academical village." Jefferson's turn to Palladian designs was more than a colonial, anti-Georgian gesture and more than a symbol of republicanism. Palladian designs are landscape oriented; they have "a remarkable capacity to harmonize visually with their natural environs."[63] In addition, among what supplies an individuality is the entrepreneurial structure of the living units for faculty and students. Each is meant to serve as a separate hotel, supplied by independent merchants.[64]

Nevertheless, the plantation, a public institution in the case of Monticello, remains the primary model for Jefferson's university. Both the house and the university share an architectural grammar. They locate both internal and external subjects, a paternal and class hierarchy within and an outward-aiming, nation-building orientation, evident in the way they construct their vistas. The university, like the villa, is not meant to be monastic or sequestered; rather, it is designed as an exoteric institution, a triumphal emblem as well as a pedagogical institution. As in his house, Jefferson organized his university to implement what Wills refers to as a "negotiation of a conversation between inner and outer worlds."[65] On the one hand, it is designed "to contribute to the inculcation in the students [of] the principles of a republican and deistic ethos."[66] But on the other, its metaphorical burden extends its function beyond pedagogy; it is to be a "microcosm" of the new nation. Internally, such features as "the pantheistic rotunda" promote "a system of socio-political values." The interior conveys "an architectural message" that "says we are all republicans, we are all federalists."[67] And with its included farm as well as with its orientation to its "natural" surroundings, the university design is a rhetorical statement of Jefferson's hope for "nature's nation" to be an expanding homogeneous, agriculturally based community.

Ultimately, while the thought-world embodied in the structure of Monticello was academically singular—it was located spatially in Jefferson's library and private quarters—the university's extension from its center toward its peripheral wings, occupied by students and faculty, as well as its outward orientation toward the landscape, constituted a relaxation of Jefferson's exclusive intellectual purchase. His university surrendered Jefferson's rigid spatial and temporal order, "gradually fading into the unstructured surrounding world."[68]

The African American University

Despite Jefferson's hopes, and his steadfast attempts to check the growth of a troubling cultural diversity, a commitment evident in both his Land Ordinance of 1785 and his architecture, his (and other Euro-American) plans have been contested, by alternative architectures as well by alternative voices. One significant locus of resistance has been the African American university. To put the issue in general terms first, it has been noted that "African-American builders, architects, and designers, since the era of southern enslavement, have carefully practiced the balancing act of accommodation, resistance, and appropriation in design and building."[69] For example, the Hampton Normal and Agricultural Institute (now Hampton University), founded in Virginia in 1868 and dedicated to "Negro education," and Native American education as well (having enrolled thousands of members of over sixty tribal groups between 1878 and 1923), embodies aspects of traditional Euro-American university architecture along with alternative and resistant cultural markers.

Planned by Euro-American architects, who collaborated with the white missionary founder, John Armstrong, the campus was designed to reproduce the existing "architectural status quo" and thereby to "maintain aesthetic standards of the contemporary white campuses."[70] But, as Bradford Grant describes the details:

The physical campus became the product of cultural interpretations and creative identity or the resistive expressions of
the Hampton students and faculty joined to the experimental
advances of the established white architects. Throughout the
campus carefully placed cultural markers can be found in the
structural and ornamental details of student- and faculty-built
halls alongside the more overt planning and designs of later African-American architects, from the playful repeating rhythms
of Kelsey Hall's brickwork to the geometrically patterned brick
panels of Armstrong Hall and the modernist buildings Harkness
and Davidson Hall by the early African-American architects
William Moses and Hilyard Robinson, these buildings collectively communicate a story of accommodation, resistance, and
appropriation.[71]

Thus, while the Institute's Memorial Church "conforms to the dictated
Romanesque Revival style of contemporary church design . . . the interior details suggest an adjusted and more culturally specific aesthetic.
Identity and pride are expressed in the corbel blocks of the arcade under the cornices . . . revealing alternative reliefs of African-American
and Native American busts—[in spaces] traditionally reserved for classical gods and Anglo faces."[72]

    In subsequent historically black colleges and universities (HB-
CUs), which had to deal with a post-Reconstruction white backlash,
the designs of the campuses did not have the same freedom as the "majority" university. Rather than turning to an architecture of building
and landscape that would serve as "a testament to the cultural power and
centrality of the institution's publicly affirmed mission," their design reflected a negotiation of their function within a hostile, white-dominated
world.[73] For example, contrasting Tuskegee University (established in
1873 and over which the Hampton-educated Booker T. Washington
presided as its first president) with the white Huntingdon College in
the same town, Ian Grandison notes that while the latter is a "Gothic
showpiece" with its hall oriented toward the main public street, the
layout of the former did not have the luxury to architecturally mark a
town-gown relationship and thus "command public attention."[74]

    HBCU campuses are "frequently . . . laid out backwards accord-
ing to the dominant paradigm"; they tend to "put their 'best' facades
inward not outward."[75] In contrast with the continuing tradition in the

architecture of majority campuses (Jefferson's University of Virginia, among others), whose main buildings are proud emblems of the institution and "gateway" buildings, visible from various approaches to campus, Tuskegee's primary buildings—for example, its Carnegie Library, which "has its back to the only public road"—reflect the historically "marginal status of blacks in American society."[76] In addition to their frequent backward orientation, the HBCU campuses tend to use other ways to sequester themselves, for as Craig Evan Barton notes, to understand the African American cultural landscape is "to understand how [Ralph] Ellison's concept of invisibility was built and spatialized."[77]

Even in cases in which a black college is facing toward the town, the tendency is for its axis to be oblique with respect to the town's grid and for its access to be interrupted by a highway or rail line.[78] Unlike the tradition of the majority university, from Jefferson's design onward, in which the campus has a unitary rhetorical force, the history of servitude visited on African Americans has imposed a different kind of architectural statement on HBCUs, a doubleness that has characterized many African American genres of expression.[79] As Grandison puts it, "[t]he facades of these campuses have a double message: one, the institution belongs here and has the right to dominate space; two, those who belong to the institution must show due respect, and those who do not belong must be reminded of it."[80]

Beyond Jefferson's Agricultural America: The City

The architecture of urban built environments and landscapes constitutes another locus of "majority" design versus "minority" reinflection or resistance.[81] On the one hand, there is the official government-approved design of the urban environment, and on the other is a vernacular architecture, which conveys alternative cultural and political statements. At a minimum, Jefferson's hope for an agricultural nation has long since been superceded by the growth of manufacturing and the development of a majority, urban population. As Leo Marx notes, "[i]t did not occur to Jefferson that the factory system was a necessary feature of technological progress."[82] Ultimately, machines, along with in-migrating and diasporic labor forces, produced an America that looks nothing like Jefferson's pastoral ideal and harmonious ethnoscape. The varying degrees of contention that have shaped American cities is well beyond the scope of this chapter. In brief compass, I want to treat three city-shaping personalities, who operated under official warrant, and juxtapose aspects of the American city's vernacular landscape.

At the official level, two architects of the American city stand out because of the relationship between their architecture and their notions of democracy. The first is Frederick Law Olmsted, whose design of Central Park in Manhattan was meant as a space of democratic egalitarian leisure for the city's working class: "It is one great purpose of the Park to supply to the hundreds and thousands of tired workers, who have no opportunity to spend their summers in the country, a specimen of God's handiwork that shall be to them, inexpensively, what a month or two in the White Mountains or the Adirondacks is, at great cost, to those in easier circumstances."[83] And the second, Louis Sullivan, who presumed that his "stark Chicago-style skyscraper . . . would help bring to fruition democracy's promise,"[84] writing, "We are on the high-road to a natural and satisfying art, an architecture that will soon become a fine art in the true, best sense of the word, an art that will live because it will be of the people, for the people, and by the people."[85]

Turning first to Olmsted, it should be recalled that the City Commission's plan for Central Park stemmed from a Jeffersonian impulse, a fear of a troubling cultural diversity. In approving the park, begun in 1853, "the commissioners said, 'While the Park is intended as a place for freedom and relaxation, for play and not for work, it has been constructed with no idea of encouraging habits of laxness, or in any way for the benefit of idlers and drones . . . its paramount object is to offer facilities for a daily enjoyment of life to the industrious thousands who are working steadily and conscientiously." However, as Sarah Miller points out: "This proviso reflected not only their deep-seated religious and economic beliefs, but also their need to control an unsettling social climate that had been developing since the 1830's. At that time, an influx of people began to racially alter the city's demographics. The old agrarian lifestyle of Jeffersonian America was being replaced by an urban industrial society, which attracted rural farm workers to cities in search of new jobs and new opportunities [as well as] displaced African Americans, freed by emancipation, manumission, or migration."[86]

Yet Olmsted's landscape architecture enacted both Jeffersonian and anti-Jeffersonian impulses. Because he shared Jefferson's romantic view of nature, he wanted to invent a park that was as natural as possible, one in which the structures blend into the landscape. And although, like Jefferson, he was involved in the design of college campuses, in his plan for Central Park (designed with the collaboration of Calvert Vaux), he resisted both geometrical patterns and grids, the former being central to Jefferson's buildings and layouts and the latter being the feature that Jefferson had imposed on the nation as a whole.[87] Avoiding both of these Jeffersonian design orientations, "[t]he landscape sequence of the Mall and Bethesda Terrace is the only straight line in Central Park."[88]

Despite continual interference by park commissioners, who tended to cater to the desire of various elites to place their signatures on the park (in monuments and clearings that would provide more open vistas than Olmsted and Vaux favored), because of Olmsted's influence the park retained an egalitarian and even vernacular quality. In spite of attempts by alternative architects whom the commissioners summoned—for example, Richard Morris Hunt (one of the architects who designed the Hampton Institute), who favored "grandiose classical monuments at the end of long urban vistas"[89]—the park remained under Olmsted's design influence and continued to cater to the "many immigrants who often spoke or read no English." It became increasingly vernacularized as "newly arriving ethnic groups began to place statues of their own folk heroes, cultural leaders, and political figures in Central Park."[90]

However successful Olmsted and Vaux were in retaining a democratic and anti-elitist version of landscape design in Central Park, their efforts at lending a democratic shape to New York pale in comparison with the elitist, anti-democratic influence of Robert Moses, who reshaped not only New York but also urban America as a whole. In the words of Lewis Mumford, "In the twentieth century, the influence of Robert Moses on the cities of America was greater than that of any other person."[91] In his specific venue, with control over a "confederation" of public authorities, especially his chairmanship of the Triborough Bridge and Tunnel Authority, Moses reshaped New York City, adding expressways, parks, and new neighborhoods. In the process of his new public construction, "he evicted the city's people, not thousands of them or tens of thousands but hundreds of thousands. . . . Neighborhoods were obliterated by his edict to make room for new neighborhoods reared at his command."[92]

Rather than reviewing Moses's various projects, I want to note simply that in contrast with the democratizing and difference-welcoming of Olmsted's landscape architecture, Moses's encouraged ethnic and class separation. Like the urban renewal and reform movements that his efforts spawned in other cities, his plan for New York, implemented with a federal-size budget of billions, created and reinforced racial and economic segregation. Apart from the bias in his "improvements"— dotting the city with swimming pools in white sections and adding only one in Harlem, and spending millions to enlarge Riverside Park, but "not a dime between 125th and 155th Streets" (which border the black community)—his plans were deliberately aimed at segregating ethnic communities.[93] He planned his expressways in a way that encircled and isolated ethnic communities, and he purposely limited access to public transportation from poorer areas to keep "colored people" (Moses's expression for "Negroes" and Puerto Ricans) from using parks in white neighborhoods, even going so far as to discourage permitting authorities from issuing permits to buses chartered by people from the black community.[94]

In contrast with Moses, Louis Sullivan, the architect responsible for shaping much of Chicago, especially its skyline, saw himself as a product of "the people." The resistance to classicism and an "imperial grandeur" model for Central Park's design exemplified by Olmsted and Vaux is also part of the democratizing ethos energizing Louis Sullivan's architecture. A "prophet of architectural modernism," Sullivan criticized the architecture of New York's skyscrapers because he viewed their historical motifs as the "negation of democracy."[95] And looking locally, he was critical of the University of Chicago's Gothic structures, which he saw as *profoundly anti-social . . .* [making] the city poorer and emptier . . . undermining American life."[96] Aware of the relationship between architecture and social space, Sullivan sought to democratize built structures: for example, in his design for the People's Saving Bank in Cedar Rapids Iowa, where, "in the interests of creating a more democratic space Sullivan tried to lower the barriers separating bank employees and customers as well as the barriers that divided employees themselves. . . .To this end the offices of bank executives were made as visible and accessible as the spaces used by bank tellers. The offices and teller spaces were organized around a central area used by the public."[97]

But Sullivan is best known for his stark and largely unadorned Chicago skyscrapers. Counter-intuitively, he regarded these structures as "natural," but in a special sense. Because he viewed the historical motifs in many of New York's buildings as anti-democratic, and because he saw the future of America (in a Jeffersonian sense) as a progressive destiny, he wanted architecture to privilege an enlightened future, free of superstition and congenial to human democratic development.[98] Accordingly, he saw his tall, steel structures (and indeed steel technology in general) as a "central expression [which] would help bring to fruition democracy's promise." He was particularly sanguine about the inter-articulation of such technology and democracy: "Ours is a wonder-ful day of ocean cables, land-lines, railways, machine tools, daily papers, printing presses. . . . The elemental dream of the age shall achieve full voice in the advent of democracy."[99]

Certainly Sullivan's optimism has been contested. The tall buildings, which he regarded as symbols of democratic newness, came to be viewed as aspects of capitalism's machine of capture, particularly of the entrapment of a white-collar worker in office cubicles. And despite his democratic proclivities, Sullivan showed little appreciation for ethnic diversity, except in a negative sense. He had Teuton envy. Like another famous Teuton admirer, the recognized founder of American political science, John Burgess of Columbia University, who wrote that "the Teuton really dominates the world by his superior political genius,"[100] Sullivan saw democracy as an outgrowth of "the individualistic spirit of the Teutonic Barbarian."[101] Thus, although he asserted that "the flow of the building we call Historical architecture [is only] the flow of the thought of the people,"[102] with a notable exception he made for "Teutons," he regarded the "people" as a homogeneous multitude and paid little heed to an actual architecture of the people (that is, to vernacular designs). His buildings were designed on the people's behalf.

Vernacular America

While at a national level the "nation" emerges as a mode of "moulding and interpreting space,"[103] there are abundant versions of a vernacular architecture that shape the spaces of the city. Just as early Euro-America was shaped in part by the above mentioned vernacular architecture of the elite Virginians, whose plantation house designs were oriented toward maintaining a local hegemony, the modern city has seen a proliferation of vernacular architectures belonging to different ethnic Americans. Often their aim has been to survive rather than dominate. Recognizing the diversity of the urban American, Dolores Hayden notes that "[i]ndigenous residents as well as colonizers, ditchdiggers as

well as architects, migrant workers as well as mayors, housewives as well
as housing inspectors, are all active in shaping the urban landscape."[104]
Similarly, in one of his New Orleans crime stories, James Sallis treats
the way in which vernacular architecture (in this case sedimented in
one structure) testifies to a public or civic as opposed to an official history: "You could read the building's transformations through the years,
manifest history, in its string of add-ons and embellishments: the colon-
naded entryway that turned it from palatial residence to luxury hotel
sometime in the fifties; redundant entrances from subsequent incarnation as apartment building with . . . at least twelve units; from its brief
time as a church, a long-unused plywood marquee."[105]

Thus, while official architects such as Louis Sullivan were shaping
parts of Chicago and other cities, at the same time, entrepreneurs, a
work force, and others were involved in the architectural production of
space. The vernacular architectural production of space was especially
prominent along the "metropolitan corridor" created by the development of the rail system.[106] Along that corridor, as well as in border and
coastal areas, the vernacular architecture of diverse indigenous and
migrant ethnic groups has articulated alternative architectural Americas, which, if read, provide what Hayden calls alternative "public histories."[107] These are histories that can be discerned, for example, in
"Chinese American neighborhoods [with their] laundries, herb shops,
seamen's boardinghouses [and in] Japanese American neighborhoods
[with their] temples, nurseries, and flower markets."[108]

The documentation of the Latino contribution to such an architecturally inscribed public history has been undertaken in Camillo Jose
Vegara's photographic studies. Treating the Mexican American house
and store, Vergara describes what distinguishes the Mexican American design presence in the contemporary United States, a preference
for exoteric, colorful display—for example, brightly painted storefronts
such as that of Jorge Moreno, who has "neatly paint[ed] on his walls
the products he sells. He is constantly cleaning off graffiti and adding
pictures of new products, such as motor oil and axles, as they are introduced in his store."[109] And certainly an urban Mexican design preference has manifested itself architecturally in "Tucson, San Antonio, El
Paso and Albuquerque," as well,[110] in a dramatic change from the original architecture of Spanish America, which was manifested in three
designs, the presidio, mission, and pueblo, which were the bases of the
original Spanish settlements.[111]

If we go back and look at architecture in America before the Anglo America conquest and subsequent and extensive continental settlement, we can discern yet another different thought-world, one in which indigenous America articulated its life-world in two kinds of buildings, the multiple family lodge—primarily a utilitarian and protective design—and the ritual buildings through which they represented their relationship with a transcendent universe. As two commentators on Native American architecture note, "[t]he buildings of Native Americans encoded not only their social order but often their tribal view of the cosmos." Many Indian narratives tell of a "Distant Time" or a Myth Age, when a "First House" was "bestowed upon a tribe as a container for their emerging culture."[112]

An Overcoded Thought-World: Native America

While there is a variety of ways to juxtapose the thought-worlds articulated in Euro versus Native American architecture, here I turn to two feature films, Alfred Hitchcock's *North by Northwest* (1959) and Jim Jarmusch's *Dead Man* (1996), because in addition to thematizing the juxtaposition (implicitly in Hitchcock's film and explicitly in Jarmusch's), they both supply narratives of the westward movement of Euro-America's architectural thought-world. Moreover, both films use as their thought vehicles two naive characters—Roger Thornhill (Cary Grant) in *North by Northwest* and William Blake (Johnny Depp) in *Dead Man*—both of whom are oblivious to the forces that have shaped and are shaping the landscapes through which they travel from the East to the West.

The urbane Roger Thornhill, whose eastern-style gray suit retains its press throughout a strenuous journey (involving both flight and fight), is a vestige of an aristocratic class. He is a relatively idle advertising executive, a Momma's boy at home and a dependent boss to a competent secretary at work. He is also blissfully unaware of a more pervasive support structure, the laboring underclass that makes his comfortable life possible. Equally is he oblivious to the cold war domestic intelligence operatives whose invented character, George Kaplan, he is mistaken for by a group of alien conspirators. And most significantly, although he is caught up in an adventure whose cinematic narrative maps an America with considerable historical depth, he remains a man "above the economy."[113] His expensive lifestyle, with designer clothes, theater tickets, etc., are part of an easily worn habitus. He is innocent of history, and is one who resists valuable information until he is forced to act, either for self-preservation or, ultimately, to save the woman who, at some ambiguous and unacknowledged level, he seems to want.

Although it is doubtless tempting for the viewer who simply follows the fate of Thornhill to enjoy the film as an amusing, picaresque adventure, the landscape sequence tells a more profound tale. At the beginning of the film, Thornhill emerges from the C. I. T. Financial building. After an abduction to a large estate and a visit to the United Nations building, his cross-country flight takes him on a long train ride to a string of hotel rooms and ultimately to Mount Rushmore, where he engages in the film's decisive confrontation with the most perverse member of the espionage ring. It is of course steel and its role in the railway system that has been the technology (optimistically welcomed and used in the "democratic" architecture of Louis Sullivan) implicated in transforming the economy and thus the midwestern and western landscapes.

Certainly the scene west of Chicago, with the attacking crop duster and the burning oil truck into which it crashes while chasing Thornhill, marks the historical shift from a small Jeffersonian nation of family farms to one with an industrialized agriculture. And perhaps most significantly from the perspective of the advance of Euro-American hegemony, what could be a more stark representation of the whitening of the American landscape than the final scene, a struggle staged on the enormous visages of Washington, Jefferson, Roosevelt, and Lincoln, carved into the face of Mount Rushmore, which looms in the midst of a landscape that is sacred to Native American nations. As I put it in chapter 3, no national monument is more thoughtlessly intrusive and forgetful about the history of imperial violence in the West than Mount Rushmore. Native Americans are thus an unseen or absent presence in Hitchcock's film, which, through Thornhill's odyssey across the American landscape, maps the process of commercialization and the architectural appropriation of their provenances.

Jarmusch's *Dead Man* is more explicit about the role of steel in the demise of the Native American ethno- and landscape. The film also features a naive character headed westward, in this case to a job as an accountant in the Dickinson steel mill in the town of "Machine" (perhaps a reference to Leo Marx's famous imagery of "the machine in the garden") in the Far West. Along the way, the plaid-suited and bowler-hatted protagonist is warned that although he has a letter con-

Dickinson steel mill in *Dead Man*. Courtesy of Miramax.

firming his employment, the job may not be available. The train's stoker (a white man with a blackened face, making him a stand-in for nonwhites) warns him before they arrive, saying, "I wouldn't trust no words written down on no piece of paper written by Dickinson out in Machine," doubtless referring not only to the fragility of the work contract but also to the broken treaties with Native Americans nations during the Euro-American westward expansion.

The oblivious William Blake, who, after finding no job and being mortally wounded, is led through a wilderness toward a Native American village by the Indian "Nobody" (Gary Farmer), consistently fails to comprehend Native American culture. Every time Nobody asks him if he has any tobacco, inquiring in effect if he is able to establish a bond through an exchange, he responds to the effect that he doesn't smoke. Without going into all the details of a complicated treatment of the destruction of Native America—for example, as the train reaches the Far West, white men in the garb of hunters shoot buffalo from the train's windows—I want to mention two scenes in which architecture is prominent. In the first, William Blake alights from the train in the town of Machine and walks slowly down the town's main street toward the Dickinson steel mill, which turns out to be a huge building full of industrial workers, an office staff, and the mill's owner, the homicidal maniac Dickinson, who chases Blake away with a shotgun.

Haida house in *Dead Man*. Courtesy of Miramax.

The second scene clearly refers to the first. At the end of the film, as William Blake nears the place where Nobody is taking him to fulfill his destiny as a dead man (like his namesake, the deceased poet William Blake), he again walks slowly down a long street. In this case it is the main thoroughfare of an Indian village, filled with destitute Native Americans (in contrast with the degenerate revelers Blake passes on his walk toward the Dickinson steel mill). At the end of his walk, he enters a large ceremonial building, where he is ushered inside by a Native American shaman. The building is a "cosmos house," looking quite like the "large plank houses of Northwest coast Indians," for example the Haida, whose dwellings were constructed to be located symbolically at the center of the universe, between the forest and beach, and with a verticality that represented three worldly zones: the sky world, the earth world, and the underworld.[114]

It would be too facile to simply assert that the juxtaposition of Blake's two walks, toward the steel mill on the one hand and the Haida spiritual house on the other, reflect the displacement of Native American spirituality by a Euro-American predatory commercial life. While certainly the Euro-American conception of investment property differs markedly from many Native American tendencies to spiritualize landscapes, the architecture of the American city, which has become the dominant feature of the modern landscape, is not wholly isolated from spiritual practices. Although, as Lewis Mumford points out, the city, "through its concentration of physical and cultural power," played a major role in the commercialization of life, "heighten[ing] the tempo of human intercourse and translat[ing] products into forms that could be stored and reproduced," it also played a role similar to that of the Native American ceremonial house: "By means of its storage facilities (buildings, vaults, archives, monuments, tablets, books), the city became capable of transmitting a complex culture from generation to generation."[115] In short, the city's buildings are also sites of historical memory. To underscore the homology between the city and Haida house (a "cosmos-house" as Nabokov and Easton describe it), it should be noted that Mumford refers to the "cosmo-city," arguing that the modern city, which is organized around central buildings, evolved from architectural forms that were seen as replicas of the universe, most notably the "royal citadel."[116] The commerce-facilitating city thus contains not only a utilitarian architecture of circulation but also a ritual architecture of cultural memory.

Certainly Jarmusch's film alerts us to a process of violent destruction and appropriation. And, in Foucault's sense, to recognize that violence is to become open to a counter-history that impugns the traditional sovereignty-oriented, social contract narrative. But my aim in emphasizing the juxtaposition is to note that inasmuch as there are alternative architectural thought-worlds, there are also alternative "public histories" (in Hayden's terms) or, as I want to emphasize, alternative architectural thought-worlds embodying varying relationships between architecture and memory. Yet my concern is not to merely point to difference but, rather, to frame a diversity-welcoming, non-closural politics of American architecture.

Conclusion: The Politics of American Architecture

To return to the earlier discussion of the architecture of the Virginia plantation in the seventeenth century, I noted that it drew on classical and Georgian idioms to manage a position of local hegemony while mollifying colonial authorities. In turn, Jefferson's Palladian, anti-Georgian (and thus anti-colonial) designs of Monticello served a larger national project, while embodying nevertheless the same coercive community as the designs of the less ambitious, earlier plantation owners. At stake for Jefferson was the relationship between historical memory and the realization of a national culture. Countering Jefferson's resistance to an ethnically diverse America, and therefore privileging an architectural imaginary that regards the adequation of architecture to memory as always incomplete, I have pointed to Daniel Libeskind's designs as exemplary. It is worth repeating Young's insight that in Libeskind's designs the "memory of historical events, which never domesticates such events, never makes us at home with them, never brings them into the reassuring house of redemptory meaning." What I want to add by way of a provisional conclusion is that the anti-redemptive cast of Libeskind's designs opens the issue of memory to avenues of otherness that the dominant architectural traditions have closed.

How might we achieve such an openness. My resort to the films of Hitchcock and Jarmusch is meant to foreground the architecturally enacted memories of those whose pasts tend to be left out of the dominant contemporary American imaginary. As Kaja Silverman has suggested, such "aesthetic work is a privileged domain for displacing us from the geometrical point [privileged, for example, in Jeffersonian designs], for encouraging us to see in ways not dictated in advance by the dominant fiction."[117] Silverman goes on to treat the way this dislocation can alert us to a remembering of "other people's memories."[118] The point, which I share with Silverman, is not merely to produce a more pluralistic and inclusive mode of memory, but to create a subjunctive "history" rather than reinforcing the official versions, which have embodied, in architecture as well as other commemorative genres, a steadfast forgetting and "the denial of other possibilities."[119] Such aesthetic displacements, finally, can remind us of what radical democratic theorist Jacques Rancière would call a history of "wrong," which continues to haunt the American democratic experiment.[120]

5 Composing America

A nation's emergence is always predicated on the construction of a field
of meaningful sounds. Just as infants babble through a welter of phonics
to achieve phonemes of a native language, so conglomerates of human
beings seeking national identity engage myriads of sounds in order to
achieve a vocabulary of *national* possibilities.

—Houston A. Baker Jr.,
Modernism and the Harlem Renaissance

What do we hear when America sings? What sounds from the
disembodied voice of a nation so traumatized and confused by its own
racial constitution? What might the music tell us that we fail to discern
in other artifacts of culture?

—Ronald Radano, *Lying Up a Nation*

Counterpoint and Ménage

Two inspirations inaugurate this investigation of "American music."
The first is the contrapuntal soundtrack of Spike Lee's 1998 film, *He
Got Game,* in which an American basketball story provides the main
narrative. An African American father, in prison on a murder conviction for killing his wife (accidently, as a flashback shows), is temporarily
paroled to try to convince his son, a high school basketball star, to sign
a letter of intent to play for the governor's alma mater. He is offered a
commuted sentence if he succeeds. The film explores a range of corrupt college recruitment practices as well as the avarice of those who
would live off the athletic skills of a young black athlete: politicians,
colleges, family members, friends, and lovers. While the film story is
focused on two major venues for the capture of the African American body, the penal system and the sports system—depicted in paral-

lel montage as the father, Jake Shuttlesworth (Denzel Washington), is shown shooting baskets in a prison exercise yard while the son, Jesus Shuttlesworth (Ray Allen), shoots baskets on a practice court—the soundtrack enacts a different contrast.

The musical background of Lee's film alternates between the vernacular-inspired symphonic music of Aaron Copland and the rap sounds and lyrics of Public Enemy. As Lee states, he selected Copland's music because "when I listen to [Copland's] music, I hear America, and basketball is America."[1] Certainly Copland aligned himself with composers who drew from vernacular sources, but he aimed at transcending specific idioms to create a uniquely American music: "Our concern was not with the quotable hymn or spiritual; we wanted to find a music that would speak of universal things in a vernacular of American speech and rhythms."[2] But which "America" does Copland's music reference? While Copland's earlier music was "reflective of his Jewish, New York, and Paris experiences," his post-1935 (and now most familiar) music, "*Billy the Kid, Rodeo, Lincoln Portrait, Fanfare for the Common Man,* and *Appalachian Spring* . . . speak to a wide breadth of American sensibilities."[3] Of course, most of the "sensibilities" within this "wide breadth" are Euro-American ones. The pieces that Lee's soundtrack incorporates are doubtless intentionally those associated with some of the spaces of white America (*Appalachian Spring*) and those associated with Euro-America's movement westward (the "Ho Down" from *Rodeo* and *Billy the Kid*). As Jessica Burr suggests, "Copland's western works are fundamental to his pre-eminence in American music because the West looms so large in the national consciousness. . . . It is well known that Copland's use of open intervals and wide spacing, clear orchestration, and plain folk-like materials has given Americans a powerful musical image of their frontier."[4]

The melodic landscapes of Copland's music, their "rising and falling pitches,"[5] articulate well with the western landscapes they accompany in the film. At the same time that big-name schools in the already-settled West (musically framed in Copland tunes) are bent on recruiting Jesus, another America, its urban venues inhabited by much of the African American population, is framed by the rap music of Public Enemy, whose staccato rhythms and inner city–directed lyrics speak to and mimic other sensibilities. And while Copland's music, with its inter-articulated vernaculars, references a comfortably shared America, Public Enemy's provides a more strident political edge; it supplies a commentary on the predatoriness of those who run a sport system that exploits young African Americans and more generally on the ever-present commerce that inflects the game. Note for example the lyrics of their "Politics of the Sneaker Pimps": "I see corporate hands up in foreign lands. With the man behind the man gettin' paid behind the man." And some of their other songs treat the pervasive inequalities that constitute the political economy of America's racial-spatial order—for example, the line "white men in suits don't have to jump."

Lee's soundtrack thus stages a contrapuntal encounter between the exemplary musical scores of two alternative American thought-worlds, connected with alternative American experiences. To situate the soundtrack's political resonances, we can heed Jacques Rancière's insight that the politics of aesthetics has its impact on "the system of self evident facts of sense perception that simultaneously discloses the existence of something in common and the delimitations that define the respective parts and positions within it."[6] In contrast with an aesthetic that aims toward fashioning the "in common" (Aaron Copland's) is a more radical political aesthetic (Public Enemy's) that, when arrayed against Copland's musical America, creates different political subjects by, in Rancière's terms, "reconfigur[ing] what are given to be facts."[7] Public Enemy's contribution to Lee's soundtrack offers a counter-aesthetic that focuses on dissensus and "establishes a grid that makes it possible to think through the forms of political dissensuality . . . by undoing the relations between the visible, the sayable, and the thinkable."[8] In short, they help reframe a sports story, making it one that addresses America's racial politics.

The second inspiration is Richard Powers's novel *The Time of Our Singing*, in which he interweaves a meditation on America's hybrid musical history with key moments in the mid-twentieth-century struggle against racial discrimination. The novel features the family of Delia Daley, an African American concert singer from Philadelphia, and David Strom, a German Jewish èmigrè physicist, who meet at an historic occasion, Marian Anderson's 1939 concert on the National Mall in Washington. They marry and raise three children in a musical environment that belies the cultural and racial divisions raging around them, as first the civil rights movement of the 1950s and 1960s and subsequently more militant forms of activism ultimately exert divisive pressures on their children.

What is especially notable about the music in their household is the contrapuntal interludes the Daley-Stroms stage in a way reminiscent of America's often fraught, interracial musical self-fashioning, running from the late nineteenth century through much of the twentieth: "After dinner they came together in tunes, Rossini while washing the dishes, W. C. Handy while drying." Delia had "come from more places than even her hybrid children could get to, and each one of those clashing places sang its signature tune." She and David often played a game called "crazed quotations" in which Delia, sitting at the piano, would begin

> playing a simple melody—say Dvorak's slow reedy spiritual "From the New World." The husband then had two repeats to find a response. The children watched in suspense as Delia's tune unfolded to see if Da could beat the clock and find a countersubject before the mother reached the double bar. . . . He rarely failed. By the time Dvorak's stolen folk song looped back around, the fellow found a way to make Schubert's *Trout* swim upstream against it. . . . The game produced the wildest mixed marriages, love matches that even the heaven of half-breeds looked sidelong at. Her Brahms *Alto Rhapsody* bickered with his growled Dixieland. Cherubini crashed into Cole Porter. Debussy, Tallis and Mendelssohn shacked up in unholy menages a trois.[9]

Like Lee's contrapuntal musical score, Powers's mixed marriage and ménage metaphors and clashes of ethnic musics provides a powerful provocation to explore the historical construction of "American" music, which in many of its forms is a product of encounters among diverse ethnic thought—and experiential worlds. The musical ménages Powers stages in the midst of the Daley-Strom family, an articulation of an intertextual music and interracial household, is echoed in some contemporary musical compositions—for example, William Bolcom's song cycle, *Songs of Innocence*, a William Blake–inspired encounter of "contraries" "that encompasses styles ranging from solemn chorales, lush romanticism, abrasive, dissonant modernism, to jazz, folk, country and rock."[10] Bolcom's commitment to combine the diverse ethnic sources of American music has a heritage that begins with Antonin Dvorak's American compositions, especially his *New World Symphony*. And inasmuch as Powers's reference to Dvorak's "stolen folk song" stems from the earliest attempt to fashion an American musical idiom that welcomes the participation of Euro-, African, and Native American traditions, he provides an appropriate threshold for a treatment of the historical encounters and initiatives that speak to the changing shapes of American music, as diverse ethnic musics reflect both centrifugal and centripetal political sensibilities, while they collide, clash, and coalesce.

Dvorak versus Tocqueville

There is a telling contrast in the responses to a multiethnic America of two famous nineteenth-century European visitors, Alexis de Tocqueville and Antonin Dvorak. As is well known, for Tocqueville the American ethnoscape was to be Euro-American dominated. He saw the "Negro" as hopelessly incapacitated and otherwise inadequate as a participant in an American democratic future, and he saw Native Americans as also unqualified participants, in their case by dint of temperament and cultural practices (although he did hold out some hope for the benefits of "racial mixing"). While he lamented the practice of slavery and the demise of Native Americans, he showed little ethnographic interest in either. He ranged as far as Minnesota to gawk at immiserated remnants of nearly destroyed Indian nations, and during his journey to the South, he looked at slaves from an even greater conceptual as well as physical distance than his plantation-owning hosts: "Habitually assum[ing] an aristocratic attitude toward American ideas and customs," his view of all aspects of America was conditioned by "the social position [that aristocrats] had lost after the french revolution." Rather than immersing himself deeply in the various dimensions of vernacular culture, what Tocqueville observed was screened through his preoccupation with his "unworked through attachments to the aristocratic tradition."[11]

In contrast, appearing on the American scene almost sixty years after the aristocratic Tocqueville, Dvorak, a descendant of farmers and tradesmen, welcomed and incorporated America's ethnic diversity into his musical compositions. Displaying an ethnographic rather than aristocratic regard, he was committed to fashioning a musical America that partook of African American and Native American, as well as Euro-American, musical idioms. As he famously stated in his 1893 *Harpers* essay, "In the Negro melodies of America I discover all that is needed for a great and noble school of music. . . . There is nothing in the whole range of composition that cannot be supplied with themes from this source." Accordingly, he "saturated himself with the spirit of the old tunes [for example, 'Swing Low, Sweet Chariot' in the second theme of his first movement] and then invented his own themes." He even used a "flatted seventh [a characteristic passed on to jazz, known as a 'blue note']."[12] And he "tried to combine Negro and Indian themes," for example, composing a largo movement for his *New World Symphony* after reading the famine scene in Longfellow's *Hiawatha*.[13]

Although Dvorak's grasp of "Indian music" was based exclusively on the degraded impressions of the music produced by Euro-Americans outside of its original contexts, his interest in the music inspired others—for example, Edward MacDowell and Arthur Farwell—to mine authentic Native American musical traditions. Although the "Indian" music was to serve as "raw material" in their own synthesizing compositions, at least they worked with "ethnographic transcriptions and recordings," derived from Indian performance venues.[14] MacDowell's "Indian Suite" was derived from his study of "the Indians, their dances and songs," but he resisted calling it "American music."[15] In contrast, Farwell, like Dvorak, wanted to appropriate Indian musics in order to craft a distinctive American music. Contrasting his appreciation of Indian music with the collection of artifacts that constituted the museum approach to Native American culture, Farwell asserted that the method of filling museum shelves with artifacts has "an aristocracy, a free-masonry about it all, that constitutes an almost impassible barrier between it and the American people." Instead, he insisted, "The only way wholly compatible with democratic ideals . . . is to bring the American people as a whole into sympathetic relation with the Indian. For through his simple, direct, poetic expression, in ritual, story and song, which he is willing to communicate to one who approaches him as a fellow man, we are able to recognize, once and for all, his humanity and wealth of interest and significance which it offers for the enrichment of our own lives."[16]

However worthy one might deem Farwell's commitment to a democratic recognition in word and musical deed, inspired by what he saw as original "musical ideas" in the Native American soundscape (he composed "Indian Melodies"[17]), a better sense of the way the Native American thought-worlds are articulated in hybrid musical forms yields itself with attention to how contemporary Native American writers, composers, and performers interpret their relationship with other

American musics. However, before turning to a treatment of the diversity that an approach to American music deserves, I want to look briefly at a notable Eurocentric, anti-diversity impulse that articulated itself in the form of an American musical nationalism early in the twentieth century.

A Reactive Yankee America and a Fraught Emergence of Jazz

At the same time that Farwell and a few others were seeking to realize Dvorak's pan-ethnic American musical vision, there existed a strong Eurocentric anti-vernacular impetus from prestigious "Yankee" composers, whose cultural version of racism remains alive in contemporary anti-immigrant texts, both popular and academic.[18] Exemplary among these composers was Daniel Gregory Mason (born in 1873), who sought to uphold what he saw as a racial inheritance, an Anglo Saxon "moral community," expressible in music, against a younger generation of composers, born between 1895 and 1900, who enacted a model of ethnic diversity in their compositions.[19] In reaction to composers who incorporated such vernacular American idioms as ragtime, Mason wrote: "It is strange and somewhat repulsive to see European musicians, with a long and intensive culture behind them, at the behest of tired nerves throwing it all away and acclaiming American ragtime, the sweepings of our streets, as the rejuvenator of their senile art."[20] However, Mason's "European musician" was selectively identified. For example, while he grudgingly acknowledged that "'the more sensuous Slav' productively counterbalances 'the more convention-beset Anglo-Saxon,'" in the production of a national music culture, he remained convinced nevertheless of the preeminence of "the Yankee composer."[21]

The virtual worship of a hierarchical view of American culture that Mason and other Yankee composers expressed as a virtual mission to transplant Anglo Saxon culture and its attendant "Victorian assumptions about music and art"[22] constitutes what MacDonald Smith Moore calls "redemptive culture." Describing themselves in terms of "race," Mason and his contemporary, Charles Ives, "believed that the true moral community of neighborliness had been born in Old New England" and that it was their job to help "reaffirm the meaning of American community for each generation." Mason, Ives, and other "Centennial composers" would fulfill their calling, Moore suggests, "if they could create through musical culture a grammar of national identity."[23]

However, as Moore's gloss on the history of American music suggests, it was ultimately an "ethnic dissonance" rather than a racist redemptive sensibility that was to have the most telling influence on
American music, especially after jazz "burst into the awareness of white
Americans at the close of World War I."[24] "The Jazz Age," he adds, "re-
pudiated an older tradition of redemptive culture."[25] Thereafter a musical culture war developed between white American subcultures, with
some, primarily Anglos, who were committed to a model of a racial
hierarchy, attempting to dismiss jazz as a remnant of an inferior culture
and others, mostly Jewish èmigrès, incorporating jazz and aspects of its
ragtime roots into a new hybrid American music in both symphonic
and musical theater genres. As Moore puts it, those involved in the
struggle sought "to control the root metaphors of their self-definition
as Americans."[26]

Among those who entered the culture war with a redemptive mentality was the automobile magnate Henry Ford, whose redemptive impulse reached into America's rural backcountry rather than, like the
Yankee composers, sorting various American inflections of European
music. The historical context for Ford's redemptive involvement with
music was "a widespread fear of the loss of white Anglo Saxon Protes-
tant hegemony in American political life and culture," which led to,
among other things, a sponsorship of an "old-time" music thought to
represent the threatened way of life.[27] Through his broadly dispersed
company dealerships, Ford sponsored music and dance events aimed
at displacing jazz with "old-time fiddling" and jazz dancing with "old-
time square and round dancing."[28] Ford and those who shared his views
disparaged not only ethnic musics but also "America's dependence on
Europe for models of artistic inspiration." For example, among this type
of musical nationalist was the composer-conductor Lamar Stringfield,
who issued a handbook through the University of North Carolina Press
in 1931 to promote a national music, disparage jazz, and identify the
centrality of American culture in a purportedly authentic American
vernacular music, thought to be the music of the common people.[29]

Rather than being concerned with the elevation of alternatives to
jazz or with musical purity, African American composers and musicians
have struggled against the appropriation of African American musical
idioms by white composers and performers. For example, an influential
critique articulated in Amiri Baraka's *Blues People* insists that the commercial appropriation of blues and bluesy jazz is a thin commercial

version of a music that has had ontological depth. African American blues and bluesy jazz, as it departed from its predominantly African-inspired vocal and rhythmic forms, according to Baraka, remained a resistant, highly coded mode of signifying musical expression of the African American "meta society."[30] It reflected the situation of a people whose music enacted their sense of difference and their struggle for solidarity. Or, in the words of Ronald Radano, "Black sounding practices identified a difference that, while constituted within the master-slave relation, gave material significance to a people under siege."[31]

For Ralph Ellison as well, "the blues is an impulse to keep the painful details and episodes of a brutal experience alive in one's aching consciousness, to finger its jagged grain, and to transcend it, not by the consolations of philosophy but by squeezing from it a near-tragic, near-comic lyricism."[32] But although he also lamented the loss of historical context in the trajectory of jazz developments, Ellison saw it as more a function of performance venue than of racial difference. He was discontent with the disconnect that had taken place between music and dance. Prizing the "palpable *physical* dimensions of the blues/jazz ritual,"[33] Ellison complains that "the thinness of much of so called modern jazz," its "loss of wholeness," can be attributed to its distance from "the small Negro public dance," which is its most authentic venue.[34]

Nevertheless, for Ellison jazz is a pan-ethnic American phenomenon, a classic expression of American vernacular music and a mèlange that defies any boundary between high and low, "that speaks eloquently to the United States's predicament as a still-forming nation, black, white, brown, and beige, that is still in the state of relative nakedness . . . but this nakedness allows for a greater degree of personal improvisation, and with the least hindrance from traditional social forms, rituals, manners, etc."[35] And he observes that "jazz seems somehow to give expression to the times much better than does classical music in the European tradition—though of course I love them both."[36]

Ellison's love of "both" has a politically significant heritage. As he reports, while a student at Mrs. Zelia N. Breaux's music school in the black school system of Oklahoma City, he was exposed to both traditions. She insisted on strictly classics by day, but by night "she was the owner/operator of the Ira Aldridge Theater where Duke and Louis reigned in the footlights, along with Bessie Smith, Ida Cox, Jimmy Rushing and the Blue Devils as creators and perpetuators of the shouts, smear, and muted rhapsodies that characterize blues and jazz."[37] The political significance of Mrs. Breaux's division of the day is parallel with another such division reported by Jacques Rancière. In Rancière's analysis of the political assemblages and writing initiatives of nineteenth-century proletarians, he refers to the way workers used their evenings to make of themselves political subjects. By devoting the night to writing, they turn the night into a political zone, a space within which to invent themselves in a way that resists the worker identity that exhausts the bourgeois conception of them.[38]

Similarly, the musical work in Mrs. Breaux's school, which by day is dominated by a Euro-American musical pedagogy, is countered by a welcoming of an African American musical idiom at night, effecting a reassertion of a musical identity that is suppressed hours earlier. The love of both to which Ellison refers is enacted in important compositions by Euro- and African American composers, although with varying political inflections. Notably, the compositions of George Gershwin and Duke Ellington are explicit attempts at combining Euro- and African American musical idioms to compose "America" in sound.

George Gershwin's Intertextual America

There is little doubt about what Gershwin thought he was up to as he worked on his *Rhapsody in Blue* (1924). Very much in tune with the spirit of Dvorak's approach to American music, he stated that *Rhapsody* "began as a purpose not a plan . . . as a sort of musical kaleidoscope of America—of our vast melting pot of our incomparable national pep, our blues, our metropolitan madness" (indeed Gershwin's initial plan was to entitle his piece "American Rhapsody").[39] Moreover, his *Rhapsody in Blue* was premiered at a concert where a prestigious committee of famous musical personalities—Sergei Rachmaninoff, Jascha Heifetz, Efrem Zimbalist, and Alma Gluck (among others)—were to decide the question, "What is American Music?"[40] And, as the January 4, 1924, *New York Herald Tribune* report continued, it was noted that "George Gershwin is at work on a jazz concerto, Irving Berlin is writing a syncopated tone poem and Victor Herbert is working on an American suite."[41]

It is tempting to impose a linear narrative on the influences shaping Gershwin's *Rhapsody,* the composition in which he saw himself as a producer of a uniquely American musical idiom. One might suppose that Gershwin, being already steeped in classical music, added a jazz inflection to create what emerged as a form of symphonic jazz. But musical thought-worlds are not simply temporally additive, moving from earlier to later compositions. If we think intertextually, we can enact a different assumption; rather than seeing Gershwin's *Rhapsody* as a product of a linear music history, in which we imagine him taking classical forms and adding blues, slide, and jazz forms, etc., we can recognize that his approach to classical forms is already shaped by his appreciation of jazz, blues, and rag forms. Thinking intertextually—about the interweaving or crossing of texts—presents a challenge to the typical idea of a linear history of musical influences. As Michael Klein puts it, "Broadly conceived, intertextuality has the potential to disrupt our notions of history and the unidirectional timeline that runs from an earlier text to a later one."[42]

In Gershwin's case the kind of "classical" forms that play a role in his compositions are romantic. His musical training is primarily in "the romantic piano literature (Chopin, Liszt, Debussy) not the symphonic classics."[43] For one familiar with the improvisational challenges to traditional musical intelligibility in the development of jazz, it is not surprising to observe a jazz-influenced composer turning to the romantics, who, initially influenced by Wagner's departures from the traditional quadratic form, created a music that violates familiar meaning conventions, especially by disrupting syntactic expectations.[44] For example, "Claude Debussy's melodic ideas are not contingent upon a rigid tonal scheme."[45] In ignoring the norms of musical periodicity, his compositions resist expectations of closure. Rejecting the authority of conventional tonality, his scales have no conventional points of beginning and ending; for example, they often have whole-note intervals, a practice that violates the tonality conventions through which musical spacing and narrative had been commonly understood.[46] In addition, Debussy uses a "reiterative phraseology" with "oscillating chords" which constitute "a mode of musical continuity that is diametrically opposed to the goal-directed syntactical harmony of traditional tonal music."[47] Instead of developing themes, Debussy creates musical fragments, a multiplicity, a nonlinear set of musical associations, and repetitive patterns that resist instead of moving toward a stable narrative or set of references.

As is the case with Debussy's music, the jazz aesthetic, which early in its development incorporated blues scales, ragtime rhythmic motifs, chromatic voicing elements, repetitive phraseology, and unconventional, polyphonic tonalities, disrupts conventional musical form and the expectations of closure with which conventional music is associated. As James Snead puts it, "Black music sets up expectations and then disturbs them."[48] While in Debussy there are no conventional beginnings and endings, in blues/jazz compositions there are many new beginnings; they are characterized by pervasive cuts and abrupt "skipping back to another beginning."[49] Gershwin's *Rhapsody* makes good use of the aesthetic homology between romantic and jazz forms, especially the swing style of jazz, which drew significantly on the "arsenal of Debussy's harmony."[50] "Debussy bequeathed his harmonies to jazz . . . [as reflected in] Gershwin, Milhaud, Constant, Lambert, and Bernstein," who wrote music that effaced the highbrow/lowbrow divide, creating a music "grounded in harmony and counterpoint."[51] Accordingly, as David Schiff points out, there is a pervasive African American musical presence in Gershwin's *Rhapsody*; its five basic tunes are "all based on the blues scale."[52] In sum, in Gershwin's *Rhapsody* there are recognizable elements of Debussy's piano music,[53] of ragtime (especially stride piano) styles, vaudeville-style comic piano motifs, and even elements of American popular songs. Apart from his classical training, Gershwin studied with Luckey (Charles Luckeyeth) Roberts, "the master ragtime pianist."[54] As a result, *Rhapsody* constructs American music as an inter-articulation of parts of a Euro-classical form and a variety of vernacular idioms and styles.[55]

Gershwin's synthesis in his *Rhapsody* is also apparent in his folk opera, *Porgy and Bess,* in which he also saw himself attempting to "forge an American musical language" while achieving an artistic unity out of a historical and ethnic diversity. He wanted his music to represent what he called the "the rhythms of these interfusing peoples . . . clashing and blending."[56] Doubtless Gershwin achieved a musical fusion or inter-articulation, but if one treats the historical depth and phenomenological significance of the different sound-worlds with which he was working, the issue of composing an inter-ethnic America defies a simple, compositional solution. Wynton Marsalis (among others) does not regard "fusion" music as jazz because "certain key elements of jazz are not addressed. First and foremost the blues."[57]

But certainly Gershwin's *Rhapsody* contains blues melodies. In his *Creole Rhapsody,* seemingly a combination of appreciation and response to Gershwin's *Rhapsody in Blue,* Duke Ellington, whose piece begins with "the same harmonic progression," goes on to render *his*

Rhapsody "bluesier." And a more radical departure among pieces that "would not have been written without the example of [Gershwin's] *Rhapsody*" is African American musician/composer James P. Johnson's *Yamekraw* (or "Negro Rhapsody"), which, Schiff notes, is "an act of ethnic definition, a pulling together of elements from the African-American musical traditions, not a bridge between those traditions and European music."[58]

In contrast, when the African American pianist/arranger Marcus Roberts interprets Gershwin's *Rhapsody*, he achieves the "clashing and blending" to which Gershwin refers. Roberts's approach effectively interweaves the kind of African American self-definition that "a jazz sensibility" reflects, without, he suggests, "destroying the essence of Gershwin's original score." It places that jazz sensibility "within a classical environment."[59] Wanting to "create a modern dialogue with the entire history of American jazz piano," Roberts's treatment of Gershwin's *Rhapsody* includes the influence of the hesitation pacing of Thelonious Monk, the "shuffle-based New Orleans groove, anchored by bassist Roland Guerin and drummer Jason Marsalis," and the kind of syncopated swing "first introduced by Louis Armstrong."[60] However, to understand the tensions between self-definition and respect for traditional form that has produced American musical traditions, one has to move beyond the mere idioms that various compositions incorporate and explore the ethnic experiential trajectories that have eventuated in such hybrid sounding practices.

Jewish American and African American Self-Definition

It is clear that the history of African American sounding practices has operated in a more constrained situation than that experienced by Gershwin and other Jewish American composers and musicians. While granting that "[a] nation's emergence is always predicated on the construction of a field of meaningful sounds," Houston A. Baker Jr. points out that the black musical contribution creates a disjuncture. He notes that the "*national* enterprise of black artists and spokes persons, since the beginning of the century," have been involved in "a mode of *sounding* reality"[61] that resists the Euro-American state's desire for unitary, nationalizing cultural productions.

In contrast, the Jewish American musical contributions have been driven for the most part by an assimilationist motivation. For example, as Andrea Most points out in her treatment of the Jewish contribution to musical theater, "the Broadway stage was a space where Jews envisioned an ideal America and subtly wrote themselves into the scenario as accepted members of the mainstream American community."[62] Nevertheless, despite what emerged as differential sensibilities operating as both ethnic groups connected with mainstream Euro-America, there is one striking homology between Jewish and Afro modernity as they articulated themselves into their respective sound-worlds. Both Jewish American and African American musical inventions owe aspects of their forms to the kinds of doubleness and masking imposed on peoples who are forced to function within cultures from which they are in varying degrees abjected. Both Jewish and Afro modernity stem from traditions in which disguise has constituted an integral part of their cultural productions.

In the Jewish case, as it is treated by Gershom Scholem, the beginning of their modern consciousness can be traced to "sixteenth century Marrano culture" and the seventeenth-century "Sabbatian movement," within which "the Marranic split between inner belief and outer identity" was "sacrilized."[63] Given the condition of a people who desired to preserve their beliefs while at the same time seeking to survive in national, Gentile-dominated environments, where their beliefs were disrespected and/or outlawed, their aesthetic forms—their humor, music, and drama (among other genres)—reflect a situation that recalls the way masking constituted many African American aesthetic forms. And, arguably, "the self-conscious role playing demanded by modernizing societies led Jews to develop talents that were highly suitable for the theater."[64] But while their aesthetic productions throughout the nineteenth century accommodated both their divided presentation of self and a recognition of divided audiences, by the twentieth century the Jewish American contribution to the Broadway musical theater was oriented toward inventing a mainstream American musical/theatrical idiom.

Certainly Irving Berlin's musical trajectory is exemplary with respect to the assimilationist cast of the Jewish American contribution to inventing a musical America. Berlin ultimately saw himself as one "writing American music."[65] Having ceased writing ethnic novelty songs by 1914, Berlin, "a gifted assimilator of a variety of musical traditions and an equally eager champion of dominant American institutions and values," composed music that contained "a vision of America devoid of all evidence of difference and conflict."[66] While there existed a musical theater that was more critical, using "flashbacks, broken timelines and the projection of a character's interiority on stage . . . to express the contingent quality of all we 'know,'"[67] Berlin was participating in a mainstream Broadway musical theater that featured simple, linear narratives and uncomplex musical voices. Aspiring to the invention of a unitary national voice, his imagined geography was national in scope. Berlin's patriotic songs "God Bless America," "The Freedom Train," and "the Song of Freedom," among others, map an ideationally undifferentiated national space,[68] and his personae are protagonists rather than antagonists. Rather than creating conflicting voices, as in the call and response mode of much of the African American musical tradition, Berlin's music tends toward an edifying process reflected in one voice. In accord with the ideological frame of the Jewish American *Bildungsroman*, Berlin's early songs were usually written as the expression of a single protagonist "whose identity," as Charles Hamm puts it, "was encoded into the text and music, then projected, clarified, or even changed in the act of performance."[69] Subsequently, the narrative trajectory of the characters in the Tin Pan Alley musicals of Jewish Americans tended to reflect a confidence in one's ability to assimilate into mainstream American culture.

By contrast, given the more intense levels of discrimination, exclusion, and rejection with which African Americans were faced, the veil or mask was a more persistent feature of the aesthetic within which their sound-world emerged. And in contrast with the macropolitical, national-level territoriality of Berlin's music, African American music recognized a split between mainstream American politics and the micropolitics of African American survival tactics (a split that, for the most part, Jewish modernity left behind in Europe). For example, the early assemblages in African American–produced musical theater featured minstrelsy and racist, denigrating "coon songs" that had been integral to the amusement of white audiences. However, in subtle ways, the songs and minstrel structure were recontextualized to give black audiences possibilities for a reception that differed from what white audiences were experiencing. Houston A. Baker Jr. puts the aesthetic problem of Afro modernity compellingly: "An African American spokesperson who wished to engage in masterful and empowering play within the minstrel spirit house needed the uncanny ability to manipulate bizarre phonic legacies. For he or she had the task of transforming the mask and its sounds into negotiable discursive currency."[70]

Baker points out that to understand the emergence of the African American aesthetic in the twentieth century, as it was articulated through both writing and musical genres, one must heed two alternative African American relationships with the aesthetic forms produced by Euro-Americans. One involves "the mastery of form," and the other, "the deformation of mastery." As an exemplar of the former, Baker treats Booker T. Washington's autobiography, *Up From Slavery*, which manages to tell a story of American racism in a way that articulates with white American modes of reception of black America's aesthetic forms while simultaneously addressing "the contours, necessities, and required programs of his own culture."[71] To do this, he self-consciously adopts "minstrel tones . . . reassuring sounds from black quarters" while at the same time engaging in a "rhetorical appropriation" that Baker calls "the mastery of form."[72]

The mastery of form to which Baker refers can be applied to the early African American musical theater, in particular to Will Marion Cook's 1898 *Clorindy: Or the Origin of the Cakewalk*. This musical comedy, with words by Paul Lawrence Dunbar, was the first all-black musical comedy with an original score.[73] Roughly one-third of the songs in the show bear a surface similarity to "coon songs: chicken mania, fancy dressing, and generally raucous behavior."[74] However, like Booker T. Washington's subtle rhetorical offerings to his African American audience, many of the Cook/Dunbar coon songs "contained topical humor that obliquely commented on the state of racial affairs":

> Dey's gwine to be colored policemen, all over dey say
> If dey do, it'll be [the] leading topic of de day,
> I'd like to see colored people rise up to de mark,
> But I'd rather not see a coon on de street or in de park,
> For it's hard enough to find a white policeman after dark.[75]

While the double level of address in Cook and Dunbar's *Clorindy* manifests Baker's "mastery of form" aspect of the African American aesthetic, some subsequent black musical theater productions exemplify the "deformation of mastery" he ascribes to such African American writing as W. E. B. Du Bois's *Souls of Black Folk*. The deformation of mastery is characterized by "distinguishing rather than concealing," and by enacting "a go(ue)rilla action in the face of acknowledged adversaries."[76] Thus, for example, in a subsequent Cook musical, *The Sons of Ham* (1900), the black audience is directly addressed, as in this narrative about a "proud southern girl" who moves north and prepares to confront different regional and class conceits:

> Ah's heard so much 'bout their high-toned ways,
> 'Bout dem actin' more like white folks ev'ry day,
> If dey tries to come it on me too gran'
> Ah'll tell 'em who I am — [77]

Yet the audiences addressed by the trajectory of African American sounding practices are only part of the identity context within which those practices have been shaped. When Duke Ellington insisted (in his first article) that "rhythmic sequences" are more important than "the show part of the band—the melody instruments," he was evoking the historical space of the jazz tradition, the dance hall, and thus also the relationship between music and the body, a reception that is experienced in movement, not merely in listening.[78] Rhythm according to Ellington is as important to musical production as it is to its reception: "Long association between players should result in their being able almost to anticipate each other's thoughts, [to] play as one man. . . . The first step to this end is to stabilise the rhythms played by the section."[79]

In addition to his concern with the bodies addressed by his music, Ellington was keenly sensitive to the interrelationships among his players. His compositions are oriented toward a recognition of both the individuality of each musician and the dynamic rapport of the ensemble. The construction of consonance and dissonance, characteristic of the jazz aesthetic that Ellington disproportionately invented, was guided by a democratizing ethos. Accordingly, it was a familiarity with Ellington orchestras, among other groups, that encouraged Ralph Ellison to assert that the jazz ensemble achieves the essence of democratic practice: "True jazz is an art of individual assertion within and against the group."[80] And Ellington himself also pointed out that what he called "Negro music" went well beyond the mere entertainment supplied by a marginalized minority. For example, addressing himself to the subject of a Langston Hughes poem, "We, Too Sing America," he insisted, "we play more than a minority role, in singing 'America'": "I contend that the Negro is the creative voice of America, is creative America. . . .

It was our voice that sang 'America' when America grew too lazy, satisfied and confident to sing."[81]

Duke Ellington's "Deformation of Mastery"

As Fred Moten puts it, "Ellington's music reconfigures the context in which everything, that is to say music, is read."[82] In contrast with an aesthetic that wore a mask, Ellington, at least in his music, was direct and confrontational. He insisted that he wanted "to take Uncle Tom out of the [musical] theater"; and after the premier of *Porgy and Bess*, he said that "the times are here, to debunk Gershwin's lampblack Negroisms."[83] To address those "times," he staged his own musical, *Jump for Joy*, with an all-black cast. In this musical, his deformations even ran to an amusing reversal, which he removed as possibly indelicate before it was performed. In the face of the Jewish actor Al Jolson's black minstrelsy-oriented role in *The Jazz Singer* (1927), the first script of Ellington's *Jump for Joy* included a scene in which there were "three colored guys sitting on a table in a tailor shop, sewing and singing Jewish songs."[84] "All the sketches had a message for the world," Ellington said, and the indictments of Uncle Tom imagery were explicit and humorous. For example the finale of the first act was "Uncle Tom's Cabin Is a Drive-In Now":

> There used to be a chicken shack in Caroline,
> But now they've moved it up to Hollywood and Vine;
> They paid off the mortgage—nobody knows how—
> *And Uncle Tom's Cabin is a drive-in now!*[85]

In its original conception, Ellington's *Jump for Joy* also satirically treated the racial-spatial order; removed from the opening of the second act was the line, "I've got a Passport from Georgia (and I'm going to the U.S.A.)"[86] Effectively, to use another of Baker's expressions (with Booker T. Washington resonances), Ellington's music was designed, like other genres belonging to the "black spokesperson," to pursue the "necessary task of employing audible extant forms in ways that move clearly *up*, masterfully and re-soundingly away from slavery."[87] Certainly Ellington pursued this move. His theater music is, in his words, "a statement of social protest . . . without saying it." "This," he insisted, "calls for the real craftsman."[88]

Shortly after writing and staging his *Jump for Joy*, Ellington undertook a longer work that would sound "the history of the American Negro," his *Black, Brown and Beige: A Tone Parallel to the History of the American Negro*. In this piece he inter-articulates history and sound to demonstrate the fortitude of a people who had moved "re-soundingly" *through* slavery as well as away from it. In his words, "The first section, 'Black,' delved deeply into the Negro past . . . the second section, 'Brown,' recognized the contribution made by the Negro to this country in blood . . . the third section, Beige . . . refer[s] to the common view of the people of Harlem, and the little Harlems around the U.S.A."[89]

Debuting at Carnegie Hall in 1943, *Black, Brown and Beige* is an exemplar of Baker's "deformation of mastery." Rather than simply reinflecting the "phonic legacies" of "conservatory trained musicians," whose music had dominated that venue, Ellington's working injunction was to write a piece "from the inside by a Negro."[90] Thus "Black," which inaugurates the musical, constructs the "Negro past" with a "Work Song" and a spiritual, "Come Sunday," a combination that refers to "the time when the workers had a church of their own."[91] Nevertheless, *Black, Brown and Beige* is a work of synthesis inasmuch as it has a European framing; it is a symphonic suite incorporating much of the history of the African American sound-world, and it required "recasting a jazz band composition for a symphony orchestra."[92]

Despite the incorporation of different ethnic musical traditions within the piece, *Black, Brown and Beige* manifests a striking disjunction. On the one hand, as a piece written "from the inside by a Negro," it explores not only evolving structures of feeling but also the spatial diaspora of African Americans, a spatial history with long global trajectories within which those structures of feeling were evinced. There is, of course, an intimate connection between structures of feeling and African American spatial history. For example, Nathaniel Mackey demonstrates that connection in his description of a moment when he and his ensemble are playing at a Thelonious Monk homage evening at the city of Oakland's club, Onaje's. As he is listening to another group playing Monk's composition *Pannonica*, he at first hears a "wistful strain" through the set; but at a certain point, he says, "Wistfulness turned into *saudade*. As I stood there I couldn't help remembering that the quality Brazilians call *saudade* goes back to the homesickness the slaves felt for Africa."[93]

On the other hand, Ellington's piece is designed for an enclosure, the concert hall, which, as Jacques Attali famously noted, displaced the earlier spaces of music that had witnessed a co-articulation of cultural life and sounding practices. The concert hall, as Attali points out, enfranchised a different kind of music; it changed both the space and the economy of music. The evolution of musical space to which Attali refers begins well before Ellington's attempt to use an enclosed space to articulate a historically and geographically extensive one. The process of enclosing and revaluing organized sound became a pervasive reality in the eighteenth century. Whereas prior to that time, "the musician, the social memory of a past imaginary, was at first common in the villages and the court, and was unspecialized; he [subsequently] became a domiciled functionary of the lords, a producer and seller of signs who was free in appearance, but in fact almost always exploited and manipulated by clients."[94]

Attali goes on to note that by the nineteenth century, the space of the concert hall was dominated by a "star system" as part of an irresistible feature of the music market. And central to this development was the piano repertory.[95] However, Ellington's approach to orchestration resisted the star system. As jazz musician Wynton Marsalis puts it, Ellington "as the inventor of the real American orchestra . . . advanced the conception of democratic creation."[96] Unlike those orchestral forms in which a featured soloist is in the foreground while other forms of instrumentation are in the background, Ellington "created a new system of harmony [in which] . . . the personality of the sound of each member of the orchestra took importance over the organization."[97] He exulted in the "freedom of expression" of each band member.[98]

Nevertheless, Ellington also prized the ability of each member of his orchestra to "anticipate each other's thoughts."[99] Again, Mackey provides a telling instance of this kind of rapport, which was in evidence at the Monk homage evening at Onaje's Oakland club. As his group was playing despite the absence of one of his band members, Penguin, "at the beginning of the second repeat . . . we heard an oboe join in from near the club's entrance, perfectly in tune and right on the beat. We looked over the heads of the audience, all of whom had turned around to see who the oboist was. And there was Penguin playing away while slowly making his way toward the stage."[100]

As Mackey has pointed out, the rapport in which jazz band members are able to anticipate what Ellington calls "each other's thoughts" operates within what is distinctive about the musical thought-world of

African American musicians. Recalling Amiri Baraka's discussion in his *Blues People* of the big-band jazz in the twenties and thirties of Fletcher Henderson, Duke Ellington, and Jimmy Lunceford, Mackey argues that the special meaning of *swing*, which functioned as a verb connoting the improvisational character of Afro-American music, became in the hands of some (white) commercial imitators "a less dynamic, less improvisatory, less blues-inflected music, and, at the political level, a containment of black mobility."[101] The improvisatory privileging of the verb in Afro-American compositions/performances, he states, connects with the more general linguistic situation "among a people whose ability to act is curtailed by racist constraints."[102]

Accordingly, through its improvisational character, Ellington's music, like that of other black composer/musicians, resists "the nounization of swing."[103] The musical innovations that restore the improvisational character of the music are part of what (the ever historically aware) Ellington called "the Marcus Garvey extension—a movement in its reaction to [the appropriated versions of] swing, from noun to verb."[104] As Ellington notes in his discussion of how his orchestra works, "we do not use any printed orchestrations. These are much too stereotyped."[105] But the political significance of Ellington's role in the dynamic phenomenology of the African American sound-world is subordinate to the politics of history to which his *Black, Brown and Beige* is addressed. That project, which is reminiscent of Dvorak's earlier attempt to make African American music a major part of the American musical canon, is an exemplar of his contribution as *the* major composer of "American music."

While Dvorak was privy to one historical African American musical idiom, the spiritual, whose musical style migrated into the blues-jazz traditions, Ellington's compositions are primarily manifestations of the swing aspect of the blues. However, in his *Black, Brown and Beige*, Ellington treats a long historical trajectory of African American musical idioms, while interconnecting the history of the American black experience with the history of their music. There are many powerful moments in the way he stages the inter-articulation of music and historical experience, but perhaps the most poignant occurs during the *Black* segment in the piece entitled "Come Sunday," originally an orchestral piece but subsequently produced in a vocal version sung by "the great spiritual and gospel singer Mahalia Jackson" (in her only appearance with a jazz group).[106]

Musically, "Come Sunday" straddles the two dimensions of the blues tradition famously distinguished by the classical and music scholar Albert Murray, the blues as feeling and the blues as music.[107] The former, he suggests, is a feeling of resignation and defeat, while the latter is a musical response to the ontological condition of African Americans. In this latter dimension, blues as music functions as "an experience-confrontation device that enables people to begin by accepting the difficult, disappointing, chaotic, absurd, which is to say the farcical or existential facts of life."[108] It moves beyond the negative facts of life to not only cope but also triumph. The orchestration of blues through jazz then becomes "a fundamental device for confrontation, improvisation, and existential affirmation . . . for improvising or riffing on the exigencies of the predicament."[109]

To understand the "predicament" to which "Come Sunday" is addressed, we have to consult Ellington's poem, in which Boola, his character who moves through the narrative of *Black, Brown and Beige*, approaches a church in which a white congregation is assembled for a service:

> Came Sunday, Boola was irresistibly drawn
> To that pretty white house with the steeple
> So tall, shining there in the sun. Everyone
> Who entered there was scrubbed and polished
> And all dressed up. How happy they seemed!
> While the white voices inside rang out
> In triumph . . . the blacks outside would grunt
> Subdued approval. When the white voices inside
> Were raised in joyous song, the blacks outside
> Hummed along, adding their own touches. . . .

Enacting this affirmation with instrumentation, Ellington's "Come Sunday" composes "short, lyrical statements by solo trombone and trumpet [to] introduce the 'song'" and includes a "typical blues style 'flatted fifth.'" And making the musical articulate with the emotional resonances of a people who are at once kept outside while nevertheless affirming the spirituality in progress inside, "the music holds still, catching its breath [as] 'the blacks outside . . . grunt/Subdued approval.'"[110] The expression, "Subdued approval," seconded by the musical resonances, speaks powerfully to Ellington's mission. His recovery of the history of "Negro music" is aimed not only at elaborating the experiences and structures of feeling within which it was spawned but also making the case that "we too sing America." "Subdued," therefore, has a double resonance; it reflects the historical fact of a people who have been subdued and it expresses their ambivalence about granting approval to a nation that has subjected African Americans to coercion and violence.

Thereafter, in the "Brown" section, the rhythms and tonalities of the spiritual follows its historical and musical migration to the blues. In this register the music features the traditional twelve-bar blues structure. Narratively, Ellington's "conceptual persona,"[111] Boola experiences the blues in the last section of "Brown," in which "Ellington's song 'The Blues,' is a masterpiece *about the blues*," as Maurice Peress puts it.[112] And by the time the narrative moves to "Beige," the character Boola morphs into Ellington, as the story shifts "from the mythical to the autobiographical" and Ellington's Harlem Cotton Club experience is at the center of the music. It is in this section that the narrative moves from a "weary blues" mood to a hopeful one that is reflected in the intellectual contributions of the Harlem Renaissance and the patriotic contributions of black America's participation in the war effort. This latter emphasis is in accord with the financial contribution of the Carnegie Hall debut of the piece, which was in support of Russian war relief. The continuing and pervasive blues element in "Beige" contains reprises from the earlier sections, as emotional (and thus tonal) vicissitudes abound, and Ellington's piano "returns in medium stride to introduce the final shout chorus [incorporating] bits and pieces from 'Come Sunday' and 'Work Song'" from "Black."[113] However one wants to construe the musical contribution of *Black, Brown and Beige* with Ellington, Dvorak's desire to locate the African American sound-world at the center of American music is realized. As Ellington puts it, "Negro music is America. It developed out of the life of the people here in this country."[114] But, at the same time, the African American sound-world creates disjuncture as much as it blends because Ellington recognizes that "Negro music" must articulate dissonance with dissonant chords. As he famously notes, "dissonance is our way of life in America. We are something apart, yet an integral part."[115]

The Blues Pervades the American Ethnoscape: *Red*

To treat one of the important implications of Ellington's creation of a place for the blues tradition at the center of American music, I want symbolically to add *Red* to his *Black, Brown and Beige.* Toward this end I treat the migration of the blues into other disjunctive musical spaces, the Native American sound and thought-worlds as they are articulated by two Native American artistic contributions, Sherman Alexie's novel, poetry, and accompanying music for his *Reservation Blues,* and John Trudell's poetry and music, especially as reflected in his *Blue Indians* recording. As is noted in my discussion of early twentieth-century efforts at composing "American music," the existence of distinctive Native American sound-worlds got the attention of both the European visitor Antonin Dvorak and subsequent "Yankee" composers who wanted to incorporate aspects of Native American music in their creation of a genuinely American soundscape. However, the so-called genuine is historically fugitive. As a result of a history of contact, the Native American soundscape has undergone significant changes. For example, after having been "[forcibly] taught to sing Christian hymns," formulated "to facilitate learning," Native American peoples created musical hybrids, adjusting and performing the hymns in "their own vocal style . . . [in] characteristically flat, nasal delivery with its glissandi . . . [as contrasted with] the European bel canto [operatic] ideal of singing."[116]

And, arguably, given the inter-ethnic associations, both voluntary and coercive, between African and Native Americans in the Southeast, well into the nineteenth century, their musical idioms had mutual impacts, especially because of some of the homologies between the percusive aspects of African and Native American ritual song forms, the existence of call and response patterns in both musics, and the intimate connections between song and dance forms in both cultures.[117] In the case of the former, Native American music becomes simply part of a vernacular-inspired melodic potpourri, while in the latter there is a blues translation with ontological depth. Accordingly, although there is a wide range of musical idioms in the history of Native American sound-worlds, my emphasis here is on the contemporary relationships between the African and Native American musics, with a special emphasis on blues. Nevertheless, it should be noted that "contemporary Native American music is rich and diverse, incorporating many tribally derived traditions, as well as popular and commercial forms and styles, including polkas, country musics, folk, rock and roll, blues, jazz, and reggae."[118]

In his novel *Reservation Blues,* Sherman Alexie pays particular attention to the potential of the impact of the blues on Native America and emphasizes its redemptive power, the characteristic that Murray ascribes to the blues as music.[119] To note the significance of the blues in the novel, however, we must recognize as well that for African Americans, the blues aesthetic has not been merely articulated in various art forms. As Clyde Woods points out (as I noted in chapter 2), it has had epistemic and ontological significance; it is a system of social explanation and a practice of identity-shaping solidarity, respectively.[120] Accordingly, when *Reservation Blues* begins with the legendary African American blues man Robert Johnson traveling to a Spokane reservation and lending his guitar to the Native American Thomas Builds-the-Fire, who ultimately plays for the Coyote Springs rock group, a linkage is established between the African American and Native American experiences of separation and political disqualification.

Alexie's assemblage of the Coyote Springs players also creates a linkage between Native and white American mythology. Thomas Builds-the-Fire expresses much of his participation in a blues aesthetic through storytelling. As a result, when the two white women, Betty and Veronica, whose names derive from the venerable Archie comic strip, join the group, two ethno-mythologies are conjoined. The narrative in *Reservation Blues* therefore constitutes a resistance to simplistic identity politics. It impugns Native American resistance to the forging of cultural and political coalitions as much as it offers a critique of the white dominance manifested by the reservation system. As is noted in the novel at the point where Robert Johnson arrives, Johnson's blues created a problem for those Spokanes who were practicing forgetfulness. At a moment when Alexie has Johnson singing about "worried blues," he writes, "The music stopped. The reservation exhaled. Those blues created memories for the Spokanes, but they refused to claim them. Those blues lit up a new road, but the Spokanes pulled out their old maps. Those blues churned up generations of anger and pain: car wrecks, suicides, murders. Those blues were ancient, aboriginal, indigenous."[121]

In addition to trying to ward off the power of the blues aesthetic, the Spokanes in Alexie's novel are resistant to accepting a culturally diverse rock group. The Wellpinit Rawhide Press, a reservation paper, carries a column in which someone writes: "Dear Tribal members, As you know, Coyote Springs, our local rock band, has just returned from Seattle with two white women. They are named Betty and Veronica, of all things. I'm beginning to wonder about Coyote Spring's ability to represent the Spokane tribe."[122] Alexie's political point works not only for the Spokanes but also for all those engaged by a blues aesthetic: For the blues to be redemptive, a people must not only claim its past but must also reclaim its relationship with an estranged otherness.

Accordingly, Alexie recognizes the disjunctive cultural forces that have assembled contemporary Native American identities. As I noted in chapter 1, as one subject to such material from mainstream American popular culture, Alexie regards his participation in a white-dominated literary culture as one among many of the "tiny treaties" to which he must add his artistic signature.[123] The music of the Coyote Springs rock group in his novel and the musical soundtrack in which he subsequently participated (as a reader) reflect the mix of white and red aesthetic idioms to which he subscribes. The "treaty" in Alexie's case is a negotiation and inter-articulation of diverse aesthetic idioms, conjoined within a blues matrix. Reflecting the historical trajectory of violated Indian-white treaties, the poem in the novel and song in the recording contain these lines (while the song itself combines traditional Native American rhythms and vocals with modern popular music):

Treaties never remember
They give and take till they fall apart
Treaties never surrender
I'm sure treaties we made are gonna break this Indian's heart

Reflecting the pervasiveness of the "tiny treaties" within Native America's contemporary habitus, Alexie's characters represent the fraught hybridity of contemporary Indianness. For example, his character Chess worries about the *"quarter-blood and eighth-blood grandchildren* [who] . . . *will get all the Indian jobs, all the Indian chances because they look white."*[124] But Alexie recognizes and accepts an Indianness that collects parts from diverse ethnicities and elements of popular culture. "Big Mom," the primary cultural icon in the novel, has made "Jimmi Hendricks, Janis Joplin, and Elvis . . . honorary members of the Spokane Tribe."[125] As Alexie has noted (treated in chapter 1), contrary to some Native American approaches to literature, he resists the "corn pollen and eagle feather school of poetry."[126] Rather than searching for authenticity, Alexie's artistic productions incorporate a model of Indianness as a ceaseless, inter-cultural becoming.

Accordingly, rather than treating Native Americans as an originary "blues people," he has them welcome and reinflect the blues in a process of cultural encounter that he represents metaphorically as a crossroad. At a crossroad, blues man Robert Johnson exchanges his soul or freedom to a stranger for a sublime musical ability. Thereafter, crossroad imagery abounds, with encounters between the blues tradition as it arose in the African American sound-world and its expression in Native American oral traditions, represented by Alexie's ever-present storytelling character, Thomas Builds-the-Fire, who in this novel receives the magical guitar from Robert Johnson at a crossroad. Reflecting different cultural codings, the guitar, which within Johnson's frame is regarded as dangerous, in Thomas's is regarded as powerful.

The Coyote Springs band becomes the carrier of a hybrid blues idiom at the center of the novel, as their lyrics reflect the individual and collective catastrophes of Native Americans. Within the novel, the blues serves as Alexie's frame for recounting oppression associated with Native American history. For example, the inability of the Coyote Springs band to get a recording contract results from their being rejected by producers named Sheridan and Wright, who are obviously named for the infamous cavalry colonels historically involved in the destruction of tribal peoples. In particular, Colonel George Wright is known for destroying over eight hundred horses after the defeat of Tilcoax of the Spokanes, a slaughter that became known as Wright's bone-yard. Accordingly, Alexie has Big Mom use a flute made from a horse's bone. Her morning songs on the flute—a reminder of the daily creation of the world—recall both the ritual significance of traditional Native American music and the historical moment associated with Wright's destruction of an Indian resource.

While Big Mom's playing serves as an emblem of the ritual past of Native American music, the Coyote Springs band plays a music that blends diverse American cultural forms. The *Reservation Blues* sound recording, with Jim Boyd's music and Sherman Alexie's readings, produced to represent the musical dimension of the novel with lyrics from the novel's poems, achieves the same musical hybridity as that of the Coyote Springs band. Songs such as "Reservation Blues," "Urban Indian Blues," and the above noted "Treaties," among others, have lyrics that address both past injustices and current catastrophes. For example, there is a reference to the infamous "Trail of Tears" in the poem/song "Indian Boy Love Song," and to alcohol addiction in "Father and Farther." The songs combine traditional tribal sounds and instruments with contemporary ones from jazz and rock ensembles (for example, oral chants combined with jazz and rock instrumentation), and some of them address the ironies in the history of white-red antagonisms, as in "99% Alike," in which we hear Alexie saying that because there is, biologically speaking, only 1 percent difference between white and red, he and Custer are 99 percent alike. Musically, like the Coyote Springs band in the novel, Jim Boyd and an occasional chorus of singers combine elements of traditional Native American and diverse contemporary popular musics. Boyd plays a cedar flute as well as guitar, bass, and keyboard, and the vocals include traditional chanting styles as well as modern popular rhythms.

The inter-cultural style of Boyd's music is not unlike that of one of the most gifted Native American poet-musicians, John Trudell, whose work combines elements of the traditional Native American soundworld with a blues idiom and tonality and a modern rock style. This latter aspect of Trudell's lyrical/musical work is inspired by the composer and singer Jackson Browne, who, with his appreciation of how to combine blues with rock and roll, has helped produce and has participated in some of Trudell's recordings. The primary thought-world that pervades Trudell's inter-articulation of a soundscape and ideoscape harks back to a Crazy Horse quotation that Trudell repeats often and which is the basis of the song "Crazy Horse" on his *Bone Days* album[127]:

> One does not sell the earth
> The people walk upon
> We are the land
> How do we sell our mother
> How do we sell the stars
> How do we sell the air . . .

Musically, Trudell's homage poem (to both Crazy Horse and the earth) is accompanied by elements of a traditional Native American soundscape—chant-style vocals by Milton "Quiltman" Sahme and drum rhythms—and of a contemporary blend of blues and rock music, played by both a slide and an electric guitar and a keyboard.

The thought-world conveyed and the musical fusion within which it is articulated achieve their first assemblage in Trudell's *Blue Indians*, which, like the Alexie/Boyd musical collaboration, translates aspects of the blues tradition into the contemporary Native American predicament. But Trudell is less eager than Alexie to see Native American culture suffused with Euro-American aesthetic forms. Although he shares Alexie's sense of ethnohistory as a story of oppression, he constructs the predicament of Native Americans in a language of authenticity and distortion rather than seeing culture as encounter and becoming. Thus, in his "Blue Indians" lyrics he says that "nothing escapes myth slayers," and adds that "Distortion streams, wearing away inside of hearts" and that cultural encounter only pulls Native Americans away from their culture:

> Blue Indians being pulled into
> Melting pots . . .
> Terminologies change
> Progress as evolution in
> Terminal strange
> Blue Indians being pulled into
> Melting pots . . . [128]

As in the subsequent *Bone People* songs, "Blue Indians" combines Trudell's reading with the traditional vocals of Milton "Quiltman" Sahme, traditional Native American-style percussion, and popular music style and instrumentation (slide and regular guitar plus organ). And in this recording, there are "backing vocals" by Trudell's musical collaborator, Jackson Browne, as well as by guitarist Billy Watts. In sum, Trudell's turn to music produces sounds that speak both to contemporary popular music consumers and to those familiar with the evolution of Native American soundscapes, while at the same time turning his poetry into exemplary blues ballads, so that a significant part of the Native American thought-world achieves musical articulation. As Neal Ullestad points out, "This isn't simply pop rock with Indian drums and chants added. It's integrated rock and roll by an American Indian with a multicultural band [reminiscent of Alexie's Coyote Springs] directed to anyone who will listen."[129]

Specifically, Trudell's music speaks of a people who achieve "power" (a spiritual identity) through a respect for and attachment to the earth. As result, "the blues," as it is manifested in word and sound, evokes a past of imperiled attachments and a present of redemptive commitment to (as Trudell has noted elsewhere) "always act for the love of the people and the earth." Waxing pedagogical, he insists, "We have to understand our role to natural power," and although he laments those Native Americans who give in to continuing brutality by "the predator," he asserts that although "we feel oppressed," unlike white America, which is not oppressed but feels powerless, "we do not feel powerless."[130]

Conclusion: "Mixing"

As I noted at the outset, the foreign visitor Alexis de Tocqueville was quite certain that Euro-American culture would remain the only one left standing in a relatively short time after his visit in the 1830s (in contrast with the view of Antonin Dvorak, who roughly sixty years later worked toward an inclusive, multiethnic musical culture). However, despite his fairly firm conviction that Euro-America would and should ultimately exhaust the cultural and political options and yield a coterminous ethnocracy and "democracy in America," Tocqueville did ponder the possibilities for mixing. But by "mixing," Tocqueville meant intermarriage, noting that because of a possible future of antagonism, "the Negroes and the whites must either wholly part or wholly mingle." Extensive mixing between whites and Native Americans or African and Native Americans seems not to have occurred to him. Expecting their extinction and abjuring their relative lack of civilizational orderliness, he saw "Indians" as incapable of adjusting to others because of their stubborn attachment to a "pretended nobility of . . . origin." As for other kinds of mixing, Tocqueville paid little attention to instances of hybrid cultural forms—musical, linguistic, or otherwise.[131]

The composers' thought-worlds—products of considerable "mixing"—addressed throughout this chapter reflect different visions of an America that is deployed across a fractionated social order. For example, given the economic and spatial segregation among diverse ethnicities, many of the inter-ethnic encounters in the typical American city are freighted with anger, violence, and hostility, seeming to confirm Tocqueville's (and Jefferson's) worst fears about a shared American ethnoscape. Paul Haggis's film Crash (2005) depicts such encounters in contemporary Los Angeles, where, among other things, white fears of black crime, black fears of white police harassment, and everyone's fear of middle eastern cultures are rampant. As the film thinks cinematically, showing how everyone's initial perceptions of other ethnicities are either blocked architecturally/spatially or screened through store and car windows, the dialogue seconds its perspective: "We are always behind this metal and glass," says a police detective (Don Cheadle) to his partner/girlfriend. The city as space seems to be designed to heighten class and ethnic alienation and, except in rare encounters, prevent people from recognizing each other's vulnerable and often sympathetic humanity.

Doubtless, soundscapes have lent themselves more readily to mixing than cityscapes. While, as noted, some of the "Yankee composers" abjured an ethnically co-invented American sound-world, music has nevertheless been a relatively active domain of cultural hybridity, thanks not only to those composers dedicated to inter-cultural creation but also to the ability of sound to permeate structures and media that have been more effective impediments to sight and movement. Historically, although the development of concert halls temporarily inhibited the deployment of music, closing it off, limiting its audience, and thus displacing it from the open spaces of ritual allegiance and cultural reproduction, subsequent technologies of recording and dissemination have once again opened up the spaces of music. Although, as Attali points out, the opening of musical space did not halt a process of commodification that changed ontological cultural forms into something controlled by exchangeable value, or, in his words, from something that had been "an affirmation of existence" to something "valorized," cultural mixing was nevertheless facilitated by music's extended reach.[132]

The impact of music's dissemination on cultural mixing is evident in the cosmopolitan perspective of the contemporary writer Salman Rushdie, who illustrates the effects in his novel *The Ground Beneath Her Feet*. Rushdie attributes his ability to think "outside the cultural frame" within which he was raised to being able to receive a variety of music and other global cultural forms from Radio Sri Lanka as he was growing up.[133] The novel maps the effects of the "earthquake songs of a fictional composer, Ormus Cama," whose songs "are about the collapse of all walls, boundaries, restraints."[134] Rushdie includes an alter ego, a photographer named Rai, who articulates an anti-nationalistic perspective. Rai's post-national perspective, like Rushdie's, is also owed to an artistic genre with global reach. It develops in the cosmopolitan city of Bombay, where he was able to view foreign films. As a result, he is motivated to use his photographic practice in a way that parallels Ormus Cama's music—in acts of creative imagination that mix cultural forms to oppose exclusionary (especially nationalistic) myths. Like Rushdie, Ormus Cama is subject to inter-cultural musical forms: "The music he had in his head during the unsinging childhood years, was not of the West except in the sense that the West was from the beginning, impure old Bombay, where West, East, North and South had always been scrambled, like codes, like eggs."[135]

As is the case with Rushdie's fictional Ormus Cama, the composers that have been my primary focus have mixed sound-worlds in ways that defy an exclusionary form of cultural nationalism. Although there are significant idiomatic differences in their compositions, they—in particular, Gershwin, Ellington, Boyd/Alexie, and Trudell/Browne et al.—are carriers of and innovators in one of the twentieth century's major musical forces, the blues. Susan McClary puts the case for the importance of the blues across America's soundscapes succinctly: "If twentieth century music has no single stream, it does have something more coherent to bequeath the future than the various trickles we grasp at. . . . I have no qualms comparing it to a mighty river. It follows a channel cut by a force known as the blues."[136]

Thus, even though America is composed musically from diverse ethnic/experiential perspectives, the blues remains a major "matrix" within which various compositions are initiated.[137] However, that said, it must be noted that while the blues has managed to leap across the fault lines of "a nation so traumatized and confused by its own racial constitution" (to repeat Ronald Radano's words from the chapter epigraph), one must acknowledge that the sounds within its compass often retain incommensurate resonances.

For example, merely hearing a blues-inflected composition might evoke for some simply the recognition of a style. On the other hand, recalling, as John Gennari does, Duke Ellington's injunction that "It don't mean a thing, if it ain't got that swing," the implication of the embodied experience that is called forth for a musician or dancer is that s/he is "making an affirmation and hence exemplary and heroic response [to the human condition] . . . to the exigencies on which [she/] he finds himself [/herself] . . . confronting, acknowledging and contending with the infernal absurdities and ever-impending frustrations inherent in the nature of all existence by playing with the possibilities that are also there."[138]

To recognize the alternative inflections of the blues as articulated within incommensurate but nevertheless mutually influencing ethnic imaginaries, we can evoke Baker's conception of the "blues matrix." Noting that "Afro-American culture is a complex, reflexive enterprise which finds its proper figuration in blues conceived as matrix [which is] . . . a web of intersecting, crisscrossing impulses always in productive transit," Baker sees this dimension of "American creativity" located in the particular spaces, historical experiences, and "material conditions" of slavery.[139] In short, the history of Afro-American culture is the mediating frame for the African American blues performance.

However, as I have noted, given some of the similarities between Afro- and Jewish American modernity, it is not surprising to see Gershwin incorporating a blues aesthetic. Although it doubtless had a different historical resonance in his version because he left behind a different world from the one experienced by African Americans (as well as being received into his new one differently), the blues' "wide appeal" could have affected him because, as Baker suggests, "it expressed a toughness of spirit and resilience, a willingness to transcend difficulties which were strikingly familiar to those whites who remembered their own history."[140] Similarly, one can understand that an aesthetic articulated as part of an "Afro-American discourse" by those seeking to successfully negotiate an obdurate "economics of slavery" and achieve "a resonant, improvisational, expressive dignity" would find its way into Native American sound-worlds, the worlds of peoples seeking to negotiate an economics of displacement.[141]

Baker's blues matrix can therefore be deployed into a variety of sub-matrices, each framing alternative but intimately interconnected aesthetics. What remains is to ponder the significance of the blues musical aesthetic, which is a major inter-cultural force, on a multiethnic democratic imaginary, which was notably absent when Tocqueville visited and wrote his still influential treatise. The answer has to be connected to the blues' role as a vehicle/genre that has carried voices articulating claims about pain and injustice within the range of our collective hearing.

To situate such a blues contribution to a multiethnic democratic imaginary, it is useful to recall a contrast I offered in chapter 1 between the contribution of the blues and the historical trajectory of American social science. As I noted, Judith Shklar, the only president of the American Political Science Association to mention chattel slavery as a major part of the American experience in her presidential address, asserted that the stain of that experience has been effectively wiped away by the social sciences within which "the democratization of values" is implicit.[142] But as Clyde Woods points out in his investigation of the post-slavery period in the Mississippi Delta region, the social sciences aided and abetted what he calls "plantation bloc explanation," which supported an anti–African American world view and provided a legitimation for continuing oppression.

Woods's elaboration of "blues epistemology," to which I have already referred, is offered as an antidote to plantation bloc explanation. What I want to note beyond what Woods's critical insights imply is that, given the migration of the blues into diverse ethnic sound-worlds, the blues provides a frame for widely distributed thinking, across deeply embedded historically engendered ethnic fault lines; it speaks to the promise of a yet unrealized American democracy. If "democracy" involves, as Jacques Rancière suggests, encounters between policing and politics, where nongrammatical excluded parts voice claims and thereby "undermine" the authorized "distribution of bodies into functions corresponding to their 'nature' and places corresponding to their functions," we have to regard the blues as a major genre of democratic expression.[143] But finally, following Duke Ellington's insistence on dissonant chords because (to repeat his remark) "dissonance is our way of life in America. We are something apart, yet an integral part," the "democracy" to which the blues contributes is one that embraces that which is both apart and an integral part.[144] That tension between being within and being apart is what Jacques Rancière refers to as dissensus. And as he suggests, a genre is political not when it addresses epic historical moments (as in the novels of Emile Zola), but rather when (as in the novels of Virginia Woolf) it is attentive to micropolitical levels of dissensus.[145] In chapter 6, I explore the place of dissensus in thinking democracy and the failures of the American democracy to live up to its promise.

6 Democracy's Risky Businesses

Pluralism and the Metapolitics of Aesthetics

Political Thinking

In this chapter on democratic theory, I seek both to rearticulate the central conceptual contributions in earlier chapters and to open up some new ground by focusing on the differential experiences of diverse ethnic Americans—in particular, Euro-, African, and Latino Americans—in their working lives. This latter focus presumes that people's daily working lives are a more important terrain for gauging the functioning of the American democracy than are the occasional episodes of public choice involved in elections, plebiscites, school board participation, and so on, which have been the basis of mainstream evaluations of democratic performance. Indeed, the ground I seek to "diagram" has been fugitive precisely because of the way the mainstream, neo-liberal preoccupation with instances of individual citizen participation effaces the differences I seek to illuminate.[1] Fortunately, some critical thinkers have treated democratic theory in ways that precede and edify my efforts here—for example, William Connolly, Gilles Deleuze, Jacque Derrida, and Jacques Rancière. Their contributions lessen the risks I am taking as I wander some distance from the canonical frames within which the American democracy is typically explored and evaluated in order to make sense of and distinguish the overlapping thought-worlds that constitute "American political thought." These thinkers, like Deleuze's version of the painter Francis Bacon, are in a battle against the "givens" that precede them. As Deleuze puts it, "An entire battle takes place on the canvass between the painter and the givens."[2] Critically oriented approaches to democracy must stage a similar battle.

Therefore, while I pursue my substantive concern with how, in the "American democracy," some ethnic Americans are subjected to extraordinary risk in their working lives, my focus is also on the meta-level risk involved in coming to terms with democracy. The main theorists of politics in general and democracy in particular upon whom I draw acknowledge the contingencies and ambiguities of grasping and evaluating a sensible world that does not partition itself conveniently. To put the matter in terms intelligible to empiricists, the "data" on Americans' democratic performance are not out there, ready to supply self-evidence. While I derive my conceptual support mostly from the genres of critical theory and philosophy, I want to point out that the recalcitrance of the world to affirming modes of sense making is especially well appreciated by those practitioners of novelistic realism who, in Jacques Rancière's words, reverse "hierarchies of representation" and adopt "a fragmented or proximate mode of focalization, which imposes raw presence to the detriment of the rational sequences of the story," thereby, as I add in the preface, presenting viewers with multiple perspectives rather than a single privileged focus.[3]

Franz Kafka's writing is exemplary in this respect. Among novelists and story writers, he, perhaps more than any other writer/thinker, conveyed a deep appreciation of the risks of thinking. He addressed himself incessantly to the fraught relationship between consciousness and world. Although there are abundant illustrations of this aspect of Kafka's perspective on the perils of consciousness, it is nowhere better exemplified than in his story "The Burrow." Presuming a radical entanglement between the inferences deployed by the operation of consciousness and the signs emitted in the world, Kafka situates his burrow in the midst of a metaphorically expressed dilemma. His story features a "creature" who is digging an intricate maze, hoping that it will serve as protection from a predator that it thinks it hears outside its burrow. As it turns out, the creature cannot distinguish "the extent to which the 'dangers' impinging on the inner space it has created are from 'the outside' or are produced by its own (interpretive) activity."[4] Ultimately, the creature, in despair about solving its dilemma, describes itself as an "old architect," one who has succumbed to the script of its consciousness: "But on my side everything is worse prepared for than it was then; the great burrow stands defenseless, and I am no longer a young apprentice but an old architect."[5] Doubtless here as elsewhere, Kafka is addressing the problem of thinking and writing. Well past his apprenticeship in life, he is pondering *his* maze, the already inscribed codes that flood one's consciousness, rendering thought and its modalities of expression risky, as likely to confound its own productiveness with what is discernible outside of it.

In contrast, going back to arguably one of the most enlightenment-committed thinkers among America's "founders," we encounter a Thomas Jefferson who thought that nature stood as thinking's guarantee. As I have repeatedly pointed out, Jefferson presumed that he had an ally in the natural world; far from enigmatic, nature seemed to warrant the design that he had in mind for his new democratic nation. In one telling instance (treated in preceding chapters), while describing a landscape seen from his Monticello plantation, he "constructs a visible scene" in which he sees the world of nature as "as an icon of historical change," as a symbolic narrative of the movement from chaos to pacified order.[6] After he remarks on the "disruption" that nature creates, he has nature promise a pacified locus of possession, asserting that what nature "presents to your eye" is a "smooth" vista "at an infinite distance in the plain country inviting you, as it were from the riot and tumult roaring around, to pass through the breach and participate in the calm below."[7] Jefferson's "nature" is seductive as well as affirming. According to his romantic historical narrative, by the eighteenth century nature was beckoning the Euro-Americans: "[W]e have an immensity of land courting the industry of the husbandmen."[8]

Less than a decade after Jefferson had ascribed the results of his own productive imagination to the external summons of nature, Immanuel Kant disqualified the possibility of such a summons. While earlier in *The Critique of Judgment*, Kant's analytic of the beautiful suggests a fit between nature and the mind, in a later section, as Jean-François Lyotard puts it, "this betrothal proper to the beautiful is broken by the sublime"; in Kant's elaboration of his analytic of the sublime, "[n]ature is no longer the sender of secret messages."[9] Kant's critical treatment of aesthetic comprehension in his analytic of the sublime constitutes an annulment of the mind-nature marriage that Jefferson assumed. Moreover, the Kantian insight constitutes a pervasive discrediting of the Jeffersonian version of enlightenment, which prescribes "highly elaborated modes of attention, observation, and description, applied to natural objects," and gives too little heed to the productive imagination in which objects are presented.[10] As Kant puts it, "true sublimity must be sought only in the mind of the [subject] judging, not in the natural object."[11]

In one of his most compelling pieces of political analysis, Jacques Derrida effects a similar critique of the conceit that the external world validates the operation of one's interpretive sensibilities. In this case it is a critique of Jefferson's scripting of Euro-America's founding document, the Declaration of Independence. Focusing on textuality rather than (a Kantian) mentality, Derrida discerns a "fabulous event."[12] He points to a temporal instability in Jefferson's document, showing how it hovers ambiguously between a description of what has been the case and a performative utterance that establishes that case. In reference to "the 'good people' who declare themselves free and independent," Derrida asserts, "one cannot decide . . . whether independence is stated or produced by this utterance."[13] To *hold* certain truths to be self-evident, from Derrida's perspective, is not merely to find a warrant for them as much as it is to constitute them. The self-evident truths to which the document refers are productively brought about by the statement.

On Derrida's reading, it is force rather than accord with an external normativity that establishes the lawfulness that the document engenders. Jefferson's Declaration can therefore be recruited into what Walter Benjamin famously called "lawmaking violence," for, as Derrida points out, the radical doubt (or aporia in his terms) of the founding document bases the American democracy on a fiction, a "founding violence" in which there is an irreducible complicity between the law and force.[14] On such a reading, Euro-America's founding is a crime story. Inasmuch as the force it deployed was on behalf of white men rather than an inclusive chromatic and gender, the founding was of a patriarchal ethnocracy rather than a democracy. Jefferson et al. were effectively "worlding" at the expense of other possible worlds. They were instituting a very exclusive "we."

As I noted in chapter 1, the implication of the document's inattention to the pluralistic context in which it is created is central to Thomas Pynchon's fictional treatment of the territorial elaboration of Euro-America's founding, where his narrator, the Reverend Wicks Cherrycoke, remarks (in reference to the surveying process of Mason and Dixon), "these times are unfriendly toward Worlds alternative to this one."[15] Effectively, Pynchon addresses a critical fiction to a nation-constituting fiction; he refigures the continental expansion of Euro-America as one that expunged the subjunctive in favor of "the ends of government" and involved "trespass"[16] and criminal acts: "Acts that in Whitehall would merit hanging."[17] To the extent that unreflective

democratic discourses—much of what is understood as "American political theory"—fail to question the constitutive fictions in founding
documents and the subsequent territorial and juridical implementa-
tions that follow, they contribute to the other violence-law relationship
to which Benjamin addresses himself—"law-preserving violence."[18]

If Derrida's brief analysis of the Declaration of Independence ges-
tures to a dimension of America's experiment in democracy that implicates a founding and a continuing crime story, how are the crimes
to be rectified? Among those who thought most rigorously about rec-
tifying the crimes of the American democracy, especially some of its
major ones, the slavery visited on those of African descent and the
discrimination and violence against successive generations of African Americans during the post-Reconstruction, Jim Crow period, was
W. E. B. Du Bois. He argued that what is required first of all is a
retelling of the American democracy's second failure, the failure of
the Reconstruction to produce the equality that had been promised.
Noting that "it was morally wrong and economically retrogressive to
build human slavery in the United States in the eighteenth century,"
and gesturing toward a broader, global level of enslavement, Du Bois
insists that "in the face of the new slavery established elsewhere in the
world under other names and guises, we ought to emphasize this lesson of the past."[19]

Du Bois's approach to rectification looked to both the past and
the future. "What is the object of writing the history of Reconstruction?" he asked; "it is simply to establish the truth, on which Right
in the future may be built."[20] The "truth" that Du Bois recovers required him to indict the way American historians "distort the facts of
the greatest critical period of American history."[21] In his critical reinterpretation of the period of the Reconstruction, he credits the role
of black Americans in their own emancipation: their crippling of the
South's war effort as they abandoned the plantation in large numbers,
and their contributions to the early economic gains under Reconstruction, when black entrepreneurs returned to the South so that "the rank
and file of black labor had a notable leadership of intelligence during
the Reconstruction period."[22] Noting that many white laborers began
to appreciate the strength that would derive from a combined labor
force and thus "bring workers of all colors into united opposition to the
employer,"[23] Du Bois aligns himself with the subjunctive so valued in
the Pynchon text I have treated; he points to a historical moment in

which parts of the South "saw a possibility of democracy across racial lines."[24] The tragic failure of Reconstruction and the reestablishment of economic exclusion—however mitigated by subsequent civil rights initiatives—remains evident in the contrasts between the extremes of the white privilege on display in wealthy suburbs and black deprivation and vulnerability in central cities, which I treat with reference to two films later in this chapter.

Given the ways in which Du Bois constructs the trajectory of the American democracy, his partitioning of the world is more compelling than that of Frederick Jackson Turner. On Du Bois's reading, it has been the color line rather than the frontier that has shaped the dominant American political realities. To situate the present level of inequality, in which alternative kinds of risk characterize the economic lives in the ethnic experiences I treat in my film analyses in this chapter, one must recover the clashing political and economic forces that Du Bois saw as playing a major role in the failure of Reconstruction: "a battle between oligarchy whose wealth and power had been based on land and slaves on the one hand; and on the other, oligarchy built on machines and hired labor."[25] Given the trajectory of mainstream historical accounts preceding Du Bois's, in which little or no black agency is in evidence, Du Bois's history of the Reconstruction is an audacious example of political thinking; it challenges the authoritative scripts that favor power and privilege by concealing its abuses and, in effect, bolstering a neo-liberal, ahistorical view of America's racial inequality.

In effect, although he asserts that he is establishing the truth, what Du Bois provides is an alternative facticity, based on an alternative spatio-temporal partitioning of the world. Within Derrida's mode of conceptualizing, one can situate Du Bois's analysis of the failure of Reconstruction in crime stories that exist at meta as well as substantive levels. While substantively Du Bois addresses the crime of a reasserted inequality, at a meta level he challenges what Derrida regards one of history's meta-level crimes, the failure to think the political. Distinguishing this kind of crime from familiar "political crimes"—for example, "those assassinations with political motivation which litter history with so many corpses"—Derrida refers to "the crime *against* the possibility of politics . . . the crime of stopping to examine politics . . . reducing it to something else and preventing it from being what it should be."[26] While Du Bois's culprits were American historians, who "make right wrong and wrong right,"[27] Derrida's are those in the history of philosophy who abrogate thinking. Democracy's condition of possibility, most notably in the contemporary world, according to Derrida, requires not mere thinking but "hyperbolically ambitious" thinking,[28] a rethinking of democracy that acknowledges today's condition in which, because "no locality remains, democracy must be thought globally."[29]

Thus, while the divisions to which Du Bois addressed himself were primarily the nation's racial fault lines, resulting from the flow of captured bodies during the period of the Atlantic slave trade and then a failure to mitigate the economic and political inequality instituted in the post-Reconstruction period, Derrida's focus is on external divisions, the national sovereignty boundaries that play the major role, bolstered by a "ruthless [global] economic war" in a "massive exclusion of homeless citizens from any participation in the democratic life of states [along with] the expulsion or deportation of so may exiles, stateless persons and immigrants from a so-called national territory."[30] To appreciate this latter and to some extent newer problematic within which the failure of democracy in the United States (among other places) can be recognized, one must abandon a "conception of the United States as a discrete national entity" and view the country instead as "a nation of overlapping diasporas."[31]

Given these two kinds of exclusion, internal and external, approaches to democracy must heed not only the contingencies of dealing with a body of people in which the count is radically unstable, but also the events in which those who have been on the pale of politics voice the demand that they be regarded as qualified political subjects. Among the approaches heeding these two conditions are those of Jacques Rancière, William Connolly, and Gilles Deleuze. In what follows, I engage those examples of democratic thinking that heed aspects of difference that are otherwise unobserved in mainstream approaches to democratic theory. I then analyze two films that, when juxtaposed, illustrate how a divided America allocates different risks to its different, racialized segments of the population, go on to examine the newer forms of exclusion and inequality that have been Derrida's focus in his later writings, and turn to a reading of yet another film, which addresses the exclusions to which Derrida refers. Finally, I treat the extravagant, new risks to which the American democracy is exposed as a result of a suspension of rights—a "state of exception" associated with a post-9/11 war on terror.[32]

Toward Radical Democracy: Rethinking Social Space and Saving Contingency

In a radical challenge to the dominant approach of traditional political theory to democracy, Jacques Rancière writes: "Democracy is not a regime or a social way of life. It is the institution of politics itself. The system of forms of subjectification through which any order of distribution of bodies into functions corresponding to their 'nature' and places corresponding to their functions is undermined, thrown back on its contingency."[33] In contrast with Anglo American approaches to democracy, which are primarily social-contract-oriented and thus concerned with a negotiation among already officially warranted political subjects, Rancière addresses the issue of democracy at a level of its pre-subjective dynamics. He deploys a grammatical figure that implicates the *becoming* of subjects as intelligible parts of the social order and extends his challenge to the social sciences, pointing out that they have historically assisted a "modern parapolitical enterprise,"[34] an effacement of the contingencies of political encounter in favor of "the problematization of origins of power and the terms in which it is framed—the social contract, alienation, and sovereignty."[35]

While, as noted, Derrida indicts philosophy, Rancière's main culprit is a social science that takes as its starting point an "individuality," where entitlement is simply "the *entitlement* of anyone at all to question the state or to serve as proof of its fidelity to its own principle."[36] In contrast, politics, in Rancière's sense, escapes the compass of social and political science's concern with policy. "The political" makes an appearance through a "polemicization,"[37] an action in which a part that has had no part makes itself manifest, an enactment of what he calls subjectivization. The political is therefore not a set of structures or a continuing process accessible to an application of disinterested knowledge. It is not based on the arithmetic distribution of identical bodies. And it is not expressed in the discourses on individual participation in modes of governance, as it is in approaches to "deliberative democracy," which partition social space ahistorically.

As I pointed out in chapter 1, Jefferson's attempt to expunge diversity, to forge a uniform national society, was spatial; his Land Ordinance of 1785 was Cartesian, a "democratic social space" that would comprise a "homogeneous cellular medium of life."[38] But apart from the impact of urbanization and capital on social life, which have radi-

cally sundered Jefferson's spatial America (his map of small independent farms), the historical forces associated with ethnic exclusion have
left a map of incommensurate spaces. While to some extent, as Philip
Fisher puts it, "the modern American suburb is another such Cartesian, democratic social space . . . equipped with the same schools and
parks for children, the same shopping centers,"[39] American democratic
space is also "damaged" by it past of slavery (Fisher's example) and also
by the Indian removal, the "irrevocable residue[s] of mistake."[40] And
some writers, who have recognized this aspect of spatial history, have
"built in the damaged space of history into democratic aesthetics."[41]

How then can one describe the ways in which "the social," filled
as it is with historically produced fault lines, can provide predicates for
thinking democracy. Rancière's and the other approaches I survey and
analyze here all resist the mythic idea of a homogeneously effected social contract to which the society as a whole accedes as the legitimating
predicate of democratic governance. Instead, they identify disparities,
diversities, and escape routes from a uniform endorsement issuing from
a consensual democratic social space. For example, Rancière rejects
the traditional meta politics within which "man and citizen are the
same liberal individual enjoying the universal values of human rights
embodied in the constitutions of our democracies."[42] Recognizing the
history of wrong involved in the founding violence of the law (for example, constitution making) and in the preservation of the law (adjudi-
cation), a form of policing or "policy" that functions within a traditional
meta politics, Rancière evokes the distinction between "a logic of subjectivization and a logic of identification."[43] The logic of identification
is the typical political arithmetic within which everyone is a subject
before the law or has a political preference to be counted along with
the others. In contrast to "the arithmetic of shopkeepers and barterers,"
Rancière speaks of "a magnitude that escapes ordinary measurement," a
"paradoxical magnitude" that escapes a logic that equates "the equality
of anyone at all with anyone else."[44] The logic of subjectivization derives from a pluralism of *disparity*. Resisting metaphysical foundations,
Rancière sees the social order as sheer contingency. There are no political parties with an existence prior to "the declaration of a wrong." Thus,
to take one of Rancière's examples: "Before the wrong that its name
exposes, the proletariat has no existence as a real part of society."[45]

But what is "society" for Rancière? How are democratic subjects
situated? Referring only indirectly to the social frame within which

democratic encounters emerge, he writes: "Real democracy would presuppose that the *demos* be constituted as a subject present to itself across the whole surface of the social body."[46] Apart from implying that the democratic subject must be socially pervasive, Rancière occasionally remarks on the economic fault lines within the social order—wryly noting, for example, the "unjustifiable and inescapable frontier separating those whom the deity destines for thinking versus those whom he destines for shoemaking"[47]—but he does not develop an elaborate structural model of segments comprising the social body. Instead of mapping a static social space, he implies that social segments are episodic; insofar as they have political significance, they arise during encounters.

While since the eighteenth century canonical political thinkers have constructed society as a regulative ideal and the legitimating basis or alibi for "the political," Rancière reverses the order of significance.[48] Politics is Rancière's regulative ideal. Politics is to be judged on the basis of a steadfast commitment to the equality of everyone and is understood as the proper regulator of social bonds. Critical of all sociological conceits, Rancière indicts political theory, sociology, and the administrative agencies of a hierarchical order, who invent "the social" and then distribute "justice" as a logical outgrowth of naturalized social arrangements.[49] Here Rancière must cope with a dilemma of intelligibility. Despite the absence of a stable referent called "society," it emerges nevertheless as one of his discursive objects. This is necessarily the case not only because ordinary grammar is recalcitrant to the instability that Rancière wants to convey, but also because however contingent and contestable social segments may be, any approach to democracy must contend with a complex history of imposed segmentation and boundary making, even if one concedes that much of what is intelligible as "the social" is epiphenomenal to a history of modes of domination. Accordingly, any radical democratic politics must necessarily challenge the reigning order of intelligibility, which is always an ambiguous achievement. On the one hand, it creates the conditions of possibility for communication, but, on the other, it achieves a unified grammar of subjectivity and objectness at the expense of the subjunctive; it pushes alternative possibilities to the margin or erases them altogether.

Thinking about the exclusions immanent in the boundary creations affirmed in reigning discourses of politics has been central to William Connolly's approach to democratic theory. His meditation on the ambiguous achievement of social and symbolic boundaries provides a particularly apt threshold for a critical treatment of foundational commitments underlying America's democratic social space. In particular, in a chapter on Alexis de Tocqueville's conception of American democracy, Connolly begins with some general observations on boundaries: "Boundaries abound. Between humanity and the gods. Between human and animal. Between culture and nature. Between life and death. Between genders, nations, peoples, times, races, classes, and territories."[50] The historical establishment of such boundaries is with power-invested, collective acts that affirm and legitimate some practices and interests and discredit others. It is through such enactments that, at an abstract level, peoples become coherent collectives, giving their worlds meaning and value and, at a more concrete level, organizing their social and political spaces. But foundational acts, however contingent and conflictual they have been, are lent transcendent necessity in founding documents and by much of "modern political thought, [which] celebrates the advantages of overcoded boundaries by suppressing the violences accompanying those codes."[51] Contemporary political theorist-apologists follow the venerable tradition of those canonical thinkers in the history of political thought who have recognized the political ambiguities of boundary-making but have been reluctant to acknowledge or, in Connolly's words, "to come to terms with them."[52]

Connolly suggests that the question of the ambiguity of boundaries is more likely to surface now, "in a world experienced by many to be without a natural design," and he goes on to explore the consequences of a hospitality to this question for democratic theory. His meditation on boundaries articulates well with significant contributions of both Rancière and Deleuze. In accord with Rancière's insistence that there are no political parties with an existence prior to "the declaration of a wrong," Connolly summons the "Indian" subject to illuminate some of the dire consequences of Tocqueville's version of American pluralism, which necessitated "the elimination of the Indian."[53] And in accord with Deleuze and Guattari's treatment of the modern state's containment of nomadism, through a deployment of apparatuses of capture,[54] Connolly points to Tocqueville's toleration of a "modest nomadism," coupled with his pessimism that the American democracy cannot evince "a viable response to forms of nomadism that cannot be eliminated by, nor are they very consonant with, the civi-territorial complex," which Tocqueville saw as essential to democracy's future.[55]

Nomadism, a way of being-in-the world that cannot be captured within contemporary society's authorized model of social segments, and other modes of constituting and inhabiting "the social" have not had conceptual leverage in the dominant empiricist-oriented approach to democracy, in which the notion of "political participation" tends to exhaust ideas about the democratic subject. Social space for empiricist social scientists and traditional theorists of democracy is constructed as a set of majorities and minorities who form around particular issues. Their objects of analysis are numerical distributions in which members of any majority or minority are assembled from undifferentiated "individuals." Moreover, they adhere to the model of the Cartesian social space that Jefferson's already discussed Land Ordinance of 1785 initiated, the gridded American landscape within which majorities versus minorities are formed and situated, a space that is "identical from point to point." Within the liberal individualist model, deployed on a homogeneous social space, every person is present to the political process in the same way. Each is a political participant in a "[d]emocratic social space [that is] a universal and everywhere similar medium in which rights and opportunities are identical, a space in which the right and even the ability to move from place to place is assured."[56]

Addressing the conceptual impoverishment rendered by participation enthusiasts, who homogenize and dehistoricize the social domain, Rancière asserts that "the idea of participation blends two ideas of different origins: the reformist idea of necessary mediations between the center and the periphery, and the evolutionary idea of a permanent involvement of citizen-subjects in every domain."[57] Similarly, Connolly is critical of the way in which the standard participatory model, which deploys freely acting agents in a homogeneous space, constitutes an attempt to "resolve ambiguity" and to press individuality and commonality "to harmonize more closely."[58] Ultimately for both Rancière and Connolly, attempts at adding up preferences fail to acknowledge the forms of difference that a democratic order must recognize—"the part of those who have no part"[59] for Rancière, whose logic of subjectivization derives from a pluralism of disparity, and "the claims of diversity" for Connolly, who privileges a pluralism that requires negotiations among persons separated by ambiguous boundaries.[60] But perhaps the most thoroughgoing critique of the majority versus minority model of democratic social orders is that of Deleuze and Guattari, who argue (as I noted in chapter 1) that no majority has an unproblematic representational value because there is no homogeneous order from which it can be drawn as a quantitative solution. Rather, such "majorities" are a product of "state power and domination." There exist instead "majoritarian 'fact[s]'" that constitute "homogeneous system[s] in which the minorities are sub groups."[61]

Rancière is similarly suspicious of the "unities" deployed by apparatuses of power, of those "social groups" or "political subjects" who are put into play within the official political discourse. Their recognition as legitimate participants is part of policing, a fixing of the terrain of individuals relative to public power,[62] rather than politics. "Politics," as Rancière conceives it, is carried on by "subjects that are not social groups."[63] And Connolly shares Rancière's resistance to a rigid model of social identity and to the familiar forms of identity politics with which it is associated. Similarly suspicious of officially imposed "unities," Connolly prescribes a moderation of the urge for "attunement" between identities and the order. Rather than adhering to the typical pluralism, which favors the inclusion of various under-represented social groups, his model of diversity is an endorsement of "a social ontology of discord,"[64] which "would require that we acknowledge and seek to articulate the elements of discordance in the unities we establish."[65]

In sum, for Rancière, Connolly, and Deleuze, social space is an unstable arena of discord. Rather than seeing society as a stable set of arrangements, they view the social arena as a domain of evolving force and counter-force. For Connolly, the significant opposing forces are ideational. One is fundamentalism, an impulse he has addressed often and characterizes in his later work as the neo-conservative platform in a culture war, which is "[t]he futile drive to reinstate the old picture through force and repression,"[66] a firming up and policing of identity boundaries and the abjection of identity types that do not fit the "old picture." The counter-force, which would enable what Connolly calls "a multidimensional pluralism of democratic life,"[67] are all those impulses toward negotiating a commonality with difference while appreciating "the constitutive ambiguity of identity."[68]

While Connolly's social arena is, in his terms, "agonistic," Rancière's is "polemical." Critical of historians of ideas whose critiques merely distinguish what is thought versus what is unthought, Rancière argues that the more basic issue is "the very right to think."[69] The contention within Rancière's polemical social space is a struggle between the forces of policing (the familiar social policies within which some bodies receive recognition as bona fide political subjects and others do not) and the forces of politics (events of subjectivization in which excluded parts of the social order demand to be heard). Articulated with a spatial idiom, such episodes disturb the institutionalized "distribution of bodies into functions" and also challenge the epistemic basis for the prior exclusion, the naturalization of the differences among bodies and of the appropriate "places" where those bodies belong; they disturb, in Rancière's terms (already quoted), "the order of distribution of bodies into functions corresponding to their 'nature' and places corresponding to their functions."[70]

As part of his conception of the episodic partitioning of social space, Rancière sees the political as arising from a continuous mobility within the social configuration. Because democracy rests not on specific leadership qualities but rather on "an absence of qualifications that, in turn, becomes the qualification for the exercise of a democratic *arche*,"[71] democratic challenges to the policing order arise from a non-place. While what is proffered by Rancière appears to be a structural phenomenon, a "democratic void" that is "a given constitutive of politics," it is also implicitly a temporal phenomenon. The moments of democratic enactment come from a supplement that arises as disconnected from that part of the population which, at any time, is regarded as politically qualified.

Because Rancière's rendering of the temporal aspect of the political is structurally embedded, his history of the political is necessarily predicated on a structural logic rather than a finite genealogy of power and resistance. The social base from which politics arises is constituted as a mobile set of "vanishing difference[s]."[72] On the one hand, this approach supplies a radical alternative to the classic contractual narratives of the political, which emphasize a mythic consensus, a politics "deduced from the necessity of gathering people into communities."[73] And it avoids identifying the political with the groupings produced by a state-centric discourse, the "well defined interest groups."[74] Against a politics of already politically enfranchised identities, Rancière insists that "there is politics as long as 'the people' is not identified with the race or a population . . . [, as long as] the poor are not equated with a particular disadvantaged sector, and as long as the proletariat is not a group of industrial workers, etc." On the other hand, although Rancière provides an exemplary episode of contention in his work on the organs articulating workers' complaints in nineteenth-century France,

his structural frame leaves a conceptual void, the absence of a treatment of how "dis-agreement" emerges in different historical periods.[75]

Although Deleuze also tends toward exemplification to treat historical forces, he does treat specifically the historical shift from the epoch dynasties or despotic orders to that of the state and thus provides
a more temporally sensitive model, a rough history of modernity. The
pre-state, despotic order is a centrally focused machine of capture,
where the social body (the "socius") is symbolically captured by "the
body of the despot," who constitutes a "detached object" that preempts
all social coding.[76] The state is also a machine of capture. But in contrast with despotic orders, that capture consists in a dense coding, the
production of rigid segmentation that displaces or overcodes former
modes of attachment and affiliation.

In response to state-imposed segmentation (citizens, ethnic major-
ities/minorities, gender and age categories, etc.)—the creation of what
Deleuze and Guattari refer to as molarities—there are flows and movements of resistance within the social field, the pursuit of lines of flight
from state-imposed modes of segmentation and coding. As they put it,
"[a] social field is always animated by all kinds of movements of decod-
ing and deterritorialization affecting 'masses' and operating at different
speeds and paces."[77] The contemporary Deleuzian society is therefore
conflictual in that a series of micropolitical initiatives are always in tension with the molar politics of the state: "From the viewpoint of micropolitics, a society is defined by its lines of flight, which are molecular.
There is always something that flows or flees, that escapes the binary organizations, the resonance apparatus and the overcoding machine."[78]
Such micropolitical forces are reflected by, among other things, alternative modes of collective assembly (effectively "subjects that are not
social groups," in Rancière's terms). For example, confronted with the
molar politics of a state's security-oriented segmentation, "[t]here is
always a Palestinian or Basque or Corsican to bring about a 'regional
destabilization of security.'"[79]

Toward a Democratic Ethos: Restoring the Subjunctive

Connolly, Deleuze, Derrida, and Rancière all see the restoration of
contingency as a prerequisite for the institution of democratic social space. For Rancière, it involves the encounter between policing
and politics, where nongrammatical excluded parts voice claims and

thereby "undermine" the authorized "distribution of bodies into functions corresponding to their 'nature' and places corresponding to their
functions."[80] Derrida invokes the contingent with respect to democracy with his conception of the contingency: "The thought of what he
calls the perhaps" is a thinking about the possibility of friendships to
come. It is a commitment that accords with Derrida's insistence that
the boundaries of democratic community remain open, resistant to the
territorial imperatives of states or other political entities.[81] Contingency
for Deleuze arises in connection with his advocacy of multiplicity, by
which he means not a simple politics of recognition, not the familiar
promotion of "diversity," but rather the creation of space for *potential*
difference, for the possibilities of becoming outside of the forms of
segmentation that are authoritative within the state-dominated socius.
Democratic social space for Deleuze therefore requires a retreat from
contemporary society's "hypersegmentation,"[82] and a move toward
what he calls a "flexible segmentarity," a contrast with state-imposed
rigid segmentarity.

Connolly's most elaborate contingency-affirming formulation is
his conception of a "deep plurality": "Incorporating deep plurality into
existing political pluralism is consonant with democracy if and when
an ethos of engagement is negotiated between numerous constituen-
cies honoring different assumptions and moral sources."[83] Accordingly,
the threat to "democracy," as Connolly conceives it, is, among other
things, "the refusal to acknowledge the contingency of one's position
and the violent assertion of one's right to protect this refusal." But I
want to return here to an earlier formulation of contingency that Connolly achieves by staging a counter-factual historical conversation, after
being inspired by one that Henry David Thoreau reports in his "The
Allegash and East Branch."

Resisting a homogeneous model of nineteenth-century social
space, Connolly notes that the reported conversation between Thoreau
and his Indian guide on a canoeing trip, Joe Polis, is one taking place
"on the edges of 'American' cultural space."[84] He then "supposes [that]
the contingencies of chance and timing had spawned an encounter between Thoreau and a Mashpee" and goes on to stage a conversation on
another part of that edge, one between Thoreau and a contemporary,
the Mashpee Pequot political philosopher William Apess, whose polemical writings reveal not only the particularities of the historically produced "Indian" locus of enunciation (in a Euro-American-dominated

political order), but also the contradictions and hypocrisies inhabiting Euro-America's democratic conceits.[85]

Connolly's staging of this counter-factual encounter articulates well with Thomas Pynchon's privileging of the subjunctive over necessity, for in Connolly's words: "The very identification of this unpursued space of historical *possibility* begins to crack the Tocquevillean/American code of moral/civilizational/territorial necessity. . . . The hypothetical Apess/Thoreau conjunction drains the presumption of necessity from the historical options between assimilation of the Indian and exclusion of the Indian from civilized land."[86]

In addition, by staging this conversation, Connolly creates an instance of subjectivization, adding a voice and thus widening the scene of "American political thought" as it developed during the nineteenth century. Like Rancière, Connolly summons the genre of the conversation to intervene in the reigning structure of intelligible politics and reconstitute the distribution of eligible political bodies. But such instances of political initiative arise in diverse genres. For example, both Connolly and Rancière have recourse to film (a genre that Deleuze has famously explored), which, for Connolly, evokes layers of subjective presence that evade ordinary consciousness, and for Rancière has a tendency to provide critical reflection on the relations of the sensible, and the sayable.[87]

To illustrate the implications of these insights for American social space, I turn to a comparison of two films, Paul Brickman's *Risky Business* and Spike Lee's *Clockers*. The frames within which the two operate—the "centrifugal space" of the suburbs in the case of *Risky Business* and the "centripetal space" of the city in the case of *Clockers*—provide telling reflections on the vagaries of America's democratic social spaces and the economies that function within and between them.[88] And because (as I note in the preface) "film is the aesthetic matrix of a particular historical experience,"[89] it is the genre that is best able to demonstrate the material conditions under which modernity's alternative public spheres develop and interact. In particular, Siegfried Kracauer offers an incisive observation about the way in which the seemingly trivial moments of slapstick comedy (which abound in *Risky Business*) speak to the contingencies of modern life. As Miriam Hansen puts it, "chance for Kracauer is a historical category, another signature of modernity." And slapstick comedy, whose "leitmotif," according to Kracauer, "is the play with danger, with catastrophe, and its prevention in the nick of time," foregrounds the role of contingency; it treats results "brought about not by divine intervention [as in the genre of tragedy] or melodramatic coincidence, but simply by chance."[90]

Brickman's *Risky Business*

The contrasts that dominate Paul Brickman's *Risky Business* are both spatial and linguistic. The spatial contrast is evoked at the beginning of the film. While the credits are being run, a lit-up downtown Chicago is viewed at night from the moving elevated train that circles Chicago's loop. The visuals and sounds, most notably the clacking of the train's wheels, convey the sights and sounds of a city that harbors diverse activities and never sleeps. Shortly after the credits are run, there is a cut to a different venue. The camera slowly moves in on a large, neo-colonial residence in the suburban North Shore above Chicago, a community that operates with different temporal rhythms. At this moment no movement or outdoor activity is in evidence. As the framing shot fixes the Goodsen family residence, the retro details of the house express an earlier time and a typical trait of upper bourgeois society, what Jean Baudrillard refers to as "the 'taste' for the bygone," which he ascribes to the desire of the "privileged classes . . . to transmute their economic status into inherited grace."[91]

The linguistic contrast is especially evident in two lessons in political economy that Joel Goodsen (Tom Cruise), the family's college-bound son, receives, one from a high school teacher running a special class for "future enterprisers," and one from Guido (Joe Pantoliano), a pimp. In one scene, the teacher is offering a litany of capitalism's economic symbols: "profit motive, competition, free enterprise," and in a subsequent scene, Guido informs him, "kid, you never, *ever* fuck with another man's livelihood." Significantly, no syntax is provided in the high school lesson in capitalism. The teacher utters a string of nouns, empty symbols belonging to the mythology of capitalism. By contrast, Guido's lesson is in the form of a sentence, which is delivered in an interactive context (at the moment of the remark, Joel is harboring Guido's livelihood—his prostitutes—in his home). This more telling lesson that Joel receives is prompted not only by some accidental encounters but also from some structural imperatives, deriving from the vulnerabilities peculiar to upper bourgeois children whose parents are pushing hard to reproduce their privilege in their offspring.

Briefly, once Joel makes an appearance, we see him as a high school student under extreme pressure. His parents expect him to be accepted to an Ivy League school, specifically Princeton. In one scene his mother quizzes him about how he has done on the SATs (scholastic aptitude tests). Upon hearing his scores (which are marginal as regards Ivy League admissions), she frowns and asks if he can take them again. The other pressures are from his hormones and his peers. As a teenager, Joel is at the age that Phillip Slater aptly describes as one of maximum stimulation and minimum fulfillment[92]; he is prey to sexual fantasies and at the same time is pushed by some of his peers, who dangle their own sexual conquests in front of him, to do something about ending his inexperience.

In desperation, Joel makes a choice that produces the subsequent drama of the film. Alone in the house while his parents are on a trip, he calls a number in the newspaper's classified section that advertises sexual services. To Joel's horror, the call is answered by Jackie, a black female impersonator. Jackie, who tellingly says (as s/he demands payment for time spent in transit plus taxi fare) "I don't usually come out this far." The remark helps to situate Joel's class and racial milieu, for "the 'most powerful *symbolic* repertoires' of bourgeois societies are situated at their 'borders, margins and edges, rather than at their accepted centers,'" and Jackie represents a tripartite margin—occupational, gender/sexual, and racial.[93] Although Jackie's services are outside of Joel's sexual imaginary, in the process of their interaction, s/he gives him the phone number for another prostitute, Lana, while making a prophetic utterance: "She's what you want; she's what all the young boys on the lake want." As it turns out, the "want" has a double resonance. In one register, a personal one that occupies the film's more obvious narrative, Lana is positioned as an effective object of desire. She turns out to be what he wants to achieve erotic consummation. His relationship with her is part of a coming-of-age process, which the camera maps by shooting their interactions with various pictures of Joel's childhood in the background.

As the relationship deepens, the sequence of pictures moves from the toddler to the teenage stage. To seal this aspect of the narrative, a glass egg on the mantle serves as the film's primary icon. It is a subject of framing and zoom shots at key moments in Joel's maturation, and at the end of the film, when Joel has seemingly succeeded in managing the parental- and system-induced achievement pressures, the egg turns out to be cracked. Joel has hatched—moved from inexperienced teenager to an adult who is more in charge of his fate. His parents both register their disappointment with Joel when they discover the damage to the glass egg, but it is unclear as to whether their consternation is over the damage to their inert property or the attenuation of their parental control over their live property.

The more subtle and significant register of the film explores a different, collectively oriented issue, which is manifested through a dynamic that references Joel's growing economic awareness. Joel's "want," to which the female impersonator/prostitute Jackie refers, can be interpreted as a lack in his ability to perceive the abundant capital value in his milieu. Joel's appreciation of the political economy of bourgeois life is wanting. Shortly after Joel and Lana have sex, they're seated at the family dining table as Lana turns over a spoon and remarks approvingly that it is belongs to an expensive silver pattern: "Reed and Barton." And while she remains in the house when Joel goes to school, she is seen turning over the corner of a Persian rug and counting the stitches. Through Lana's observations, it becomes evident that Joel and the rest of the teenagers in his milieu are oblivious to the accumulated value surrounding them. Once the marginal sexual economy of the city migrates to Joel's suburb, the accumulated value surrounding the lives of Joel and his friends becomes a central part of the story.

When Joel first has sex with Lana, and finds himself unable to pay with his remaining cash on hand, he goes to the bank to cash in a bond that (a camera shot tells us) was a gift from his grandparents. Thereafter, when Lana and her friends set up a bordello in Joel's house, Joel's friends are shown going into and out of the bank, cashing *their* bonds to pay for the sexual services. The movement of the downtown enterprise to the suburbs turns out to be a much more lucrative "enterprise" than the trivial initiatives of the students in the "future enterprisers" club at Joel's high school. And, most significantly, Joel, whom Lana at one point refers to as "one hot shit future enterpriser," gets admitted to Princeton, even though, in the words of the recruiter who visits him in his home in the midst of the prostitution enterprise, his record though "respectable . . . is not quite Ivy League, now is it?" Subsequently, however, the recruiter turns out to be so impressed with his economic acumen that Joel receives a letter saying that Princeton needs his kind of student. It is implied that while America may be a meritocracy, the ability to manipulate capital trumps educational achievement as a mechanism for advancement.

Interestingly, despite the many markers of political economy throughout *Risky Business*, some critics have succumbed to the temptation to treat the film as a comedy. For example, there is a comic scene in which Lana has jumped into Joel's car to get away from her pimp/manager Guido. As Guido's car is chasing them through the city, Joel's friend in the back seat remarks, "I've got a trig midterm tomorrow and I'm being chased by Guido the killer pimp." But apart from the comedic situation in which this remark is the highlight, what is illustrated is an alternative approach to value. Guido is seeking to secure his primary business resource, his key employee, while Joel's friend is fixated on a moment in his credentialing process, one that will ultimately locate him in a different, more privileged and secure sector of the economy. In the risky business of bourgeois advancement, the schools—both the secondary schools and colleges—that privileged children attend are the key screening institutions. While the banks are the storage and investment nodes of the accumulation of wealth of the privileged classes, the schools are the institutions of control. Some the film's demonstration of the controlling aspect of schooling are subtle. For example, each time Joel rushes into the school because he is delayed by his relationship with Lana, he tries the middle door and finds it locked (in two scenes). Less subtly, he is asked for a pass when he rushes down the hall, and when he takes an exam, he and the others are commanded to put their books on the floor and are regulated by a clock.

In addition to the institutional controls exerted by the system of education, there is an ideational control that sits in the interface between culture and economy. Joel's entry into the management of prostitution is initially inhibited by his commitment to a moral economy—to crotchets about what are and what are not morally appropriate as objects of exchange. To become the kind of enterpriser required to run a bordello, Joel must cross a major cultural and spatial fault line, one that divides participation in mainstream versus marginal sectors of the economy. Moreover, his crossing reflects the exchanges that occasionally occur across that line. As Franco Moretti has shown in his spatial reading of Charles Dickens's novels, especially *Our Mutual Friend*, by the nineteenth century, literature began to treat the interaction of class spaces. Moretti demonstrates the treatment with, among other examples, the connections that Dickens creates between the London of the West End and that of the East End. "The spatial system of *Our Mutual Friend* unites the city," as the friend in question "is caught between the fraudulent arrogance of the West End and the physical violence of the docks."[94] And, in a parallel insight with the illusions of the privileged classes in Brickman's *Risky Business*, Dickens has his character in *Our Mutual Friend* "withdraw to the counter-world of the suburbs, to protect his moral illusions."[95] Ultimately, however, in Joel's case desperation draws him out of the illusions associated with the spatial and moral segregation of his suburb. After he incurs a huge bill because he has submerged his father's sports car in Lake Michigan, Lana supplies an analysis that induces his decision to run a bordello. Her remark, "look at it this way Joel, you're making good money and providing your friends with a valuable service," helps him to overcome his moral economy-induced inhibitions that divide legitimate business from illegitimate, marginal enterprise. And ironically, by crossing the line into the domain of illicit exchange, Joel is able to win entry to the credential that will help him move up into the licit one. In the process of treating the interaction between the two levels of economy, the film therefore maps the inequalities that obtain within the American political economy and at the same time displays the hypocrisies associated with neo-liberal commitments to meritocracy. It shows, moreover, that what is central to the American democracy is the institutionalized tendency for privilege to reproduce itself, while it illustrates the attendant preoccupation of the privileged classes with making sure that it does.

Nevertheless, much of the significance of that part of the American life world treated in *Risky Business* cannot be effectively discerned without comparison with another part. Spike Lee's *Clockers* supplies an exemplary contrast because of the many parallels between the two films, not the least of which is *Clockers*'s treatment of another risky business, drug dealing. In addition, its main character, Strike (Mekhi Phifer), is also a teenager who is under stress while sharing other features with Joel; both of them are involved in sales and both have model train sets. A film that combined the two characters' stories and made use of parallel montage to effect a comparison between alternative American life worlds would go far toward illustrating the fault lines in the American political and economic worlds that the films present. Such a film technology can serve to denaturalize those worlds, for as film technique matured it provided a critical approach to social space, forcing the viewer to deal with unexpected juxtapositions: "the yoking together of noncontiguous spaces thorough parallel editing forced a certain denaturalization of the filmic discourse."[96] In the absence of such a film, I can nevertheless read these two together and note the contrasting yet parallel scenes in order to effect the denaturalization that parallel montage can achieve.

Clockers with Risky Business

Apart from the obvious vocational fact that both are engaged in risky businesses—prostitution and drug dealing, respectively—the most evident similarity between Joel in *Risky Business* and Strike in *Clockers* is the stress under which both operate. In Joel's case, as noted, the pressure comes from the expectations in his milieu. He is pressured to grow up sexually and to gain the credential necessary to reproduce the level of privilege enjoyed by his parents. He is temporarily induced into a risky business while trying to deal with the stresses associated with the institutionalized risks that pertain to his privileged milieu. In contrast, Strike is in a risky business for want of other lucrative alternatives. As Manthia Diawara's analysis of black versions of film noir suggests, the crime vocations of African American characters can be understood as "an opportunity to beat the [vocational] system that is inhospitable to them."[97] Thus Strike's risk is not simply a failure to be effectively credentialed. He is subject to the forces that surround drug dealing: harassment and arrest by policing authorities at a minimum and death at the hands of the drug dealer for whom he works at worst. Looking at the two films together, it becomes evident that, among other things, while many privileged white parents are worrying about making sure that their children reproduce their level of privilege, many black parents are worrying about keeping their children alive. Hence, the two scenes that bear comparison in this regard are the one in which Joel's mother queries him about his SAT scores and the one in which Strike's mother watches from the project window while Strike is being roughly frisked by narcotics officers and being surveilled by his drug dealer, Rodney, who drives by during the shakedown. Scene by scene the two films focus on the very different risks across the fault lines in the economies that pertain to America's racial-spatial order.

Recalling the opening framing shot (after the credits and tracking shots of downtown Chicago from the elevated train) of Joel's upper bourgeois single family home in a suburban neighborhood, a cut to the opening shot in *Clockers* presents another framing shot: it is a view of the Brooklyn projects, where Strike's family lives. Given the difference

Joel's mother saying "Can you take them [the SATs] again?" in *Risky Business*. Courtesy of Warner Home Video.

Strike's mother in the window watching the police shakedown in *Clockers*. Courtesy of Warner Home Video.

in the narratives of Joel's and Strike's lives, these shots are telling. Joel is aiming to achieve the lifestyle that the house represents; he is expected to end up in a similar house and neighborhood (and to acquire the other accouterments that go with it, emphasized in a scene in which his father tells him to lay off the stereo until he is responsible enough to use it correctly). In contrast, Strike and his older brother, Victor, are striving to get out of the projects, Victor by working two jobs and Strike by trading his loyalty to his drug dealer/boss Rodney in exchange for Rodney's promise that he will ultimately let Strike get off the benches.

The pervasive shots of the benches in front of the projects—Strike's place of business—take on an added significance if we cut to the bank scenes in *Risky Business*, where the teenagers run to cash in bonds to pay for sex. The enclosed space of the bank evolved from its forerunner with the same name. In France there was a slow historical movement from the *bancs* or benches where the money changers sat in the proximity of outdoor markets to the *banques*, or *"encaisseurs de l'argent,"* where such exchanges could operate within a more secure, enclosed space. The juxtaposition of such shots therefore carries historical depth. It is a juxtaposition of levels of risk to which the architecture of the modern bank was addressed. In addition, the institutions of law enforcement have served to protect the banks where accumulations of wealth are held and to put pressure on alternative economies. The contrast is evident in one of the early scenes in *Clockers*. Strike's *banc*/bench is a focus of police surveillance and assault. Shortly after a drug sale is made to an undercover cop, a squad of narcotics police descend on the projects, subjecting Strike and the other clockers to physical abuse and threat of arrest, even though all the crackdowns have relatively little effect on this sector of the economy.

Foucault's analysis of the way the law works as part of "the general tactics of subjection" is apropos here: "[P]unishment in general is not intended to eliminate offenses, but rather to distinguish them, to distribute them, to use them. . . . [The administering of penalties is involved in] laying down the limits of tolerance, of giving free reign to some, of putting pressure on others, of excluding a particular section, of making another useful, of neutralizing certain individuals, and of profiting from others."[98]

It becomes clear in the film that some of the police exploit what Foucault refers to as the usefulness of law-enforcement-created domains of "delinquency." But to give institutional form to Foucault's contrast between those who have free reign and those who are pressured requires a contrast of institutions. We can cut from the police raid on Strike's bench to the college recruiter's visit to Joel's home while Joel is being "one hot shit future enterpriser." That scene, along with one of the last scenes, in which Joel's father delivers the letter of

acceptance from Princeton, exemplifies the free reign given to predatory capitalism as contrasted with the pressure and exploitation visited
on the marginal economy.

One of the most compelling juxtapositions of the life worlds of Joel
and Strike consists in the social agencies with which they must deal.
Joel's most stressful moments take place in his high school, especially
one in which he begs an administrator to overlook the fact that he
is late for an exam, noting that his entire future depends on how he
performs on it. The appropriate cut from this school scene in *Risky
Business* would be to the police station where Strike is interrogated by
Detective Rocco, who pressures him to admit to Daryl Adams's murder. Strike's very appearance at the station, where he finally implicates
Rodney in the chain of events leading to the killing, threatens to end
Strike's future. After that encounter with Rocco at the station and Rodney's subsequent arrest, Rodney orders his henchman to kill Strike.

Reading the two films together serves therefore to highlight the
different institutional ecologies within which the enterprising young
men function.[99] While college recruiters play a role in judging and
rewarding the results of Joel's enterprise and a secure bank guards his
accumulated proceeds, Strike has to try to hide his transactions within
the vulnerable public exposure of his benches, and rather than dealing
with college recruiters, his enterprise is judged by policing authorities.
And although policing is in some ways positively connected to illicit
enterprise, the enactment of policing judgments has far more dire consequences than the judgments connected to college admissions.

In addition to a differing institutional context, the comparative
pressures on Joel and Strike are also a result of spatial differences. Joel's
business takes place within the protection of his home, while Strike's is
outside. As a result, exacerbating the riskiness of Strike's open-air bank
is its surveillance by Rodney, who is shown driving by, checking on his
enterprise and employees in several scenes. Shortly after one of the police raids on the benches, Strike is seen doubled over in pain. Because
his degree of risk is much greater than Joel's, his stress is more palpable;
he has a stomach ulcer, which he tries to mitigate with a milk-based
chocolate drink. And as the story progresses he is subjected to greater
pressures from both sides of the police-crime divide. Briefly, Strike is
pressured by Rodney to earn his departure from the benches by killing
Daryl Adams, a former clocker and current manager of a food establishment. When Strike tells his brother, Victor, of the dilemma (once

Strike does the killing, Rodney will have complete control over him), Victor does the killing to save his brother, leading Strike to believe that an anonymous person has done it. As a result, however, the pressure on Strike is increased because the primary investigating homicide detective, Rocco (Harvey Keitel), who cannot conceive of Victor as a murderer, suspects Strike and pressures him continually and publicly, so much so that Rodney ultimately orders a hit on Strike to make sure that he does not turn. Strike's preteen friend, Tyrone, finds Strike's gun and kills the hit man, and ultimately with Rocco's help, Victor's shooting of Daryl is mitigated, Tyrone is exonerated, and Strike is taken to Penn Station, where he takes a train westward to escape from Rodney.

When we locate the different filmic stories in the critical space that a parallel montage can effect, we must heed not only contrasting venues and the connections between them but also the icons. One similarity and one significant contrast stand out when we view the two films together. Treating the contrast first: while the most telling icon in *Risky Business* is the glass egg on the Goodsen family mantle piece, the most telling icons in *Clockers* are guns. The most powerful parallel montage one could effect, therefore, would be the framing shots of the egg followed by cuts to shots of guns. As I have noted, the egg shows up at key moments in the film narrative of *Risky Business*, each time implying something about the maturation process that changes Joel from a striving-to-succeed bourgeois/capitalist apprentice to one positioned to achieve an effective credential. In *Clockers* there is a pervasive series of shots of guns. The first is a cartoon version, flashed during the credits, and the second is a gun logo on the t-shirt of one of Strike's fellow clockers during the first scene in which they are assembled on and by the benches. Thereafter, guns are shown at many points in the film narrative, each time implying that death from a gunshot haunts everyday life in the projects. While *Risky Business*'s Joel is merely threatened with less than an Ivy League college admission, Strike is constantly threatened with death. Perhaps the best parallel montage would be a cut from the moment when the Princeton recruiter tells Joel that his record is not quite Ivy League to the moment in Rodney's car in which an irate Rodney is sticking his gun in Strike's mouth.

Finally, the two films display a remarkable parallel with differing implications. Both Joel and Strike have model train sets. In *Risky Business*, there are two significant train scenes. In the first, Joel is shown playing briefly with his model train set; the second, which is a referential montage that recalls the previous model train scene, is a transitional moment that takes place on one of Chicago's elevated trains. Joel and Lana make love on the train in a scene that marks the transition of Lana from a prostitute serving a client to a girlfriend and the transition of Joel from an inexperienced teenager to a self-confident lover. While the train scenes in *Risky Business* are vehicles for the coming-of-age narrative of Joel to an adult and inchoate capitalist, the train scenes in *Clockers* have a much deeper historical resonance.

As Diawara points out, trains "are associated with escape and freedom for black people."[100] Strike's strong attachment to trains is shown not only in the scene in which he is displaying his very extensive model train system to his sometime protégé (who turns out to be Strike's protector), Tyrone, but also in a scene where an undercover police detective blathers about how interested in basketball Strike must be. Strike tells him that he is interested in trains, not sports, and shows him a train logo on his t-shirt. When ultimately, with Rocco's assistance, Strike is shown heading into a western landscape on a train, the scene evokes the historical role of the Underground Railroad that helped African Americans escape slavery. In this case, the train is the vehicle for Strike to escape the violence of the inner city. While Joel's risky business prepared him for a life as a future entrepreneur, a privileged location in America's economy, Strike's risky business almost ended his life. The risks turn out to be incommensurate. The fault lines in the American political economy are connected with very different worlds with respect to "life, liberty, and the pursuit of happiness."

Transnational Political Economy and Another Risky Business

The encounter that Connolly staged between William Apess and Henry Thoreau took place, he said, on the "frontiers of cultural space." Those frontiers moved westward well into the nineteenth century, as Euro-America established its control over the continent, they now exist *within* national space, not only as cultural but also as economic difference. In particular, a growing number of Mexican American workers who participate in the economy do so without benefit of the protections of legal citizens. They risk exploitation in the process of crossing the U.S.-Mexican border and further exploitation by the enterprises that take advantage of their precarious status. To evoke the spatial perspective on democracy that Derrida develops, they are forced to survive in a "democracy" that fails to extend its hospitality to people crossing national boundaries. Derrida's recognition, in many of his investigations, of the dependence of identity on its others, and Connolly's recognition of "the constitutive ambiguity of identity," undercut a long history of cultural protection, famously evoked again in Samuel Huntington's cultural essentialist lament about the threat of immigration to America's "core" or "Anglo-Protestant culture."[101]

In contrast with Huntington, Derrida is committed to hospitality rather than a model of cultural abjection that fails to appreciate the historical contribution of "the foreigner" to constructive criticism of systems of national authority. He sees the threat as precisely one of cultural monologism. The foreigner, as Derrida puts it, "shakes up the threatening dogmatism of the paternal *logos*: the being that is and the non-being that is not."[102] Moreover, as Derrida emphasizes throughout his later political writings, in which he addresses what he terms the "democracy to come," democratic practice necessitates the extension of justice across national jurisdictions, based on a deconstruction of the metaphysical and onto-political commitments that essentialize national boundaries.

Paul Laverty's screenplay for the Ken Loach-directed *Bread and Roses*, based on his firsthand acquaintance with a "Justice for Janitors" campaign in Los Angeles in the 1990s, enacts Derrida's spatio-temporal extension of the idea of democracy. The film is based on a particular historical episode. The publicity attending a police crackdown on a union-organized march aimed at publicizing the plight of janitors who had short-term contracts, no health coverage, and low wages led to a breakthrough for immigrant workers. The exploitative cleaning companies for which they worked in LA's Century City building backed down.[103] The series of events that resulted in Laverty's screenplay also exemplify the conceptions of democracy to which Rancière has addressed himself; they comprise, in Laverty's terms, one of "those hidden episodes when, even in brief flashes, people showed the ability to resist, to join together, occasionally to win."[104] Like Derrida, who locates the potential of democracy in those events that effectuate a "polemical space,"[105] Rancière locates democracy in those moments of refusal when, for example, workers step out of their accustomed role, altering their activities and effacing the boundaries between work and leisure and between work and politics.

One episode in the film version of *Bread and Roses* exemplifies Rancière's conception of a democratic moment. One of the janitors, Ruben, who has the aspiration of earning a college diploma, arrives at work early to read and write. One of his coworkers chides him for simply copying, word for word, passages from a book. He could simply use a copy machine he says, mockingly, to the other assembled workers. However, as Rancière suggests, after close attention to the polemical moments that have arisen in labor history in the nineteenth century in France, in the case of workers, *any* writing subverts the identity within which they are kept in thrall: "It is . . . a matter of producing something other than the wrought objects in which the philosophy of the future sees the essence of man-the-producer being realized, at the price of losing some time in the ownership of capital."[106] Even if the workers' discourse consists of "borrowed words," it is the *fact* that a tailor or a shoemaker writes that politicizes their existence, according to Rancière.[107] Moreover, inasmuch as the janitors in the film, who end up participating in the Justice for Janitors campaign, make use of the time outside of their working hours to organize, they effect the democratic political action that Rancière characterizes. The sense of the "night," to which Rancière refers in his investigation, is its juxtaposition with working hours. Those workers who used the time outside of work to write were inventing themselves in a way that resisted the worker identity that exhausted the bourgeois conception of them.

But workers at times have assistance. In a passage about an activist blacksmith, Rancière refers briefly to a type that is central to the Laverty/Loach film: "Between the smith and his image, between the image that recalls him to his place and the image that invites him to revolt, we get a slight twist: unexpected meetings and fleeting conversations between our marginal workers who want to learn the secret of noble passions and the marginal intellectuals who want to minister to the sorrows of labor."[108] A key character in *Bread and Roses*, Sam Shapiro (Adrien Brody) is a labor organizer who convinces the janitors to organize and pressures the tenants of the building in which they work to force the cleaning company to provide health benefits and a better salary. He is the one who "minister[s] to the sorrows of labor," but his role exceeds that of a mere exhortation and moralizing that Rancière's "minister" term implies.

Although Sam turns out to be a friend to those who have had no friends in an environment that is inhospitable to Mexican migrant labor in Los Angeles, it is ultimately the friendship bestowed by one of the most vulnerable workers, Maya (Pilar Padilla), that has the most profound effect. With her sister's recommendation, she obtains work as a janitor in the building, after being threatened by the brutal coyotes who smuggle her across the border. Then she has her first month's salary extorted by the foreman who hires her. Maya and Sam meet when she hides him in her cleaning cart, while he is avoiding the building's security guards. Subsequently, despite resistance from some of the workers, her sister, Rosa, among others, Maya becomes the most implacable supporter of the workers movement. And she makes the ultimate gesture of friendship, robbing a convenience store to fund Ruben's college tuition, because he can no longer afford it, after he is fired by the building's management. That gesture of friendship gets Maya deported by the end of the film, unable to participate in labor's victory.

Two aspects of *Bread and Roses* speak to the lament that structures much of Derrida's *Politics of Friendship*, the phallogocentric or patriarchal tenor of the friendship discourse that has been the primary vehicle for constituting conceptions of democratic intimacy since Aristotle. The first aspect is Adrien Brody's body. His Sam Shapiro is a dramatic contrast to the macho, hyper-masculinity of the coyotes, security guards, and personnel managers who threaten and exploit the women who work as janitors, both economically and sexually. Second, the pri-

Sam and Maya in *Bread and Roses.* Courtesy of Lions Gate.

mary friendships that sustain the workers are among women, and the toughest and most steadfast friend is the young woman Maya.

Ultimately, *Bread and Roses* speaks to one of the American democracy's most duplicitous contemporary crimes, the crime of exploitation. By on the one hand erecting a border security that renders the workers who cross the economic and cultural frontier subject to exploitation, and on the other allowing enterprises to exploit them once they succeed in entering, the security policy creates a class whose relationship with America's business is the most risky and whose poorly remunerated toil is their only recognizable identity within the U.S. political culture. While Derrida's deconstructive reading of the Declaration of Independence reminds us of one of the original crimes (a representational violence) associated with Euro-America's founding, his analyses of friendship and hospitality alert us to what must come if the crime story is to be mitigated.

Conclusion: Theorizing "Democracy in America" in a Time of Danger

In a prescient statement, Michel Foucault said, "War is the motor behind institutions and order. In the smallest of its cogs, peace is waging a secret war. . . . To put it another way, . . . peace itself is coded war."[109] And writing in an earlier time of danger, when an authoritarian, anti-democratic Fascism was descending on Europe, Walter Benjamin quoted a line from Franz Kafka's *The Castle* that is strikingly apropos today: "We have a saying here that you may be familiar with: Official decisions are as shy as young girls."[110] The current threat afflicting America's democracy, the location of control over life and death, freedom and captivity outside of publicly exposed political and legal processes, is succinctly summarized by Judith Butler in an analysis of the post-9/11 "state of emergency" imposed by the U.S. government under George W. Bush's presidency: "The state of emergency returns the operation of power from a set of laws [juridical] to a set of rules [governmental], and the rules reinstate sovereign power: rules that are not binding by virtue of established law or modes of legitimation, but fully discretionary, even arbitrary, wielded by officials who interpret them unilaterally and decide the condition and form of their invocation."[111]

Certainly the September 11, 2001, attacks on the World Trade Center and Pentagon were attacks on the American democracy, by intention as well as implication. While much of the animus behind those who plotted the attacks was a desire to counter the U.S. global hegemony, there was also an expressed desire to strike a blow against America's democratic secularism and cultural pluralism. In the sobering aftermath of a vulnerability that had been poorly anticipated, there was an opportunity to reflect on and, where necessary, enhance or repair the democratic pluralism that allegedly enraged democracy's dogmatic antagonists. However, instead America went to war both against antagonists with tenuous connections to the 9/11 attackers and against itself. The implementation of the Patriot Act, which allows for pervasive surveillance and the suspension of juridical protections, and the frequent complicity of an often suborned and docile media establishment, have constrained the range of disagreement and dissent that are primary features of democratic politics. As a result, added to the historical failures that have haunted the American democracy—inequalities and exclusions with respect to who is a politically recognized subject and can engage in qualified political speech—have been new official and unofficial constraints on "what will and will not count as a viable speaking subject."[112]

Far more ominous than the constraints on political expression are the "states of exception" that, by executive order, institute a radically exclusionary biopolitics. Those designated as "enemy combatants," who become "detainees" sent to incarceration in the United States' Guantanamo Bay base in Cuba, and even American citizens accused of direct or indirect acts of terrorism and detained in the United States or elsewhere, become politically and juridically disqualified bodies. They are placed outside the law to exist in what Giorgio Agamben calls "a space devoid of law, a zone of anomie in which all legal determinations—and above all the very distinction between public and private—are deactiviated."[113]

Without belaboring the obvious, what has taken place is a set of legal and extralegal governmental initiatives, located ambiguously in a space between the exercise of an extrajuridical dimension of sovereignty and a new governmentality, that are reminiscent of earlier episodes of the suspension of democratic due process—for example, the McCarran Act of 1950, which included a provision for building concentration camps to hold subversives. Astute analyses of the anti-democratic dimensions of the current, increasingly institutionalized state of emergency proliferate.[114] Because here as elsewhere in the text one of my

198 Deforming American Political Thought

major concerns is to dislodge essentialist approaches to facticity, my
focus is limited to the ways in which an approach to a self-evident facticity is accompanying the dismantling of the American democracy.

In his treatment of the new states of exception inaugurated by President Bush's administration, Agamben notes how, during the "de facto
proceedings [under states of exception], which are in themselves extra-
or antijuridical . . . juridical norms blur with mere facts."[115] Insofar as
governmental judgment about necessity has the force of overruling the
law, "law is suspended and obliterated in fact."[116] Historically, there
has been a tradition of juridical thinking—rampant in the first half of
the twentieth century and famously articulated in the writings of Carl
Schmitt—that has deemed "necessity as the foundation of the validity
of decrees having the force of law issued by the executive in the state
of exception."[117] In contrast with those who naively treat the so-called
necessities as "an objective situation" are juridical thinkers who have
recognized that "far from an objective given," necessity derives from
subjective judgment—for example, Balladore-Pallieri notes that "the
concept of necessity is an entirely subjective one . . . the recourse to
necessity entails a moral or political (or in any case, extrajuridical) eval-
uation."[118] In challenging the pre-Kantian notion of facticity used to
legitimate the current state of exception and permit a rule by executive
prerogative that initiates a new legality with its source in a self-evident
necessity, Agamben sides with Benjamin's treatment of lawmaking
violence. He, among others, realizes that there is no more important
time to run the risks of engaging in what Derrida calls "hyperbolically
ambitious" thinking. Otherwise, we accompany the crimes of the executive branch of the U.S. government with the meta-level crime that
Derrida, as noted, ascribed to much of the trajectory of the history of
ideas, the failure to think the political. In this text, I enact my concern
with "thinking the political" as a theorist/crime fighter, by wresting a
segment of the history of ideas—that comprising "American political
thought"—from its privileged exclusivity.

Notes

Preface

1. I offer a critique of the social sciences in chapter 1, "Social Science, Comparative Politics, and Inequality," in Michael J. Shapiro, *Methods and Nations: Cultural Governance and the Indigenous Subject* (New York: Routledge, 2004).

2. Sheldon Wolin, "Political Theory as a Vocation," *American Political Science Review* 63:4 (December 1969): 1062–82.

3. See Arjun Appadurai, *Modernity at Large: Cultural Dimensions of Globalization* (Minneapolis: University of Minnesota Press, 1997), 27–47. I am indebted to Appadurai's terms each time I use the ending "scape" on any word except landscape—for example, ethnoscape, ideoscape, peoplescape.

4. My references to Shklar's address are from the version in *Redeeming American Political Thought*, a posthumously assembled volume edited by her Harvard colleagues Stanley Hoffman and Dennis F. Thompson (Chicago: University of Chicago Press, 1998), 91–108.

5. Their respective texts are: Gilles Deleuze, *Francis Bacon: The Logic of Sensation*, trans. Daniel W. Smith (Minneapolis: University of Minnesota Press, 2003), and Houston A. Baker Jr., *Modernism and the Harlem Renaissance* (Chicago: University of Chicago Press, 1987).

6. Jacques Rancière, "The Politics of Aesthetics," http://theater.kein.org/node/99, accessed May 18, 2005.

7. The quoted expression is from Miriam Bratu Hansen's "Introduction" to Siegfried Kracauer's *Theory of Film* (Princeton, N.J.: Princeton University Press, 1997), x.

8. Benjamin's remark about the moral shock effect of film is in his "The Work of Art in the Age of Mechanical Reproduction," trans. Harry Zohn, in *Illuminations*, ed. Hannah Arendt (New York: Schocken, 1968), 238. It should be noted, however, that Benjamin thought that film's shock effect often led to defensive reactions whereby the audience became anaesthetized rather than activated and critical. On this dimension of his thought, see Susan Buck-Morss, "Aesthetics and Anaesthetics: Walter Benjamin's Artwork Essay Reconsidered," *October* 62 (fall 1992): 3–41.

9. These concise representations of Siegfried Kracauer's ideas on film belong to Hansen, "Introduction," xv and xiii, respectively.

10. Jacques Rancière, *La Fable Cinematographique* (Paris: Editions Du Seuil, 2001), 22.

11. Alain Badiou, *St. Paul: The Foundation of Universalism*, trans. Ray Brassier (Stanford, Calif.: Stanford University Press, 2003), 33.

12. See Jacques Rancière, *The Politics of Aesthetics*, trans. Gabriel Rockhill (New York: Continuum, 2004), 24.

13. See M. M. Bakhtin, "Discourse and the Novel," in *The Dialogic Imagination*, trans. Caryl Emerson and Michael Holquist (Austin: University of Texas Press, 1981), 259–422. The quoted expression, "verbal-ideological decentering," is on page 370.

14. Roberto Calasso, *K*, trans. Geoffrey Brock (New York: Alfred A. Knopf, 2005), 33.

15. See Edward P. Jones, *The Known World* (New York: HarperCollins, 2003), 16.

16. Thomas Pynchon, *Mason & Dixon* (New York: Henry Holt, 1997), 345.

17. See Fredric R. Jameson, "On Raymond Chandler," in *The Poetics of Murder: Detective Fiction and Literary Theory*, ed. Glenn W. Most and William W. Stowe (New York: Harcourt Brace Jovanovitch, 1983), 129–30.

18. Toni Morrison, *Playing in the Dark: Whiteness and the Literary Imagination* (New York: Vintage, 1993), 5.

19. Jamaica Kincaid, *My Garden Book* (New York: Farrar, Straus, and Giroux, 1999), 122.

20. For a review of the perspectives on new ethnicities, see Amritjit Singh and Peter Schmidt, "On the Borders between U.S. Studies and Postcolonial Theory," in *Postcolonial Theory and the United States*, ed. Amritjit Singh and Peter Schmidt (Jackson: University Press of Mississippi, 2000), 29–30.

21. I use the term ethnogenesis in the way it is applied in William Boelhower, "Stories of Foundation, Scenes of Origin," *American Literary History* 5:3 (fall 1993): 392.

22. Erwin Panofsky, *Gothic Architecture and Scholasticism* (New York: Meridian, 1958).

23. See Jacques Rancière, *The Nights of Labor: The Workers' Dream in Nineteenth-Century France*, trans. John Drury (Philadelphia: Temple University Press, 1989).

24. Jacques Attali, *Noise: The Political Economy of Music*, trans. Brian Massumi (Minneapolis: University of Minnesota Press, 1985).

25. David Michael Hertz, *The Tuning of the Word: The Musico-Literary Poetics of the Symbolist Movement* (Carbondale: Southern Illinois University Press, 1987).

26. The quotation is from Jurgen E. Grandt, "Kinds of Blue: Toni Morrison, Hans Janowitz, and the Jazz Aesthetic," *African American Review* 38:2 (summer 2004): 303.

27. The texts are: MacDonald Smith Moore, *Yankee Blues: Musical Culture and American Identity* (Bloomington: Indiana University Press, 1985); David Schiff, *Gershwin: Rhapsody in Blue* (Cambridge, U.K.: Cambridge University Press, 1997); and Maurice Peress, *Dvorak to Duke Ellington* (New York: Oxford University Press, 2004).

28. Duke Ellington, "Interview in Los Angeles: On *Jump for Joy*, Opera and

Dissonance," in *The Duke Ellington Reader*, ed. Mark Tucker (New York: Oxford University Press, 1993), 150.

29. Gilles Deleuze and Felix Guattari, *Anti-Oedipus: Capitalism and Schizophrenia*, trans. Robert Hurley, Mark Seem, and Helen R. Lane (New York: Viking, 1977), 216.

1. Securing the American Ethnoscape

This chapter is a revised version of my article with the same title in *Worlds and Knowledges Otherwise* 1:1 (fall 2004), http://www.jhfc.duke.edu/wko/dossiers/1.1/contents.php (2004), accessed July 20, 2005.

Epigraphs. Thomas Pynchon, *Mason & Dixon* (New York: Henry Holt, 1997), 359; Philip Fisher, "Democratic Social Space: Whitman, Melville, and the Promise of American Transparency," *Representations* 24 (fall 1998): 100.

1. Judith Shklar, *Redeeming American Political Thought*, ed. Stanley Hoffman and Dennis F. Thompson (Chicago: University of Chicago Press, 1998), 91–108.

2. Ibid., 94.

3. Ibid., 92.

4. Ibid., 93–94.

5. I am borrowing the hyphenated term "thought-world" from Peter Brown, who points out that the architectural expression of the public culture of Christian elites in the age of Constantine manifested a pagan-Christian hybridity. Referring to the "thought-worlds" of the ancients, he points out that "throughout the fifth century, Christianity and paganism worked together in such public representations as architectural detail and decoration; in the ancients' 'thought-worlds,' potentially exclusive explanatory systems coexisted": Peter Brown, *Authority and the Sacred* (New York: Cambridge University Press, 1995), 69.

6. Shklar, *Redeeming American Political Thought*, 95. A general indictment of the objectivity view of the social sciences is beyond the scope of this essay. I address the issue at length in Michael J. Shapiro, *Methods and Nations: Cultural Governance and the Indigenous Subject* (New York: Routledge, 2004).

7. Shklar, *Redeeming American Political Thought*, 96.

8. This bifurcated Jeffersonian legacy is described in Malcolm Kelsall, *Jefferson and the Iconography of Romanticism* (New York: St. Martin's Press, 1999), 43.

9. The concept of the colonial divide and its epistemic significance is introduced and elaborated in Walter Mignolo, *Local Histories/Global Designs: Coloniality, Subaltern Knowledges, and Border Thinking* (Princeton, N.J.: Princeton University Press, 2000).

10. See Catherine Holland, "Notes on the State of America: Jeffersonian Democracy and the Production of a National Past," *Political Theory* 29:2 (April 2001): 190–216.

11. See Thomas Jefferson to John Adams, November 25, 1816, in *The Complete Correspondence between Thomas Jefferson and Abigail and John Adams*, ed. Lester J. Cappon (Chapel Hill: University of North Carolina Press, 1959), 498.

12. Joyce Appleby, "Recovering America's Historical Diversity: Beyond Exceptionalism," *Journal of American History* 79:2 (September 1992): 430.

13. Ibid., 431.

14. Ibid., 427.

15. Ibid., 428.

16. Thomas Jefferson, *Notes on the State of Virginia*, ed. William Peden (Chapel Hill: University of North Carolina Press, 1954; originally published in 1781–82), 87.

17. Michel Foucault, *The Order of Things* (New York: Vintage, 1970), 130.

18. Myra Jehlen, *American Incarnation: The Individual, the Nation, and the Continent* (New York: W. W. Norton, 1986), 44.

19. Kelsall, *Jefferson and the Iconography of Romanticism*, 88.

20. Jefferson, *Notes on the State of Virginia*, 19.

21. Ibid., 164.

22. Pascal Bonitzer, "Hitchcockian Suspense," in *Everything You Always Wanted to Know About Lacan . . . But Were Afraid to Ask Hitchcock*, ed. Slavoj Zizek (New York: Verso, 1992), 23.

23. Lauren Berlant, *The Queen of America Goes to Washington City: Essays on Sex and Citizenship* (Durham, N.C.: Duke University Press), 226.

24. See Christine Accomando, "'The Laws Were Laid Down to Me Anew': Harriet Jacobs and the Reframing of Legal Fictions," *African American Review*, 32:2 (summer 1998), 136.

25. Quotation from Bruce Burgett, *Sentimental Bodies* (Princeton, N.J.: Princeton University Press, 1998), 138.

26. William Apess, "Eulogy to King Philip," in *On Our Own Ground*, ed. Barry O'Connell (Amherst: University of Massachusetts Press, 1992), 275–76.

27. David Walker, *Appeal in Four Articles; Together with a Preamble, to the Colored Citizens of the World, but in Particular, and Very Expressly to Those of the United States of America*, ed. Sean Wilenz (New York: Hill and Wang, 1965).

28. The quotation is from Elizabeth McHenry's historical treatment of African American literary societies: *Forgotten Readers* (Durham, N.C.: Duke University Press, 2002), 27.

29. Clyde Woods, *Development Arrested: Race, Power, and the Blues in the Mississippi Delta* (New York: Verso, 1998), 4–5.

30. Ibid., 50.

31. Ibid., 205.

32. See *Land Ordinance of 1785*, http://www.statelib.lib.in.us/www/ihb/resources/docldord.html, accessed April 5, 2005.

33. As above, I am quoting Foucault on natural history: *The Order of Things*, 130.

34. Irene de Sousa Santos, "American Exceptionalism and the Naturalization of 'America,'" *Prospects: An Annual of American Cultural Studies*, ed. Jack Salzman 19 (1994): 10.

35. The quotations are from Fisher, "Democratic Social Space," 62.

36. Enrique Dussel, "World-System and 'Trans'-Modernity," *Nepantla: Views from the South* 3:2 (2002): 229.

37. Quotation from William Boelhower, *Through a Glass Darkly* (New York: Oxford University Press, 1987), 51.

38. *Black Elk Speaks* (as told to John G. Neihardt) (Lincoln: University of Nebraska Press, 1961), 9.

39. See *Black Hawk: An Autobiography* (1833), ed. Donald Jackson (Urbana: University of Illinois Press, 1955).

40. Ibid., 80.

41. Ibid., 71.

42. Ibid., 79.

43. Quotation from Boelhower, *Through a Glass Darkly*, 67.

44. Pynchon, *Mason & Dixon*, 345.

45. Ibid., 395.

46. Ibid., 80.

47. Ibid., 646.

48. Ibid., 650.

49. Ibid., 608.

50. Ibid., 350.

51. Ibid.

52. Ibid., 349.

53. See Gilles Deleuze and Felix Guattari, *What Is Philosophy*, trans. Hugh Tomlinson and Graham Burchell (New York: Columbia University Press, 1994). As Deleuze and Guattari put it, "Socrates is the principal conceptual persona of Platonism" (63).

54. Pynchon, *Mason & Dixon*, 283.

55. Ibid., 478.

56. Ibid., 451.

57. Ibid., 487.

58. J. B. Harley, "Maps, Knowledge, and Power," in *The Iconography of Landscape*, ed. Denis Cosgrove and Stephen Daniels (New York: Cambridge University Press, 1988), 279.

59. Pynchon, *Mason & Dixon*, 257.

60. Ibid., 551.

61. Ibid., 359.

62. Ibid., 568.

63. Ibid., 692.

64. Ibid., 307.

65. Ibid., 469.

66. Ibid., 323.

67. Ibid., 470.

68. Ibid., 586.

69. Ibid., 511.

70. The quotations are from Arthur Salzman's reading of *Mason & Dixon*: "'Cranks of Ev'ry Radius,'" in *Pynchon and* Mason and Dixon, ed. Brook Horvath and Irving Malin (Newark: University of Delaware Press, 2000), 69.

71. Antigua's sugar production began near the end of the seventeenth century, inaugurated by the entrepreneurial Sir Christopher Coddington, who made his initial visit in 1684. "By the middle of the 18th century the island was dotted with more than 150 cane-producing windmills." As a result of the Coddington-initiated

enterprise, "[m]ost Antiguans are of African lineage, descendants of slaves brought to the island . . . to labor in the sugarcane fields." Information and quotations on the web at: http://www.geographia.com/antigua-barbuda/aghis01.htm (2001), accessed April 17, 2004.

72. David Eltis, "Introduction," in *Coerced and Free Migration: Global Perspectives,* ed. David Eltis (Stanford, Calif.: Stanford University Press, 2002), 40.

73. Jamaica Kincaid, *My Garden Book* (New York: Farrar, Straus, and Giroux, 1999), 123.

74. Jamaica Kincaid, "The Little Revenge from the Periphery," *Transition* 73 (1997): 70.

75. Kincaid, *My Garden Book,* 134.

76. Ibid., 122.

77. Ibid.

78. Ibid.

79. In *Mason & Dixon,* Pynchon also treats the gap between the names Linnaeus imposes and extant vernacular understandings. See pages 431–32 on Linnaeus's *Gymnotus,* which is popularly known as the electric eel.

80. Kincaid, *My Garden Book,* 120.

81. Ibid., 8.

82. For an analysis of the counter-memory function in Kincaid's *My Garden Book* and elsewhere, see Louise Bernard, "Counter-Memory and Return: Reclamations of the (Postmodern) Self in Jamaica Kincaid's *The Autobiography of My Mother* and *My Brother," Modern Fiction Studies* 48:1 (spring 2002): 113–38. Bernard notes, "The garden for Kincaid is also tied to the power of the written word. . . . [It is] a display of entitlement to be symptomatic of the erasure and revision that informs the grand scheme of imperialism" (113–14).

83. Pynchon, *Mason & Dixon,* 693.

84. Stephen Daniels, *Fields of Vision: Landscape Imagery and National Identity in England and the United States* (New York: Polity, 1993), 6.

85. Michael Neill, "Broken English and Broken Irish: Nation, Language, and the Optics of Power in Shakespeare's Histories," *Shakespeare Quarterly* 45:1 (spring 1994): 3.

86. The quotations are from David Mackay, "Banks, Bligh and Breadfruit," *New Zealand Journal of History* 8:1 (1974): 61.

87. For an elaborate treatment of the European influences on Jefferson's gardening, see Frederick Doveton Nichols and Ralph E. Griswold, *Thomas Jefferson, Landscape Architect* (Charlottesville: University Press of Virginia, 1978).

88. Kincaid, *My Garden Book,* 132.

89. Ibid., 143.

90. Ibid., 150.

91. Ibid., 137.

92. Ibid., 7–8.

93. Ibid., 153.

94. For example, Pierre Bourdieu regards speech acts as constrained by the socially governed system of intelligibility; to speak, according to Bourdieu, is to appropriate a socially recognized style or idiom. Accordingly, he treats the creativity

of writers such as Flaubert as constrained by the forces at work within the genesis and structure of the social space in which creativity is possible. However, Bourdieu fails to heed the extent to which there is a fractionated diversity, a social space with historical rifts. To appreciate that spatio-temporal diversity, we need to replace Bourdieu's model·of the social field, which he renders as a hierarchical system of social "fractions," with a model of a fractal social order, a historically effected collage of diverse life worlds that have been coercively assembled by a history of state-directed "nation-building" and its attendant forms of political economy. I address this issue in my essay "Bourdieu, the State, and Method," *Review of International Political Economy* 9:4 (November 2002): 610–18.

95. Michelle Cliff, "History as Fiction, Fiction as History," *Ploughshares* 2:2–3 (fall 1994): 199.

96. Michelle Cliff, *Free Enterprise* (New York: Dutton, 1993), 7.

97. The quotation is from Kincaid, *My Garden Book*, 123.

98. As Mary N. Layoun puts it, the novel "quickly predominated as a privileged narrative form" in the third world, but it soon became reconfigured as a site of resistance rather than a vehicle for imposing European civilizational and cultural conceits. See her *Travels of a Genre: The Modern Novel and Ideology* (Princeton, N.J.: Princeton University Press, 1990), xii.

99. For a treatment of the contribution that "thought from the outside" lends to critical thinking, see Michel Foucault, "The Thought from the Outside," in *Foucault/Blanchot*, trans. Jeffrey Mehlman and Brian Massumi (New York: Zone Books, 1989).

100. See Michelle Cliff, "Notes on Speechlessness," in *Sinister Wisdom* (1978) and "A Journey into Speech," *Graywolf Annual: Multicultural Literacy*, ed. Ricki Simonson and Scott Walker (St. Paul, Minn.: Graywolf, 1988), 57.

101. Michelle Cliff, *No Telephone to Heaven* (New York: Dutton, 1987).

102. Quotation from Marian Aguiar, "Decolonizing the Tongue: Reading Speech and Aphasia in the Work of Michelle Cliff," *Literature and Psychology* 47½ (2001): 108.

103. Sherman Alexie, "Indian Country," *New Yorker*, March 13, 2000, 82.

104. Ibid., 77.

105. Ibid., 78.

106. M. M. Bakhtin, *Problems of Dostoevsky's Poetics*, trans. Caryl Emerson (Minneapolis: University of Minnesota Press, 1984), 59. The application of this Bakhtinian phrase to Alexie can also be found in Jerome Denounce, "Slow Dancing with Skeletons: Sherman Alexie's *The Lone Ranger and Tonto Fistfight in Heaven*," *Critique* 44:1 (fall 2002): 86.

107. Sherman Alexie, "Death in Hollywood," *Literary Cavalcade* 53:8 (May 2001): 2.

108. Sherman Alexie, *First Indian on the Moon* (New York: Hanging Loose, 1993), 98.

109. Sherman Alexie, "Sherman Alexie, Literary Rebel," interview with John and Carl Belante, *Bloomsbury Review* 14 (1994): 15.

110. John Newton, "Sherman Alexie's Autoethnography," *Contemporary Literature* 42:2 (2001): 415.

111. See Alexie's poems "Tiny Treaties" and "Seven Love Songs Which Include the Collected History of the United States of America," in *First Indian on the Moon*, 56–57 and 62–65, respectively.

112. Toni Morrison, *Playing in the Dark: Whiteness and the Literary Imagination* (New York: Vintage, 1993), xiii.

113. Quotation from Madhu Dubey, "The Politics of Genre in *Beloved*," *Novel: A Forum on Fiction* 32:2 (1999): 188.

114. Ibid.

115. Toni Morrison, *Paradise* (New York: Plume, 1999). The quotations are from Pierre Bourdieu, "Rethinking the State: Genesis and Structure of the Bureaucratic Field," in *Practical Reason: On the Theory of Action* (Stanford, Calif.: Stanford University Press), 40.

116. Abdellatif Khayati, "Representation, Race and the 'Language' of the Ineffable in Toni Morrison's Narrative," *African American Review* 33:2 (summer 1999): 315.

117. Bourdieu, "Rethinking the State: Genesis and Structure of the Bureaucratic Field," 40.

118. Michael Kammen, *In the Past Lane: Historical Perspectives on American Culture* (New York: Oxford University Press, 1997), 175.

119. The quotation is from David Noble, *The Eternal Adam and the New World Garden* (New York: George Braziller, 1968), ix. The exceptionalist ideology has been subject to numerous critiques—for example, David Veysey's, in which he dismisses the notion of an American distinctiveness and asserts that contrary to the presumption of a generalized, unique, and singular American character (and mission), "we are but one fractional (and internally fractionated) unit in a polyglot world, and that social history is composed of a vast number of separate and distinct pieces, like a mosaic that seldom stops at international boundary lines" (quoted in Kammen, *In the Past Lane*, 179).

120. My reading of Morrison's novel here is a slight revision of the one in my *Methods and Nations*.

121. Morrison discovered the basis for her story when, as she says, "I was looking at the book of photographs *Ghost Towns of Oklahoma*" and noticed that "it scarcely mentions any of the black ones" (quoted in Christopher Hitchens, "Morrison's West," *Vanity Fair* 450 [February 1998], 144).

122. Morrison, *Paradise*, 194.

123. Ibid., 217.

124. From Toni Morrison's Nobel lecture, http://nobelprize.org/literature/laureates/1993/morrison-lecture.html (1993), accessed May 30, 2005.

125. For a thorough treatment of the concept of the "colonial divide," see Mignolo, *Local Histories/Global Designs*.

126. Gilles Deleuze and Felix Guattari, *A Thousand Plateaus*, trans. Brian Massumi (Minneapolis: University of Minnesota Press, 1987), 105. My analysis of the position benefits from Paola Maratti's treatment of Deleuze and Guattari's politics. See his "Against the Doxa: Politics of Immanence and Becoming Minoritarian," in *Micropolitics of Media Culture: Reading the Rhizomes of Deleuze and Guattari*, ed. Patrica Pister (Amsterdam: Amsterdam University Press, 2001), 205–20.

127. Maratti, "Against the Doxa," 207.

128. See Gilles Deleuze and Felix Guattari, *Kafka: Towards a Minor Literature*, trans. Dana Polan (Minneapolis: University of Minnesota Press, 1986).

129. See Miguel Vatter, "The Machiavellian Legacy: Origin and Outcomes of the Conflict between Politics and Morality in Modernity," Working Paper SPS No. 99/2 (Florence: European University Institute, 1999).

130. Ibid., 12.

131. Ibid., 13.

132. Foucault's insights here are especially influenced by Immanuel Kant's essay on the enlightenment. See Michel Foucault, "What Is Enlightenment?" in *Interpretive Social Science: A Second Look*, ed. Paul Rabinow and William M. Sullivan (Berkeley: University of California Press, 1987), 171.

133. Jacques Derrida, "Nietzsche and the Machine: Interview with Jacques Derrida by Richard Beardsworth," *Journal of Nietzsche Studies* 7 (1994): 48.

134. Vatter, "The Machiavellian Legacy," 27.

135. Ibid., 28.

136. Ibid., 49.

2. The Micropolitics of Crime

1. I am using the past tense to avoid grammatical awkwardness. Shklar is deceased, but Wolin, who has retired from teaching, remains an active scholar.

2. Sheldon Wolin, "Political Theory as a Vocation," *American Political Science Review* 63:4 (December 1969): 1062–82.

3. Judith Shklar, *Redeeming American Political Thought*, ed. Stanley Hoffman and Dennis F. Thompson (Chicago: University of Chicago Press, 1998).

4. See Gilles Deleuze, *Francis Bacon: The Logic of Sensation*, trans. Daniel W. Smith (Minneapolis: University of Minnesota Press, 2003).

5. Jacques Rancière, "The Thinking of Dissensus: Politics and Aesthetics," paper presented at the conference "Fidelity to the Disagreement: Jacques Rancière and the Political," Goldsmith College, London, U.K., September 16–17, 2003, 6.

6. Colson Whitehead, *The Intuitionist* (New York: Anchor, 2000).

7. Ibid., 255.

8. Wolin, "Political Theory as a Vocation," 1073.

9. Ibid., 1064.

10. See Gilles Deleuze, "Kant: Synthesis and Time," lecture of March 14, 1978, trans. Melissa McMahon, http://www.webdeleuze.com/php/sommaire.html, accessed January 6, 2004.

11. See Immanuel Kant, *The Critique of Pure Reason*, trans. Paul Guyer and Allen W. Wood (New York: Cambridge University Press, 1999). And for a discussion of the delicate balance between passivity and activity in the Kantian subject, see Gilles Deleuze, *Kant's Critical Philosophy*, trans. Hugh Tomlinson and Barbara Habberjam (Minneapolis: University of Minnesota Press, 1984), 14–15.

12. Heidegger's initial explication and critique of the Kantian reformulation of empiricism's question is in his *What Is a Thing?*, trans. W. B. Barton and Vera Deutsch (Chicago: Henry Regnery, 1967).

13. See for example, Jean-François Lyotard, *The Differend: Phrases in Dispute*, trans. Georges Van Den Abbeele (Minneapolis: University of Minnesota Press, 1988).

14. Recognizing that the sublime imperils his attempt to derive the harmonious agreement or *sensus communis* toward which his *Critique* of aesthetic judgment is aimed, Kant admits that while "the necessity of a universal agreement that is thought in a judgment of taste is a subjective necessity" (94), and while encounters with the "numberless beautiful things in nature [allow us to presume] . . . and even expect, without being widely mistaken, the harmony of everyone's judgment with our own, . . . in respect of our judgment upon the sublime in nature, we cannot promise ourselves so easily the accordance of others." See Immanuel Kant, *The Critique of Judgment*, trans. J. H. Bernard (Amherst, N.Y.: Prometheus Books, 2000), 130.

15. My discussion here benefits from Daniel Smith's concise explication of the Kantian synthesis in his "Translator's Introduction" to Deleuze, *Francis Bacon*, xv–xvi.

16. The quotation is from ibid., xvii.

17. Deleuze, "Kant: Synthesis and Time."

18. Ibid.

19. Wolin, "Political Theory as a Vocation," 1064.

20. Deleuze, *Francis Bacon*, 71.

21. Ibid., 71–72.

22. Bacon quoted in David Sylvester, *The Brutality of Fact: Interviews with Francis Bacon* (New York: Thames and Hudson, 1981), 40.

23. Deleuze, *Francis Bacon*, 14.

24. Ibid., 6.

25. Ibid., 59.

26. See Dashiell Hammett, *The Maltese Falcon* (New York: Vintage, 1992; originally published in 1929), 62–64. My reference to the Flitcraft episode as a parable is encouraged by Paul Auster's characterization of it. Inspired by Hammett's Flitcraft, Auster creates a character with a similar story in his *Oracle Night* (New York: Henry Holt, 2003).

27. Hammett, *The Maltese Falcon*, 63.

28. Ibid., 64.

29. Sean McCann, *Gumshoe America* (Durham, N.C.: Duke University Press, 2000), 4.

30. See Raymond Chandler, *Farewell My Lovely* (New York: Vintage, 1992).

31. Michel Foucault, *Discipline and Punish: The Birth of the Prison*, trans. Alan Sheridan (New York: Pantheon, 1977), 272.

32. The quotations are from D. A. Miller's Foucauldian analysis of nineteenth-century crime novels, "The Novel and the Police," in *The Poetics of Murder: Detective Fiction and Literary Theory*, ed. Glenn W. Most and William W. Stowe (New York: Harcourt Brace Jovanovitch, 1983), 316.

33. The quoted expressions belong to Robert Crooks, who sees the African American crime story in terms of a spatial divide that compares with that generated between Euro- and Native Americans in westerns. See his "From the Far

Side of the Urban Frontier: The Detective Fiction of Chester Himes and Walter Mosley," *College Literature* 22:3 (October 1995): 68–91.

34. M. M. Bakhtin, "Discourse and the Novel," in *The Dialogic Imagination*, trans. Caryl Emerson and Michael Holquist (Austin: University of Texas Press, 1981), 370.

35. M. M. Bakhtin, "Epic and Novel," in *The Dialogic Imagination*, 37.

36. The quoted expression belongs to Theodore O. Mason Jr., who also applies Bakhtinian insights to Mosley's fiction. See his "Walter Mosley's Easy Rawlins: The Detective and Afro-American Fiction," *Kenyon Review* 14:4 (fall 1992): 176.

37. Walter Mosley, *Devil in a Blue Dress* (New York: Simon and Schuster, 1990).

38. Manthia Diawara, "*Noir* by *Noirs*: Toward a New Realism in Black Cinema," in *Shades of Noir: A Reader*, ed. Joan Copjec (New York: Verso, 1993), 262.

39. Eric Lott, "The Whiteness of Film Noir," in *National Imaginaries, American Identities*, ed. Larry J. Reynolds and Gordon Hutner (Princeton, N.J.: Princeton University Press, 2000), 159.

40. The term "transcode" belongs to Fredric Jameson, who also addressed himself, in the same place, to adding history to a film's surface problems, in a discussion of allegory in Hitchcock. See his "Allegorizing Hitchcock," in *Signatures of the Visible* (New York: Routledge, 1992), 100.

41. Quotations are from Foucault, *Discipline and Punish*, 279.

42. Mosley, *Devil in a Blue Dress*, 5.

43. Foucault, *Discipline and Punish*, 280.

44. Ralph Ellison, "An Extravagance of Laughter," in *Going to the Territory* (New York: Random House, 1986), 148.

45. My commentary here is drawn from Dana Brand's discussion in *The Spectator and the City in Nineteenth-Century American Literature* (New York: Cambridge University Press, 1991), 79–82.

46. Ibid., 99.

47. The quotations are from Franco Moretti's mapping of the city in nineteenth-century novels in his *Atlas of the European Novel* (London: Verso, 1998), 134–35.

48. Ibid., 136.

49. Ibid., 86.

50. See Stephen F. Soitos, *The Blues Detective: A Study of African American Detective Fiction* (Amherst: University of Massachusetts Press, 1996).

51. Houston A. Baker Jr., "Figurations for a New American Literary History," in *Ideology and Classic American Literature*, ed. Sacvan Berkovitch and Myra Jehlen (New York: Cambridge University Press, 1986), 160.

52. Ibid.

53. Charles Dickens, *Our Mutual Friend* (London: Harmondsworth, 1977), 159.

54. Mosley, *Devil in a Blue Dress*, 48.

55. See *An act declaring the Negro, Mulatto, and Indian slaves within this dominion, to be real estate*, http://www.law.du.edu/russell/lh/alh/docs/virginiaslaverystatutes.html, accessed April 2, 2004. Section II reads: "*Be it enacted, by the*

governor, council and burgesses of this present general assembly, and it is hereby enacted by the authority of the same; That from and after the passing of this act, all negro, mulatto, and Indian slaves, in all courts of judicature, and other places, within this dominion, shall be held, taken, and adjudged, to be real estate (and not chattels;) and shall descend unto the heirs and widows of persons departing this life, according to the manner and custom of land of inheritance, held in fee simple."

56. Mosley, *Devil in a Blue Dress*, 62.

57. Pauline Hopkins, "Hagar's Daughter," in *The Magazine Novels of Pauline Hopkins* (New York: Oxford University Press, 1988), 62.

58. Pauline Hopkins, "Of One Blood," in ibid., 441–621.

59. The quotation is from Wlad Godzich's "Afterword," in Samuel Weber, *Institution and Interpretation* (Minneapolis: University of Minnesota Press, 1987), 161.

60. This scenario is encouraged by some insights in Slavoj Zizek's "Enjoy Your Nation as Yourself," in *Tarrying with the Negative* (Durham, N.C.: Duke University Press, 1993), 72.

61. See G. W. F. Hegel's master-slave dialectic in his *Philosophy of Right*, trans. T. M. Knox (New York: Oxford University Press, 1967), and Jacques Lacan's "Aggressivity in Psychoanalysis," in *Ecrit*, trans. Alan Sheridan (New York: W. W. Norton, 1977), 8–29.

62. Frederic R. Jameson, "On Raymond Chandler," in *The Poetics of Murder: Detective Fiction and Literary Theory*, ed. Glenn W. Most and William W. Stowe (New York: Harcourt Brace Jovanovitch, 1983), 129–30.

63. Ibid., 130.

64. Stephen Haymes, *Race, Culture, and the City* (Albany: SUNY Press, 1995), 70.

65. Michel de Certeau, *Practices of Everyday Life*, trans. Steven Randall (Berkeley: University of California Press, 1984), 35–36.

66. Clyde Woods, *Development Arrested: Race, Power, and the Blues in the Mississippi Delta* (New York: Verso, 1998), 30.

67. The quotations are from Soitos, *The Blues Detective*, 29.

68. Quotations in ibid., 31.

69. Jacques Derrida, *Politics of Friendship*, trans. George Collins (New York: Verso, 1997), 19.

70. Ibid., 14.

71. The quotation is from Stephen Graham and Simon Marvin, *Splintering Urbanism: Networked Infrastructures, Technological Mobilities and the Urban Condition* (New York: Routledge, 2001), 383.

72. Derrida, *Politics of Friendship*, viii.

73. James Welch, *Fools Crow* (New York: Penguin, 1986), 3.

74. Andrea Opitz, "James Welch's *Fools Crow* and the Imagination of Precolonial Space," *American Indian Quarterly* 24:1 (winter 2000): 129.

75. Ibid., 126.

76. Ibid., 131.

77. Ibid., 133.

78. Patricia Linton, "The Detective Novel as Resistant Text," in *Multicultural Detective Fiction: Murder from the Other Side,* ed. Adrienne Johnson Gosselin (New York: Garland, 1999), 19.

79. William V. Spanos, "The Detective and the Boundary: Some Notes on the Postmodern Literary Imagination" *Boundary 2* 1:1 (1972): 21 (cited in Linton, "The Detective Novel as Resistant Text," 20).

80. Linda Hogan, *Mean Spirit* (New York: Ballantine, 1990), 127.

81. Ibid., 177.

82. Ibid., 170.

83. Gilles Deleuze, *Proust and Signs,* trans. Richard Howard (Minneapolis: University of Minnesota Press, 2000), 26–27.

84. M. M. Bakhtin, *Problems of Dostoevsky's Poetics,* trans. Caryl Emerson (Minneapolis: University of Minnesota Press, 1984), 7.

85. Hogan, *Mean Spirit,* 13.

86. Ibid., 341.

87. Ibid., 234.

88. Ibid., 341.

89. Ibid., 361.

90. Ibid.

91. Alexis de Tocqueville, *Democracy in America,* trans. Henry Reeve, 2 vols. (New York: Vintage, 1990), 1:9.

92. Ibid.

93. Data provided in Alan Rosenus, *General Vallejo and the Advent of the Americans* (Berkeley, Calif.: Heyday Books, 1995), 35.

94. Text of a Vallejo speech reported in Joseph Warren Revere, *A Tour of Duty in California* (New York: C. S. Francis and Co., 1849), quoted in Rosenus, *General Vallejo and the Advent of the Americans,* 90–91.

95. Lucha Corpi, *Cactus Blood* (Houston, Tex.: Arte Publico Press, 1995), 173.

96. Ramon Saldivar, *Chicano Narrative: The Dialectics of Difference* (Madison: University of Wisconsin Press, 1990), 5.

97. Joy M. Lynch, "'A Distinct Place in America Where All *Mestizos* Reside': Landscape and Identity in Ana Castillo's *Sapogonia* and Diana Chang's *The Frontiers of Love,*" *Melus* 26:3 (fall 2001): 121.

98. Ibid., 120.

99. The quotation is from José David Saldívar, "Nuestra América's Borders," in *José Martí's "Our America,"* ed. Jeffrey Belnap and Raul Fernandez (Durham, N.C.: Duke University Press, 1998), 156.

100. The quotations are from Rosaura Sanchez and Beatrice Pita's "Introduction" to Maria Amparo Ruiz de Burton, *The Squatter and the Don* (Houston: Arte Publico Press, 1997), 7.

101. Ruiz de Burton, *The Squatter and the Don,* 66.

102. Corpi, *Cactus Blood,* 21.

103. Lucha Corpi, *Eulogy for a Brown Angel* (Houston, Tex.: Arte Publico Press, 1992), 109.

104. Corpi, *Cactus Blood,* 173.

105. The quotations are from Rafael Perez-Torres, "Chicano Ethnicity, Cultural Hybridity, and the Mestizo Voice," *American Lierature* 70:1 (March 1998): 154.

106. Dale Furutani, *Death in Little Tokyo* (New York: St. Martins, 1996).

107. Jameson, "On Raymond Chandler," 130.

108. Furutani, *Death in Little Tokyo*, 122.

109. Ibid., 87.

110. Ibid., 81.

111. Ibid., 157.

112. Rancière, "The Thinking of Dissensus: Politics and Aesthetics," 6.

3. Deforming America's Western Imaginary

Portions of this chapter are revisions of my article "The Demise of International Relations: America's Western Palimpsest," *Geopolitics* 10:2 (2005): 222–43. For a more elaborate reading of westerns, see chapter 5, "Film and Nationhood," in Michael J. Shapiro, *Methods and Nations: Cultural Governance and the Indigenous Subject* (New York: Routledge, 2004).

1. It is in Thomas Hobbes's *Leviathan* that the quoted phrase exists. See Thomas Hobbes, *Leviathan*, ed. Richard Tuck (New York: Cambridge University Press, 1991), 88.

2. See Michel Foucault *"Society Must Be Defended": Lectures at the Collège de France, 1975–1976*, trans. David Macey (New York: Picador, 2003).

3. Richard Slotkin, *Gunfighter Nation: The Myth of the Frontier in Twentieth-Century America* (New York: Atheneum, 1992).

4. Robert Burgoyne, *Film Nation: Hollywood Looks at U.S. History* (Minneapolis: University of Minnesota Press, 1997), 48.

5. See, for example, Cheryl Walker's *Indian Nation* (Durham, N.C.: Duke University Press, 1997), where she notes that not only was "America" an encounter of alternative nationhoods (for Native Americans had not understood nations as the Euros had come to define them (4), but also that America emerged as a political entity as a result of significant Native American participation in discussions of national identity.

6. For a treatment of this shift, see John Borneman, "American Anthropology as Foreign Policy," *American Anthropologist* 97:4 (December 1995): 662–67.

7. Ibid., 665.

8. John C. Cremony, *Life Among the Apaches* (New York: Indian Head Books, 1991), 13–14.

9. The term "ethnogenesis" comes from William Boelhower, "Stories of Foundation, Scenes of Origin," *American Literary History* 5:3 (fall 1993): 392.

10. The quotations are from Barry Langford, "You Cannot Look at This: Thresholds of Unrepresentability in Holocaust Film," *Journal of Holocaust Education* 8:3 (winter 1999): 29, 23–41.

11. The concepts (of frontier and region) and quotations are from William Cronon, George Miles, and Jay Gitlin, "Becoming West," in *Under an Open Sky: Rethinking America's Western Past*, ed. William Cronon et al. (New York: W. W. Norton, 1992), 18–23.

12. See John Agnew, *Geopolitics: Re-Visioning World Politics*, 2nd ed. (New York: Routledge, 2003).

13. Shapiro, *Methods and Nations*, 142.

14. This part of the plot follows that of the novel by Friedrich Durrenmatt (which treats the murder of a young girl in one of Switzerland's eastern cantons), the prototype for the film script; Friedrich Durrenmatt, *The Pledge*, trans. Richard Winston and Clara Winston (Alfred A. Knopf, 1959).

15. Gilles Deleuze, *Cinema 1*, trans. Hugh Tomlinson and Barbara Habberjam (London: Athlone, 1992), 65.

16. Ibid., 121.

17. American Indians made up almost 50 percent of the sixteen thousand-plus Nevada population in the early 1860s. Now, in the Reno area, which is representative, they currently compose slightly more than 1 percent of the population (see http://dmla.clanlib.nv.us/docs/nsla/archives/political/historical/hist18.htm, accessed December 15, 2004).

18. The "perception-image" is another of Gilles Deleuze's categories in *Cinema 1*, 66–68.

19. The so-called civilized tribes from the East, who were removed to Oklahoma, brought black slaves and black relatives with them ("thousands of Negroes were neighbors or slaves of the Five Civilized Tribes"), and many became cowboys. See Philip Durham and Everett L. Jones, *The Negro Cowboys* (New York: Dodd, Mead and Co., 1965), 18–19. As for the all-black towns, novelist Toni Morrison discovered their history in Oklahoma while researching her novel *Paradise*. As she notes, "I was looking at the book of photographs *Ghost Towns of Oklahoma*" when she noticed that "it scarcely mentions any of the black ones" (quoted in Christopher Hitchens, "Morrison's West," *Vanity Fair* 450 [February 1998], 144).

20. In his biography of Ford, Scott Eyman states that from his earliest films, Ford was already "making the landscape a character." See his *Print the Legend: The Life and Times of John Ford* (New York: Simon and Schuster, 1999), 73.

21. Deleuze, *Cinema 1*, 146.

22. Ibid., 148.

23. For an analysis of the Cooper-Wister contrast and its influence on westerns, see John Cawelti, *The Six-Gun Mystique Sequel* (Bowling Green, Ohio: Bowling Green University Popular Press, 1999), 66.

24. See Theodore Roosevelt, *The Winning of the West* (New York: G. P. Putnam's Sons, 1889).

25. Lewis H. Morgan, *Houses and House-Life of the American Aborigines*, ed. Paul Bohannan (Chicago: University of Chicago Press, 1965; originally published in 1881), xxiv.

26. Alan Nadel, *Containment Culture: American Narratives, Postmodernism, and the Atomic Age* (Durham, N.C.: Duke University Press, 1995), 195.

27. Tag Gallagher, "Angels Gambol Where They Will: John Ford's Indians," in *The Western Reader*, ed. Jim Kitses and Gregg Rickman (New York: Limelight, 1998), 273.

28. Virginia Wright Wexman, "The Family on the Land: Race and Nation-

hood in Silent Westerns," in *The Birth of Whiteness,* ed. Daniel Bernardi (New Brunswick, N.J.: Rutgers University Press, 1996), 129.

29. On the anti-diegetic aspects of experimental cinema, see Andre Gardies, *Le Cinema de Robbe-Grillet: Essai Semiocritique* (Paris: Albatross, 1983).

30. The quotations are from Altman's response to David Breskin's query, "Do you think there's a politics to your style, to the style itself?" in David Breskin, *Inner Views: Filmmakers in Conversation* (New York: Da Capo, 1997), 287.

31. Gilles Deleuze, *Francis Bacon: The Logic of Sensation,* trans. Daniel W. Smith (Minneapolis: University of Minnesota Press, 2003), 71.

32. Ibid., 71–72.

33. Quoted at http://www.wordlookup.net/mc/mccabe-and-mrs.-miller.html, accessed March 14, 2005.

34. See Wexman, "The Family on the Land," 131.

35. For this version of the typical strong stranger who must remain outside of society, see Will Wright's structural reading of classic westerns in his *Six Guns and Society* (Berkeley: University of California Press, 1975).

36. The quoted section is from Susan Armitage, Elizabeth Jameson, and Joan Jensen, "The New Western History: Another Perspective," *Journal of the West* 32:3 (1993): 5–6.

37. Graham Fuller, "Altman on Altman," in *Robert Altman: Interviews,* ed. David Sterritt (Jackson: University Press of Mississippi, 2000), 195.

38. Deleuze, *Francis Bacon,* 14.

39. Ibid., 6.

40. The convenient albeit partial review is a quotation from Pam Cook, "Women and the Western," in *The Western Reader,* ed. Kitses and Rickman, 293–94.

41. See Deleuze, *Cinema 1,* 87–88.

42. See Noël Burch, "Spatial and Temporal Articulations," in *Theory of Film Practice,* trans. Helen Lane (New York: Praeger, 1973), 17.

43. The quotations are from an interview with Altman by Bruce Williamson, "Altman," in *Robert Altman: Interviews,* ed. Sterritt, 38–39.

44. Fuller, "Altman on Altman," 198.

45. The idea that the gun is "the moral center of the Western" is expressed in Robert Warshow, "Movie Chronicle: The Westerner," in *The Western Reader,* ed. Kitses and Rickman, 37.

46. Fuller, "Altman on Altman," 198.

47. Altman quoted in Harry Kloman and Lloyd Michaels with Virginia Wright Wexman, "A Foolish Optimist," in *Robert Altman: Interviews,* ed. Sterritt, 113.

48. Gene M. Bernstein, "Robert Altman's *Buffalo Bill and the Indians, or Sitting Bull's History Lesson*: A Self-Portrait in Celluloid," *Journal of Popular Culture* 13:1 (summer 1979): 17.

49. Among the most effective recent treatments is Vincent Amiel's *Le Corps au Cinema: Keaton, Bresson, Cassavetes* (Paris: Presses Universitaire de France, 1998).

50. The quotation is from a commentary on Amiel's approach to the cinematographic body: Jerome Game, "Cinematic Bodies," *Studies in French Cinema* 1:1 (2001): 50–51.

51. The phrase belongs to Peter Handke in *A Writer's Afternoon*, trans. Ralph Manheim (New York: Farrar, Straus, and Giroux, 1989), 3.

52. Certainly Sam Shepard, who wrote the screenplay, is known for his psychological, Freudian-oriented plots. But at the same time, his stories and vignettes explore historical landscapes. See, for example, his western musings in *The Motel Chronicles* (San Francisco: City Lights, 1982), which contains imagery that anticipates aspects of his screenplay for *Paris, Texas*. For a treatment that offers a psychoanalytic reading of the film, see Donald L. Carveth, "The Borderland Dilemma in *Paris, Texas*: Psychoanalytic Approaches to Sam Shepard," *Psyart: A Hyperlink Journal for Psychological Study of Arts*, http://www.clas.ufl.edu/ipsa/journal/1997_carveth01.shtml (1997), accessed October 10, 2003.

53. Conversation with Alain Bergala in Wim Wenders, *Written in the West* (Munich, Germany: Shirmer, 1987), 11.

54. Ibid.

55. Ibid., 9.

56. Ibid., 13.

57. Ibid., 16.

58. The "location scouting" stills can be seen in *Wim Wenders-Sam Shepard: Paris, Texas*, ed. Chris Sievernich (Nordlinger, Germany: Greno, 1984), 98–99.

59. Peter Handke, *The Long Way Around*, one of three novelettes in *Slow Homecoming* (New York: Farrar, Straus, and Giroux, 1985), 76. Both authors of the screenplay of *Paris, Texas*, Wenders and Sam Shepard, are familiar with Handke's novels. Wenders worked with Handke on a screenplay for one of Handke's earlier novels (*The Anxiety of the Goaltender During the Penalty Kick*), and Shepard reviewed *Slow Homecoming* in the *New York Times Book Review*.

60. This expression and its implications are well developed in Jacques Derrida's "Violence and Metaphysics," in *Writing and Difference*, trans. Alan Bass (Chicago: University of Chicago Press, 1978).

61. Joy M. Lynch, "'A Distinct Place in America Where All *Mestizos* Reside': Landscape and Identity in Ana Castillo's *Sapogonia* and Diana Chang's *The Frontiers of Love*," *Melus* 26:3 (fall 2001): 120.

62. This is the interpretive resort of Robert Phillip Kolker and Peter Beicken, in their excellent reading of the film, "Paris, Texas: Between the Winds," in their *The Films of Wim Wenders: Cinema as Vision and Desire* (New York: Cambridge University Press, 1993), 125.

63. Handke, *Slow Homecoming*, 114.

64. This apt expression is in Kolker and Beicken, "Paris, Texas: Between the Winds," 120.

65. Quotations from Slotkin, *Gunfighter Nation*, 212.

66. Joseph Conrad, "Geography and Some Explorers," in his *Last Essays* (New York: Doubleday, Page and Co., 1926), 1–21.

67. Cecilia Tichi, *Embodiment of a Nation: Human Form in American Places* (Cambridge, Mass.: Harvard University Press, 2001), 2.

68. See Jacques Rancière, *Dis-agreement*, trans. Julie Rose (Minneapolis: University of Minnesota Press, 1998).

69. Ibid., 27.

70. The quotations are from B. D'Arcus's excellent analysis of the spatial strategies of the Wounded Knee insurgency: "Contested Boundaries: Native Sovereignty and State Power at Wounded Knee, 1973," *Political Geography* 22:4 (May 2003): 416.

71. Ibid., 421.

72. Pascal Bonitzer, "Hitchcockian Suspense," in *Everything You Always Wanted to Know About Lacan . . . But Were Afraid to Ask Hitchcock,* ed. Slavoj Zizek (New York: Verso, 1992), 23.

4. Constructing America

An earlier version of this chapter appeared under the same title in *Theory and Event* 7:4 (2004).

1. See Gilles Deleuze, *Bergsonism,* trans. Hugh Tomlinson and Barbara Habberjam (New York: Zone Books, 1991), for an elaborate analysis of how the past remains a grammatical present in Bergson's thought.

2. For the history of Libeskind's diminishing control over the design process, see Robin Pogrebin, "The Incredible Shrinking Daniel Libeskind," *New York Times,* http://www.nytimes.com/2004/06/20/arts/design/20POGR.html, accessed June 20, 2004.

3. Kirk Johnson, "The Very Image of Loss: The Pit at Ground Zero as Icon of Absence," *New York Times* (New York Report Section, page 26, Sunday, March 2, 2003).

4. Ibid.

5. Ibid.

6. For a review of the controversies and media events surrounding the design process, see Philip Nobel, *Sixteen Acres: Architecture and the Outrageous Struggle for the Future of Ground Zero* (New York: Henry Holt and Company, 2005).

7. James E. Young, *At Memory's Edge: After-Images of the Holocaust in Contemporary Art and Architecture* (New Haven, Conn.: Yale University Press, 2000), 155.

8. Daniel Libeskind, *The Space of Encounter* (London: Thames and Hudson, 2001), 19.

9. Ibid., 20.

10. See Marc-Alain Ouaknin, *The Burnt Book: Reading the Talmud,* trans. Llewellyn Brown (Princeton, N.J.: Princeton University Press, 1995), xi–xii.

11. Ibid., 170–71.

12. See Erwin Panofsky, *Gothic Architecture and Scholasticism* (New York: Meridian, 1958), 27.

13. Ibid., 43.

14. Ibid., 13.

15. Ibid., 45.

16. Ibid., 16–17.

17. Ibid., 45–46.

18. Ibid., 50.

19. Ibid., 68.

20. Ibid., 69–70.

21. Dell Upton, "Vernacular Domestic Architecture in Eighteenth-Century Virginia," in Dell Upton and John Michael Vlach, *Common Places: Readings in American Vernacular Architecture* (Athens: University of Georgia Press, 1986), 317.

22. Gilles Deleuze, *Difference and Repetition*, trans. Paul Patton (New York: Columbia University Press, 1994), 186.

23. Upton, "Vernacular Domestic Architecture in Eighteenth-Century Virginia," 318.

24. Ibid., 332.

25. Ibid., 325.

26. Ibid., 323.

27. Ibid., 320.

28. See Durand de Dauphiné, *A Huguenot Exile in Virginia: or, Voyages of a Frenchman Exiled for his Religion, with a Description of Virginia and Maryland*, trans. and ed. Gilbert Chinard (New York: Press of the Pioneers, 1934), 119–20 (cited in Upton, "Vernacular Domestic Architecture in Eighteenth-Century Virginia," 317).

29. Upton, "Vernacular Domestic Architecture in Eighteenth-Century Virginia," 320.

30. Ibid.

31. Ann Bermingham, "System, Order, and Abstraction: The Politics of English Landscape Drawing around 1795," in *Landscape and Power*, ed. W. J. T. Mitchell (Chicago: University of Chicago Press, 1994), 83.

32. The quotation is from Buford Pickens, "Mr. Jefferson as Revolutionary Architect," *Journal of the Society of Architectural Historians* 34:4 (December 1975): 263.

33. Thomas Jefferson, *Notes on the State of Virginia*, ed. William Peden (Chapel Hill: University of North Carolina Press, 1954; originally published in 1781–1782), 164.

34. Malcolm Kelsall, *Jefferson and the Iconography of Romanticism* (New York: St. Martin's Press, 1999), 88.

35. Jefferson, *Notes on the State of Virginia*, 19.

36. Quotation from William Boelhower, *Through a Glass Darkly* (New York: Oxford University Press, 1987), 67.

37. Michel Foucault *"Society Must Be Defended": Lectures at the Collège de France, 1975–1976*, trans. David Macey (New York: Picador, 2003), 77.

38. Ibid., 72.

39. Ibid., 78.

40. Ibid., 78.

41. Ibid., 81.

42. See Jefferson, *Notes on the State of Virginia*, 163.

43. The quotation is from Bruce Dain's reaction to Jefferson's *Notes on the State of Virginia* in his *A Hideous Monster of the Mind* (Cambridge, Mass.: Harvard University Press, 2002), 20.

44. Jefferson, *Notes on the State of Virginia*, 43. Subsequent to his remark about the inferiority of African Americans, Jefferson admitted that his observa-

tions may be unreliable and that blacks may only appear to be inferior because of the "degraded condition" in which they are kept. See his letter to the Marquis de Condorcet in *Thomas Jefferson, Political Writings*, ed. Joyce Appleby and Terence Ball (New York: Cambridge University Press, 1999), 485–86.

45. Kelsall, *Jefferson and the Iconography of Romanticism*, 112.

46. Pickens, "Mr. Jefferson as Revolutionary Architect," 273.

47. Fiske Kimball's argument about the revivalist tendency in Jefferson's Monticello is in his "Thomas Jefferson and the Origins of the Classical Revival in America," *Art and Archaeology* 1 (May 1915), 219–27.

48. Ibid., 278.

49. William Howard Adams, *Jefferson's Monticello* (New York: Abbeville, 1983), 263.

50. Kelsall, *Jefferson and the Iconography of Romanticism*, 129.

51. Ibid., 138.

52. See ibid., 138–39.

53. Isaac Jefferson, *Memoirs of a Monticello Slave: As Dictated to Charles Campbell in the 1840's by Isaac, one of Thomas Jefferson's Slaves*, ed. Sarah Dean Link (Charlottesville: University of Virginia Press, 1951), 29.

54. Quoted in Kelsall, *Jefferson and the Iconography of Romanticism*, 165.

55. Quotation from William M. Kelso, "The Landscape Archaeology at Thomas Jefferson's Monticello," in *Earth Patterns: Essays in Landscape Archaeology*, ed. William M. Kelso and Rachel Most (Charlottesville: University of Virginia Press, 1990), 16.

56. Quotation from Kelsall, *Jefferson and the Iconography of Romanticism*, 132.

57. See ibid., 107, on the retreat dimension of the prior country house design in Virginia.

58. Libeskind quoted in Young, *At Memory's Edge*, 175.

59. Quotation from Gerard Le Coat, "Tomas Jefferson et l'architecture metaphorique: le Village Academique a l'Univerite' de Virginie," *RACAR: revue d'art canadienne* 3:2 (1976): 19 (my translation, here and below).

60. From Andrew A. Lipscombe and Albert E. Bergh, *Writings of Thomas Jefferson*, Monticello ed., 12 vols. (Washington, D.C.: Thomas Jefferson Memorial Association, 1903), 12:387.

61. The quoted expression is from Garry Wills, *Mr. Jefferson's University* (Washington, D.C.: National Geographic, 2002), 8.

62. Ibid., 17.

63. Quotation from Denis Cosgrove, *The Palladian Landscape* (University Park: Pennsylvania State University Press, 1993), 4.

64. See ibid., 64.

65. Ibid., 75.

66. Le Coat, "Tomas Jefferson et l'architecture metaphorique: le Village Academique a l'Univerite' de Virginie," 16.

67. Quoted in ibid., 20. The expression is from Jefferson's first inaugural address.

68. The expression is Wills's, in *Mr. Jefferson's University*, 84.

69. Bradford Grant, "Accommodation, Resistance, and Appropriation in African-American Building," in *Sites of Memory: Perspectives on Architecture and Race*, ed. Craig E. Barton (New York: Princeton Architecture Press, 2001), 9.

70. Ibid., 110.

71. Ibid., 112–13.

72. Ibid., 114.

73. The quotations are from Kendrich Ian Grandison, "Negotiated Space: The Black College Campus as a Cultural Record of Postbellum America," in *Sites of Memory*, ed. Barton.

74. Ibid., 63.

75. Ibid., 75–76.

76. The "gateway" term is used to describe Antoine Predock's administration building, the "Cal Poly Building," on the California State University at Pomona campus. See Juliet Robbins and Brad Collins, *Antoine Predock* (New York: Rizzoli, 1994), 148. The other quotations are from Grandison, "Negotiated Space," 78–79.

77. Craig E. Barton, "Duality and Invisibility," in *Sites of Memory*, ed. Barton, 1.

78. Grandison, "Negotiated Space," 82–83.

79. Doubleness, a rhetoric of "assertions and counter-assertions," is a trope within what Henry Louis Gates Jr. calls "the African American discursive forest." See his *The Signifying Monkey: A Theory of Afro-American Literary Criticism* (New York: Oxford University Press, 1988), 52.

80. Ibid., 80.

81. As I note in chapter 1 with reference to Deleuze and Guattari's argument, there are no natural majorities or minorities; to designate a group as either requires the application of an arbitrary norm.

82. Leo Marx, *The Machine in the Garden: Technology and the Pastoral Ideal in America* (New York: Oxford University Press, 1964), 146.

83. Olmsted quoted in Sarah Cedar Miller, *Central Park* (New York: Harry N. Abrams, 2003), 19.

84. Quotation from: James R. Abbott, "Louis Sullivan, Architectural Modernism, and the Creation of Democratic Space," *American Sociologist* 31:1 (spring 2000): 63.

85. Louis Sullivan, "The Tall Office Building Artistically Considered" [1896], in *Louis Sullivan: The Public Papers*, ed. Robert Twombly (Chicago: University of Chicago Press, 1988), 113.

86. Miller, *Central Park*, 18.

87. See Lee Hall, *Olmsted's America: An "Unpractical" Man and His Vision of Civilization* (Boston: Little, Brown, 1995), 142.

88. Miller, *Central Park*, 29.

89. Ibid., 56. It should be noted that its was Hunt who developed the more classical features of Hampton University.

90. Ibid., 22.

91. Quoted in Robert A. Caro, *The Power Broker: Robert Moses and the Fall of New York* (New York: Vintage, 1974), 12.

92. Ibid., 5

93. Quotations from ibid., 318.

94. See ibid.

95. The quotations are from Abbott, "Louis Sullivan, Architectural Modernism, and the Creation of Democratic Space," 77.

96. Ibid., 73.

97. Ibid., 78.

98. Thus Sullivan was a Jeffersonian in only in a certain sense. He shared with Jeffersonians not only the belief in the "'sovereignty of the present generation' (i.e., its independence of past philosophies and institutions), but also the idea that it was in the ideal and perfect mechanism of nature that man would discover all he needed to know concerning his moral and social goals." He affirmed this position with a quotation from the writing of Daniel Boorstin on Jefferson: "What Jefferson 'asked of his political theory . . . was no blueprint for society, but a way of discovering the plan implicit in nature'" (from Daniel Boorstin's *Lost World of Thomas Jefferson*, quoted in David S. Andrew, *Louis Sullivan and the Polemics of Modern Architecture* [Urbana: University of Illinois Press, 1985], 73). Moreover, Sullivan, like Jefferson, essayed an organic defense of the relationship between architecture and nature (see ibid.).

99. From Louis Sullivan, *Democracy: A Man-Search*, quoted in Andrew, *Louis Sullivan and the Polemics of Modern Architecture*, 46.

100. See John W. Burgess, *The Foundations of Political Science* (New Brunswick, N.J.: Transaction, 1994), 6.

101. Sullivan, quoted in Abbott, "Louis Sullivan, Architectural Modernism, and the Creation of Democratic Space," 49

102. Sullivan, *Kindergarten Chats*, in ibid., 228–29.

103. The quotation is from Colin Williams and Anthony D. Smith, "The National Construction of Social Space," *Progress in Human Geography* 7:4 (December 1983): 504.

104. Dolores Hayden, *The Power of Place* (Cambridge, Mass.: MIT Press, 1995), 15

105. James Sallis, *Eye of the Cricket* (New York: Walker and Company, 1997), 105.

106. Hayden, *The Power of Place*, 22.

107. Ibid.

108. Ibid., 34–35.

109. Camillo Jose Vergara, "El Nievo Mundo: Latinos in La-La Land," *California Journal* 31:1 (January 2000): 85.

110. See Lawrence A. Herzog, *From Aztec to High Tech: Architecture and Landscape across the Mexico-United States Border* (Baltimore: Johns Hopkins University Press, 1999), 1–3.

111. See *The Making of an American Landscape*, ed. Michael Conzen (Boston: Unwin Hyman 1990), 57.

112. Peter Nabokov and Robert Easton, *Native American Architecture* (New York: Oxford University Press, 1989), 38.

113. The quoted expression is from Murray Pomerance's reading of the film: "The Consumer Perversity of Roger Thornhill," *Quarterly Review of Film and Video* 17:1 (March 2000): 4.

114. This description of the Haida plank house is from Nabokov and Easton, *Native American Architecture*, 39.

115. Lewis Mumford, *The City in History* (New York: Harcourt Brace Jovanovich, 1961), 569.

116. Ibid., 49.

117. Kaja Silverman, *The Threshold of the Visible World* (New York: Routledge, 1996), 184.

118. Ibid., 186.

119. Ibid., 188.

120. See Jacques Rancière, *Dis-agreement*, trans. Julie Rose (Minneapolis: University of Minnesota Press, 1998), 21–42.

5. Composing America

Epigraphs. Houston A. Baker Jr., *Modernism and the Harlem Renaissance* (Chicago: University of Chicago Press, 1987), 71; Ronald Radano, *Lying Up a Nation: Race and Black Music* (Chicago: University of Chicago Press, 2003), 2.

1. Quoted in William Brooks, "Simple Gifts and Complex Accretions," in *Copland Connotations*, ed. Peter Dickinson (Woodbridge, U.K.: Boydell Press, 2002), 104.

2. Aaron Copland, *Music and Imagination* (Cambridge, Mass.: Harvard University Press, 1952), 101.

3. Quotations are from Alan Howard Levy, *Musical Nationalism: American Composers' Search for Identity* (Westport, Conn.: Greenwood Press, 1983), 110.

4. See Jessica Burr, "Copland, the West and American Identity," 27, in ibid.

5. The concept of a melodic landscape is treated in John Snydal and Marti Hearst, "ImproViz: Visual Explorations of Jazz Improvisato," http://www.offhand-designs.com/jon/docs/snydal_improViz.pdf, accessed April 27, 2005.

6. Jacques Rancière, *The Politics of Aesthetics*, trans. Gabriel Rockhill (New York: Continuum, 2004), 12.

7. Ibid., 64.

8. Ibid., 65.

9. Richard Powers, *The Time of Our Singing* (New York: Farrar, Straus, and Giroux, 2003), 11, 143, 13.

10. The quotation is from Edith Eisler's description of the work, performed and recorded at its twentieth anniversary in 2004 by the University of Michigan orchestra and choirs under the direction of Leonard Slatkin, http://www.softforall.com/shop/William_Bolcom_-_Songs_of_Innocence_and_of_Experience_(William_Blake)___Slatkin,_University_of_Michigan_School_of_Music-B000641YZK.html, accessed February 17, 2005.

11. The quotations are from Donald Pease, "José Martí, Alexis de Tocqueville, and the Politics of Displacement," in *José Martí's "Our America,"* ed. Jeffrey Belnap and Raul Fernandez (Durham, N.C.: Duke University Press, 1998), 29–30.

12. Quotations are from Maurice Peress, *Dvorak to Duke Ellington* (New York: Oxford University Press, 2004), 25.

13. Ibid., 23.

14. Quotations are from Tara C. Browner, *Transposing Cultures: The Appropriation of Native North American Musics, 1890–1990* (Ph.D. diss., University of Michigan, 1995), 8–9.

15. Quotations are from Francis Brancaleone, "Edward MacDowell and the Indian Motives," *American Music* 7:4 (winter 1989): 359.

16. Arthur Farwell, "Wanderjahre of a Revolutionist," in *Wanderjahre of a Revolutionist and Other Essays on American Music*, ed. Thomas Stoner (Rochester, N.Y.: University of Rochester Press, 1995), 6.

17. Ibid., 79.

18. See, for example, Samuel Huntington's anti-immigration polemic, *Who Are We?: The Challenges to America's National Identity* (New York: Simon and Schuster, 2004). I treat parts of the history of anti-immigration perspectives in chapter 2, "Narrating the Nation, Unwelcoming the Stranger," in Michael Shapiro, *Cinematic Political Thought: Narrating Race, Nation, and Gender* (New York: NYU Press, 1999).

19. See MacDonald Smith Moore, *Yankee Blues: Musical Culture and American Identity* (Bloomington: Indiana University Press, 1985).

20. Daniel Gregory Mason, *The Dilemma of American Music and Other Essays* (New York: Macmillan, 1928), 140.

21. Quotations are from Nicholas M. Evans, *Race, Nationalism, and Modern Culture in the 1920s* (New York: Garland Publishing, 2000).

22. Moore, *Yankee Blues*, 5.

23. Ibid., 44.

24. Ibid., 66.

25. Ibid., 88.

26. Ibid., 67.

27. Quotations are from Richard A. Peterson, *Creating Country Music: Fabricating Authenticity* (Chicago: University of Chicago Press, 1997), 59.

28. Ibid., 60.

29. Ibid., 64–65. The anti-pluralist and racist fantasy of authenticity that spawned this brief redemptive movement is thoroughly lampooned in the Coen Brothers' feature film *O Brother, Where Art Thou?* (2000). The main singers in the film, three escaped convicts who become the Soggy Bottom Boys and record a hit bluegrass song that becomes wildly popular without their realizing that it has hit the airwaves, are not the film's actual singers. The gap between the songs and the singers is one of several ways that the film critiques the idea of an authentic music. Suffused with the rural music of the South, mainly country and bluegrass—for example, a version of the country singer Jimmie Rodgers's "In the Jailhouse Now"—the film presents stereotypical versions of the southern experience (revivals, Klan rallies, a river baptism) and a panorama of stereotypical characters, among whom is a racist Klan member and mayoral candidate who rails against "miscegenated" music.

30. Leroy Jones (Amiri Baraka), *Blues People* (New York: Morrow, 1999), 57.

31. Radano, *Lying Up a Nation*, 63.

32. *Living with Music: Ralph Ellison's Jazz Writings*, ed. Robert G. O'Meally (New York: Modern Library, 2002), 103.

33. The quotation is from Robert G. O'Meally's "Introduction" in ibid., xxv.

34. Ralph Ellison, "Remembering Jimmie," in ibid., 47.

35. Quotation from a conversation with O'Meally, in ibid., xii.

36. Ibid., 260.

37. Ibid., 17.

38. See Jacques Rancière, *The Nights of Labor: The Workers' Dream in Nineteenth-Century France*, trans. John Drury (Philadelphia: Temple University Press, 1989).

39. Quoted in David Schiff, *Gershwin: Rhapsody in Blue* (Cambridge, U.K.: Cambridge University Press, 1997), 12.

40. The January 4, 1924, article in the *New York Herald Tribune* is the first public mention of Gershwin's *Rhapsody in Blue*. The headline read, "Whiteman Judges Named: Committee Will Decide 'What is American Music.'" Cited in Robert Wyatt and John Andrew Johnson, *The George Gershwin Reader* (New York: Oxford University Press, 2004), 44.

41. Ibid., 45.

42. See Michael L. Klein, *Intertextuality in Western Art Music* (Bloomington: Indiana University Press, 2004), 11.

43. David Schiff, *Gershwin: Rhapsody in Blue*, 28. Most of my discussion of the various elements in *Rhapsody* are indebted to his observations.

44. For a treatment of Wagner's innovations and his influence on French symbolists, see David Michael Hertz, *The Tuning of the Word: The Musico-Literary Poetics of the Symbolist Movement* (Carbondale: Southern Illinois University Press, 1987).

45. Ibid., 117.

46. I am indebted to the ethno-musicologist Ricardo Trimelos for these insights into Debussy's liberties with tonality.

47. John R. Clevenger, "Debussy's Rome Cantatas," in *Debussy and His World*, ed. Jane Fulcher (Princeton, N.J.: Princeton University Press, 2001), 16.

48. James N. Snead, "On Repetition in Black Culture," *Black American Literature Forum*, 15:4 (winter 1981): 151.

49. Ibid., 150.

50. The quotation is from music theorist Ernst Krenek, who saw the Debussy-jazz/swing connection but expressed much contempt for what he regarded as the swing arranger's despoiling and banalization of Debussy's innovations; see Ernst Krenek, *Music Here and Now*, trans. Barthold Fles (New York: Russell and Russell, 1939), 249.

51. The quotations are from Roger Scruton, *The Aesthetics of Music* (Oxford, U.K.: Clarendon Press, 1997), 500–501.

52. Schiff, *Gershwin: Rhapsody in Blue*, 14.

53. See ibid., 38.

54. Quotation from Maurice Peress, *Dvorak to Duke Ellington* (New York: Oxford University Press, 2004), 68.

55. Ibid., 34–39.

56. The quotations are from David Horn, "From Catfish Row to Granby Street: Contesting Meaning in *Porgy and Bess*," *Popular Music* 13:2 (March 1994): 170.

57. Wynton Marsalis in Lolis Eric Elie, "An Interview with Wynton Marsalis," *Callaloo* 13:2 (spring 1990): 281.

58. Schiff, *Gershwin: Rhapsody in Blue*, 77.

59. The quotations are from Marcus Roberts's liner notes that accompany his *Portraits in Blue* (New York: Sony, 1996).

60. Ibid.

61. Baker, *Modernism and the Harlem Renaissance*, 71.

62. Andrea Most, *Making Americans: Jews and the Broadway Musical* (Harvard University Press, 2004), 1–2.

63. The quotations are from Andrea Most's discussion of Scholem's argument in ibid., 13.

64. Ibid., 14.

65. Berlin quoted in John Lahr, "Revolutionary Rag," *New Yorker*, March 3, 1999, 78. These observations on Berlin are elaborated in Michael J. Shapiro, *Methods and Nations: Cultural Governance and the Indigenous Subject* (New York: Routledge, 2004), 80–81.

66. Quotations are from Christian Appy, "'We'll Follow the Old Man': The Strains of Sentimental Militarism in Popular Films of the Fifties," in *Rethinking Cold War Culture*, ed. Peter J. Kuznick and James Gilbert (Washington, D.C.: Smithsonian Institution Press, 2001), 8.

67. See David Monod, "Disguise, Containment and the *Porgy and Bess* Revival of 1952–1956," *Journal of American Studies* 35:2 (August 2001): 285.

68. See *The Songs of Irving Berlin: Patriotic Songs* (Milwaukee, Wisc.: Hal Leonard, 1991).

69. Charles Hamm, "Genre, Performance and Ideology in the Early Songs of Irving Berlin," *Popular Music* 13:2 (May 1994): 145.

70. Baker, *Modernism and the Harlem Renaissance*, 24.

71. Ibid., 33–36.

72. Ibid., 32–33.

73. See Schiff, *Gershwin: Rhapsody in Blue*, 55.

74. Thomas L. Riis, *Just Before Jazz: Black Musical Theater in New York, 1890–1915* (Washington, D.C.: Smithsonian Institution Press, 1989), 51.

75. Ibid., 52.

76. Baker, *Modernism and the Harlem Renaissance*, 50–51.

77. Riis, *Just Before Jazz*, 86–87.

78. Duke Ellington, "The Duke Steps Out," *Rhythm* (March 1931), reprinted in *The Duke Ellington Reader*, ed. Mark Tucker (New York: Oxford University Press, 1993), 46.

79. Ibid., 47.

80. Ralph Ellison, "The Charlie Christian Story," in *Living with Music*, ed. O'Meally, 267.

81. Duke Ellington, "We, Too Sing 'America,'" in *The Duke Ellington Reader*, ed. Tucker, 147.

82. Fred Moten, *In the Break: The Aesthetics of the Black Radical Tradition* (Minneapolis: University of Minnesota Press, 2003), 30.

83. Quoted in Michael Denning, *The Cultural Front: The Laboring of Ameri-*

can Culture in the Twentieth Century (New York: Verso, 1996), 313; quoted in Joseph P. Swain, *The Broadway Musical* (New York: Oxford University Press, 1990), 56.

84. See Duke Ellington, *Music Is My Mistress* (New York: Doubleday, 1973), 176.

85. Ibid.

86. Ibid.

87. Baker, *Modernism and the Harlem Renaissance*, 101.

88. Ellington, *Music Is My Mistress*, 180.

89. Ibid., 181–82.

90. The Ellington quotations are from Harvey G. Cohen, "Duke Ellington and *Black, Brown and Beige*: The Composer as Historian at Carnegie Hall," *American Quarterly* 56:4 (December 2004): 2006.

91. Ellington, *Music Is My Mistress*, 181.

92. The quotations are from Peress, *Dvorak to Duke Ellington*, 171. The discussion of the piece by Peress, who scored it for symphony orchestras after its 1963 publication and sought, in his words, "to capture the inflections, phrasing, and coloration of Duke's own magnificent orchestra" (172) is my guide through this section.

93. Reported in Nathaniel Mackey, *Atet A. D.* (San Francisco: City Lights Books, 2001), 3–4.

94. Jacques Attali, *Noise: The Political Economy of Music*, trans. Brian Massumi (Minneapolis: University of Minnesota Press, 1985), 46.

95. Ibid., 68–69.

96. Wynton Marsalis, "Ellington: Sweets," *Down Beat* 58:6 (June 1991): 17.

97. Ibid., 19.

98. Among the places that Ellington uses this expression is *Music Is My Mistress*, 118. But see his remarks about the special character of each of his band members throughout this autobiographical text.

99. Ellington, "The Duke Steps Out," 47.

100. Mackey, *Atet A. D.*, 5.

101. Nathaniel Mackey, "Other: From Noun to Verb," *Representations* 39 (summer 1992): 52.

102. Ibid., 53.

103. Ibid., 61.

104. Ibid., 59.

105. Ellington, "The Duke Steps Out," 48.

106. See Peress, *Dvorak to Duke Ellington*, 182.

107. See Albert Murray, *Stomping the Blues* (New York: McGraw-Hill, 1976).

108. Albert Murray, *The Hero and the Blues* (Columbia: University of Missouri Press, 1973), 104.

109. Albert Murray, *The Blue Devils of Nada: A Contemporary American Approach to Aesthetic Statement* (New York: Vintage, 1997), 15.

110. Quotations from Peress, *Dvorak to Duke Ellington*, 182–83.

111. The concept of conceptual personae comes from Gilles Deleuze and Felix Guattari, *What Is Philosophy?* trans. Hugh Tomlinson and Graham Burchell (New York: Columbia University Press, 1994).

112. Peress, *Dvorak to Duke Ellington*, 186.

113. Ibid., 188.

114. Duke Ellington, "Interview in Los Angeles: On *Jump for Joy*, Opera and Dissonance," in *The Duke Ellington Reader*, ed. Tucker, 151.

115. Ibid., 150.

116. Quotations are from Thomas Vennum Jr., "The Changing Soundscape in Indian Country," in *American Musical Traditions*, vol. 1, ed. Jeff Todd Titon and Bob Carlin (New York: Schirmer, 2002), 107.

117. Gospel music is one among many examples of a history of musical commingling between African and Native Americans. See, for example, Malinda Maynor, "Making Christianity Sing," in *Confounding the Color Line*, ed. James F. Brooks (Lincoln: University of Nebraska Press, 2002), 321–45.

118. The quotation is from Neal Ullestad, "American Indian Rap and Reggae: Dancing 'To the Beat of a Different Drummer,'" *Popular Music and Society* 23:2 (summer 1999): 63.

119. See Sherman Alexie, *Reservation Blues* (New York: Warner Books, 1996).

120. See Clyde Woods, *Development Arrested: Race, Power, and the Blues in the Mississippi Delta* (New York: Verso, 1998).

121. Alexie, *Reservation Blues*, 174.

122. Ibid., 175.

123. See Alexie's poems "Tiny Treaties" and "Seven Love Songs Which Include the Collected History of the United States of America" in Sherman Alexie, *First Indian on the Moon* (New York: Hanging Loose, 1993), 56–57 and 62–65, respectively.

124. Alexie, *Reservation Blues*, 283.

125. Ibid., 201.

126. Sherman Alexie, "Sherman Alexie, Literary Rebel," interview with John and Carl Belante, *Bloomsbury Review* 14 (1994): 15.

127. John Trudell, *Bone Days* (New York: Daemon Records, 2001).

128. John Trudell, *Blue Indians* (New York: Americana Records, produced by Jackson Browne, 1999).

129. Ullestad, "American Indian Rap and Reggae," 73.

130. John Trudell, *Stickman: Poems, Lyrics, Talks a Conversation* (New York: Inanout Press, 1994), unpaginated.

131. Quotations from Pease, "José Martí, Alexis de Toqueville, and the Politics of Displacement," 373, 334.

132. See Attali, *Noise*, 36.

133. See Salman Rushdie, *Imaginary Homelands* (New York: Penguin, 1992), 14.

134. Salman Rushdie, *The Ground Beneath Her Feet* (New York: Henry Holt, 1999), 24.

135. I do a more extensive reading of Rushdie's *The Ground Beneath Her Feet* in *Methods and Nations*, 69–70; Rushdie, *The Ground Beneath Her Feet*, 95–96.

136. Susan McClary, *Conventional Wisdom: The Content of Musical Form* (Berkeley: University of California Press, 2000), 32.

137. The matrix expression applied to the blues belongs to Houston A. Baker Jr., in his *Blues, Ideology, and Afro-American Literature* (Chicago: University of Chicago Press, 1984).

138. See John Gennari, "Jazz Criticism: Its Development and Ideologies," *Black American Literary Forum* 25:3 (fall 1991): 4.

139. Baker, *Blues, Ideology, and Afro-American Literature*, 10–11.

140. Ibid., 11.

141. Quotations from ibid., 13.

142. The piece in which I cite Shklar's address is "Securing the American Ethnoscape: Official Surveys and Literary Interventions," in *Worlds and Knowledges Otherwise* 1:1 (fall 2004), http://www.jhfc.duke.edu/wko/dossiers/1.1/contents. php, accessed February 17, 2005.

Shklar's address appeared originally in the *American Political Science Review* in March 1991. The quotation is from the version that was subsequently reprinted in Judith Shklar, *Redeeming American Political Thought*, ed. Stanley Hoffman and Dennis F. Thompson (Chicago: University of Chicago Press, 1998), 92.

143. See Jacques Rancière, *Dis-agreement*, trans. Julie Rose (Minneapolis: University of Minnesota Press, 1998), 101.

144. Ellington, "Interview in Los Angeles: On *Jump for Joy*, Opera and Dissonance," 150.

145. See Rancière, *Politics of Aesthetics*, 25.

6. Democracy's Risky Businesses

1. My use of the concept of the diagram follows Gilles Deleuze's discussion in his treatment of Francis Bacon. To diagram, for Deleuze, is to create a "violent chaos in relation to the figurative givens" (*Francis Bacon: The Logic of Sensation*, trans. Daniel W. Smith [Minneapolis: University of Minnesota Press, 2003], 83). In my usage, it is at a minimum to remap and refigure the traditional field of meaning and in some cases to disrupt and create what Deleuze often calls another "possibility of fact" (ibid.).

2. Deleuze, *Francis Bacon*, 81.

3. Jacques Rancière, *The Politics of Aesthetics*, trans. Gabriel Rockhill (New York: Continuum, 2004), 24.

4. The quoted section is from my treatment of the story in another place: "The Politics of Fear: Don DeLillo's Postmodern Burrow," in Michael J. Shapiro, *Reading the Postmodern Polity: Political Theory as Textual Practice* (Minneapolis: University of Minnesota Press, 1992), 123.

5. Franz Kafka, "The Burrow," trans. Willa and Edwin Muir, in *Collected Stories* (New York: Schocken, 1971), 357.

6. Malcolm Kelsall, *Jefferson and the Iconography of Romanticism* (New York: St. Martin's Press, 1999), 88.

7. Thomas Jefferson, *Notes on the State of Virginia*, ed. William Peden (Chapel Hill: University of North Carolina Press, 1954; originally published in 1781–1782), 19.

8. Ibid., 164.

9. Jean-François Lyotard, *The Inhuman*, trans. Geoffrey Bennington and Rachel Bowlby (Stanford, Calif.: Stanford University Press, 1991), 137.

10. The quotation is from Lorrain Daston, "Attention and the Values of Nature in the Enlightenment," in *The Moral Authority of Nature*, ed. Lorrain Daston and Fernando Vidal (Chicago: University of Chicago Press, 2004), 101.

11. Immanuel Kant, *The Critique of Judgment*, trans. J. H. Bernard (Amherst, N.Y.: Prometheus Books, 2000; originally published in 1790), 117.

12. Jacques Derrida, "Declarations of Independence," trans. Thomas Keenan and Tom Pepper, *New Political Science* 15 (summer 1986): 10.

13. Ibid., 9.

14. See Walter Benjamin, "Critique of Violence," in *Reflections*, trans. Edmund Jepthcott (New York: Schocken, 1978), 287.

15. Thomas Pynchon, *Mason & Dixon* (New York: Henry Holt, 1997), 359. My extended treatment of Pynchon's novel is in "Securing the American Ethnoscape: Official Surveys and Literary Interventions," *Worlds and Knowledges Otherwise* 1:1 (fall 2004), http://www.jhfc.duke.edu/wko/dossiers/1.1/contents.php, accessed February 17, 2005.

16. Pynchon, *Mason & Dixon*, 608.

17. Ibid., 478.

18. Benjamin, "Critique of Violence," 287.

19. W. E. B. Du Bois, *Black Reconstruction: An Essay Toward a History of the Part Which Black Folk Played in the Attempt to Reconstruct Democracy in American, 1860–1880* (New York: Harcourt, Brace and Company, 1935), 714.

20. Ibid., 725.

21. Ibid.

22. Ibid., 350.

23. Ibid., 353.

24. Ibid., 352.

25. Ibid., 349.

26. Jacques Derrida, *Politics of Friendship*, trans. George Collins (New York: Verso, 1997), ix.

27. Du Bois, *Black Reconstruction*, 725.

28. Jacques Derrida, "Nietzsche and the Machine," in *Negotiations*, trans. Elizabeth Rottenberg (Stanford, Calif.: Stanford University Press, 2002), 254.

29. Ibid., 251.

30. Jacques Derrida, *Specters of Marx: The State of the Death, the Work of Mourning, and the New International*, trans. Peggy Kamuf (New York: Routledge, 1994), 81.

31. Robin D. G. Kelly, "How the West Was One: The African Diaspora and the Re-Mapping of U.S. History," in *Rethinking American History in a Global Age*, ed. Thomas Bender (Berkeley: University of California Press, 2002), 123.

32. The "state of exception" phrase is taken from Giorgio Agamben's analysis of the U.S. government's suspensions of legal protection following the September 11, 2001, acts of terrorism in Washington, D.C., and New York, its establishment of spaces "devoid of law." See his *State of Exception*, trans. Kevin Attell (Chicago: University of Chicago Press, 2005).

33. Jacques Rancière, *Dis-agreement*, trans. Julie Rose (Minneapolis: University of Minnesota Press, 1998), 101.

34. Ibid., 75.

35. Ibid., 77.

36. Ibid., 79.

37. For an application of Rancière's insights under this rubric, see Benjamin Arditi and Jeremy Valentine, *Polemicization* (Edinburgh, U.K.: Edinburgh University Press, 1999).

38. Quotations from Philip Fisher, "Democratic Social Space: Whitman, Melville, and the Promise of American Transparency," *Representations* 24 (fall 1998): 62.

39. Ibid., 65.

40. Ibid., 98.

41. Ibid., 99.

42. Jacques Rancière, "Politics, Identification, and Subjectivization," *October* 61 (summer 1992): 63.

43. Ibid. The concepts of founding and preserving violence are borrowed from Walter Benjamin's challenging treatment of the law-violence relationship: "Critique of Violence," in *Reflections*, trans. Edmund Jepthcott (New York: Schocken, 1978), 277–300.

44. Rancière, *Dis-agreement*, 15.

45. Ibid., 39.

46. Jacques Rancière, *On the Shores of Politics*, trans. Liz Heron (New York: Verso, 1995), 39.

47. Jacques Rancière, *The Nights of Labor: The Workers' Dream in Nineteenth-Century France*, trans. John Drury (Philadelphia: Temple University Press, 1989), 22.

48. Foucault's brief genealogy of the political is in his essay "Governmentality," in *The Foucault Effect*, ed. Graham Burchell, Colin Gordon, and Peter Miller (London: Harvester Wheatsheaf, 1991), 87–104.

49. See Rancière, *Dis-agreement*, 91–93.

50. William E. Connolly, *The Ethos of Pluralization* (Minneapolis: University of Minnesota Press, 1995), 163.

51. Ibid., 167.

52. Ibid., 163. Connolly specifically mentions Rousseau as one who "recognizes the ambiguity involved in the founding of a people" (165).

53. Ibid., 170. Rancière's characteristic examples focus on the historical wrongs visited on proletarians: "Before the wrong that its name exposes, the proletariat has no existence as a real part of society" (*Dis-agreement*, 39).

54. See Gilles Deleuze and Felix Guattari, *A Thousand Plateaus*, trans. Brian Massumi (Minneapolis: University of Minnesota Press, 1987), 424–73.

55. Connolly, *The Ethos of Pluralization*, 172.

56. The quotations are from Fisher, "Democratic Social Space," 64.

57. Rancière, *On the Shores of Politics*, 60.

58. William E. Connolly, *Politics and Ambiguity* (Madison: University of Wisconsin Press, 1987), 5–6.

59. Rancière, *Dis-agreement*, 11.

60. William E. Connolly, *Identity/Difference: Democratic Negotiations of Political Paradox*, expanded ed. (Minneapolis: University of Minnesota Press, 2002), 81.

61. Quotation from Paola Maratti, "Against the Doxa: Politics of Immanence and Becoming Minoritarian," in *Micropolitics of Media Culture: Reading the Rhizomes of Deleuze and Guattari*, ed. Patrica Pister (Amsterdam: Amsterdam University Press, 2001), 207.

62. Rancière, *Dis-agreement*, 31.

63. Jacques Rancière, "Post-Democracy, Politics and Philosophy: An Interview with Jacques Rancière," *Angelaki* 1:3 (1995): 178.

64. Connolly, *Politics and Ambiguity*, 160

65. Ibid., 157.

66. William E. Connolly, *Neuropolitics: Thinking, Culture, Speed* (Minneapolis: University of Minnesota Press, 2002), 160.

67. Ibid., 165.

68. William E. Connolly, *Why I Am Not a Secularist* (Minneapolis: University of Minnesota Press), 155.

69. Jacques Rancière, "Literature, Politics, Aesthetics: An Interview by Solange Guenoun and James H. Kavanagh," *SubStance* 29:2 (2000): 13.

70. Rancière, *Dis-agreement*, 101.

71. Jacques Rancière, "Ten Theses on Politics," *Theory and Event* 5:3 (2001): 5.

72. Ibid., 8.

73. Ibid.

74. Ibid.

75. For Rancière's analysis of nineteenth-century worker movements, see his *Nights of Labor*.

76. See Gilles Deleuze and Felix Guattari, *Anti-Oedipus: Capitalism and Schizophrenia*, trans. Robert Hurley, Mark Seem, and Helen R. Lane (New York: Viking, 1977), 194.

77. Deleuze and Guattari, *A Thousand Plateaus*, 220.

78. Ibid., 216.

79. Ibid., 215.

80. Rancière, *Dis-agreement*, 101.

81. Derrida, *Politics of Friendship*, 26–48.

82. Gilles Deleuze, "Postscript on Societies of Control," *October* 59 (winter 1992): 3.

83. Connolly, *Why I Am Not a Secularist*, 158.

84. Connolly, *The Ethos of Pluralization*, 175.

85. Ibid., 177.

86. Ibid., 177–78.

87. For Connolly on film, see various sections in his *Neuropolitics*. For Rancière on film, see Solange Guenoun, "An Interview with Jacques Rancière: Cinematographic Image, Democracy, and the Splendor of the . . . ," *Sites* 4:2 (fall 2000): 1–7.

88. On centrifugal and centripetal spaces of the suburbs and central city,

respectively, see Edward Dimendberg, *Film Noir and the Spaces of Modernity* (Cambridge, Mass.: Harvard University Press, 2005).

89. The expression belongs to Miriam Hansen in her "Introduction" to Siegfried Kracauer's *Theory of Film* (Princeton, N.J.: Princeton University Press, 1997), x.

90. Ibid., xxii.

91. Jean Baudrillard, "Sign Function and Class Logic," in *For a Critique of the Political Economy of the Sign,* trans. Charles Levin (St. Louis: Telos Press, 1981), 43.

92. See Phillip Slater, *The Pursuit of Loneliness: American Culture at the Breaking Point* (Boston: Beacon Press, 1971).

93. The quotation is from Eric Lott, "The Whiteness of Film Noir," in *National Imaginaries, American Identities,* ed. Larry J. Reynolds and Gordon Hutner (Princeton, N.J.: Princeton University Press, 2000), 161. The inside quotations are Lott quoting Peter Stallybrass and Allon White, *The Politics and Poetics of Transgression* (London: Methuen, 1986), 20.

94. Franco Moretti, *Atlas of the European Novel* (London: Verso, 1998), 117.

95. Ibid., 120.

96. Mary Ann Doane, *The Emergence of Cinematic Time: Modernity, Contingency, the Archive* (Cambridge, Mass.; Harvard University Press, 2002), 194.

97. Manthia Diawara, "*Noir* by *Noirs*: Toward a New Realism in Black Cinema," in *Shades of Noir: A Reader,* ed. Joan Copjec (New York: Verso, 1993), 272.

98. Michel Foucault, *Discipline and Punish: The Birth of the Prison,* trans. Alan Sheridan (New York: Pantheon, 1977), 272.

99. The expression "institutional ecologies" is part of Manuel De Landa's analysis of the institutional collaborations involved in contemporary modes of militarization. See Manuel De Landa, "Economics, Computers, and the War Machine," in *Ars Electronica: Facing the Future,* ed. Timothy Druchrey (Cambridge, Mass.: MIT Press, 1999), 319.

100. Diawara, "*Noir* by *Noirs*," 269.

101. Samuel Huntington, *Who Are We?: The Challenges to America's National Identity* (New York: Simon and Schuster, 2004).

102. Jacques Derrida, *Of Hospitality,* trans. Rachel Bowlby (Sanford, Calif.: Stanford University Press, 2000), 5.

103. See Paul Laverty, "Introduction," in Paul Laverty and Ken Loach, *Bread and Roses* (Los Angeles: Screenpress Books, 2000), xiii–xiv.

104. Ibid., xv.

105. See Matthias Fritsch's reading of Derrida on "the democracy to come" for a treatment of polemical space in Derrida: "Derrida's Democracy to Come," *Constellations* 9:4 (2002): 579.

106. Rancière, *Nights of Labor,* 8.

107. Ibid., 15.

108. Ibid., 20.

109. Michel Foucault, *Society Must Be Defended,* trans. David Macey (New York: Picador, 2003), 50–51.

110. Walter Benjamin, "Franz Kafka," trans. Harry Zahn, in *Illuminations* (New York: Schocken, 1968), 114.

111. Judith Butler, *Precarious Lives: The Powers of Mourning and Violence* (New York: Verso, 2004), 62.

112. The quotation is from ibid., xix.

113. Agamben, *State of Exception*, 50.

114. In addition to Butler's *Precarious Life* and Agamben's *State of Exception*, see Derek Gregory, *The Colonial Present* (Malden, Mass.: Blackwell, 2004).

115. Agamben, *State of Exception*, 29.

116. Ibid.

117. Ibid., 26.

118. Quoted in ibid., 30.

Index

Adams, William Howard, 113
aesthetics: in African American
culture, 144–46, 163; in blues,
155–56, 163; for Deleuze, Gilles,
35–36, 63, 88; democratic,
173; for Ellington, Duke, 147;
ethnically mixed, 156, 163; Euro-
American, 159; genres of, 82;
in jazz, 141–42, 147; in Jewish
culture, 144; for Kant, Immanuel,
34–35, 63; for Lyotard, Jean-
Francois, 34; as mode of
comprehension, 32, 34–36, 40,
167; for Panofsky, Erwin, 108;
politics of, 133, 165; for Rancière,
Jacques, 32, 63; for Silverman,
Kaja, 130
Agamben, Giorgio, 197, 198
AIM (American Indian Movement),
102
Alabama, 43
Alexie, Sherman, 20, 22–24, 26, 28,
154–59, 162
Allen, Ray, 132
Altman, Robert, 67, 82–97, 101
America (Euro), 11, 18, 24, 59, 65–66,
75, 82, 94, 97–98, 100–101, 123,
125, 132, 144, 160, 168, 181, 192,
196
America (indigenous), 9, 125
Amiel, Vincent, 93
Anderson, Marian, 133
Antigua, 16, 19, 203–4n71
Apess, William, 7, 180–81, 192
Appleby, Joyce Oldham, 4
Aristotle, 52

Armstrong, John, 117
Armstrong, Louis, 144
Attali, Jacques, 150, 161
attendants, 36–38, 41, 45, 58, 63, 88,
95. *See also* Deleuze, Gilles

Bacon, Francis (artist), 36–38, 83, 88,
165
Bacon, Sir Francis, 115
Baker, Houston A., Jr.: on aesthetics
of Afro modernity, 145–46; on
African American writing, 46–47;
on black musical contributions,
143; on blues matrix, 163; on
deformation of mastery, 149; on
mastery of form, 146, 148; on
sound and meaning, 131
Bakhtin, M. M., 23, 41, 57
Banks, Joseph, 19
Baraka, Amiri, 138–39, 151
Barton, Craig Evan, 119
Baudrillard, Jean, 182
Beatty, Warren, 84
Benjamin, Walter: on Kafka, Franz,
196; on law-violence relationship,
168–69, 198; on translation, 100
Berlant, Lauren, 6
Berlin, Irving, 141, 144–45
Bermingham, Ann, 111
Black Elk, 9, 22
Black Hawk, 9–10
Blue Devils, 139
blues, 51, 138–39, 141–43, 151–53;
Baker, Houston A., on, 163;
Blues People (Baraka), 138, 151;
detectives, 46, 51; Ellison, Ralph,

Opitz, Andrea, 54
Owens, Louis, 54

Padilla, Pilar, 195
Palladio, Andrea, 113
Panofsky, Erwin, 107–9
Pantoliano, Joe, 182
Paris, Texas (film), 67, 82, 96–101
Patriot Act, 197
Penn, Robin Wright, 70
Penn, Sean, 67, 69, 101
Peress, Maurice, 153
Phifer, Mekhi, 186
Philadelphia, 16
Picken, Buford, 113
plantations: bloc, 7, 51, 164; economy
    of, 4, 169; factory as extension
    of, 47; of Jefferson, Thomas, 5,
    109–10, 112–14, 116, 167; legacy
    of, 7; as system of explanation, 8,
    164; Virginia planters, 111, 123,
    129
Plato, 13
Pledge, The (film), 67–74
Poe, Edgar Allen, 44
political economy: American, 186,
    192; forms of, 27; history of,
    19, 26; in *McCabe and Mrs.
    Miller* (Altman), 90; of racial-
    spatial order, 133; in *Risky
    Business* (Brickman), 182–85;
    transnational, 192
political science, 1–3, 31, 68, 123,
    163, 172
political theory, 26, 32, 53, 174;
    American, 1–4, 7, 10, 27, 31, 169;
    canonical, 53, 65; and political
    science, 31; traditional, 172;
    vocations of, 31; western, 65
political thought, 1, 28; and aesthetic
    comprehension, 40; American,
    10, 20, 30, 165, 181, 198; history
    of, 175; modern, 175
power: of blues aesthetic, 155; of
    boundaries, 175; class, 43;
    cultural, 118; for Du Bois, W. E.

B.,170; foreign, 51; genealogy of,
    178; of kings, 112; of languages,
    27; origins of, 172; of the Peraltas,
    62; public, 177; for Rancière,
    Jacques, 177–78; redemptive,
    155; relations of, 23; sovereign,
    196; state, 27, 177, 196; structure
    of (white), 48; for Trudell, John,
    159–60; of Vallejo, Mariano, 60;
    of whiteness, 49
Powers, Richard, 133–34
Pretty Baby (film), 37–38
Public Enemy, 132–33
public policy, 8, 105
public sphere, 6, 24, 181
Pynchon, Thomas, 1, 10–16, 18–19,
    27, 168–69, 181

race, 47; Foucault, Michel, on,
    112–13; Jefferson, Thomas, on,
    112–13; at Monticello, 112–14;
    and Native Americans, 66; in
    Paris, Texas (Wenders), 98; and
    politics of crime, 43, 53, 63;
    Tocqueville, Alexis de, on, 59;
    Yankee composers and, 137
Rachmaninoff, Sergei, 140
racism, 50, 85, 112–14, 137, 146
Radano, Ronald, 131, 139, 162
Rancière, Jacques: on bodies, 178–79;
    on contingency, 173, 179; on
    democracy, 164, 172–73, 178,
    193–94; on democratic theory,
    130, 165, 175; on dissensus, 164;
    on film, 181; on participation,
    176; on political subjects, 102,
    133, 171, 177; on political
    theory, 174; on politics, 102,
    172, 174, 177–78; on politics
    of aesthetics, 32, 63, 133, 166;
    on social identity, 177; on
    social science, 172; on social
    space, 174, 177, 179; on society,
    173–74; on sociology, 174; on
    subjectivization, 173, 176; on
    workers' writing, 194